W9-CRA-656

American Images of China

1931-1949

T. CHRISTOPHER JESPERSEN

Stanford University Press
Stanford, California

Stanford University Press
Stanford, California

© 1996 by the Board of Trustees of the
Leland Stanford Junior University

Printed in the United States of America

CIP data appear at the end of the book

For Theresa

Acknowledgments

This book is an example of what can happen if you drop out of college. I left the University of North Carolina at Chapel Hill in the middle of my junior year, not knowing what I wanted to do. But before leaving, I had the good fortune of enrolling in a course on United States foreign policy taught by Michael Hunt. Although Professor Hunt had nothing directly to do with this project, I think in some indirect way he did influence my thinking. I certainly find myself coming back to his work time and again, though I do not mean to burden him with any responsibility for what I have written here.

What I quickly discovered outside of college was that I had no inclination to make being busboy or bartender a career. Thus, the decision to return to college was an easy one. Because I came from New Jersey, Rutgers seemed the logical choice, mostly because it was affordable for a state resident. It was there that things came together. During the spring 1985 semester, I enrolled in a course on America and Vietnam. Two positive developments came out of that class. The first occurred when the professor agreed to work with me on a senior honors thesis for the following academic year and later took me on as a graduate student; the second I only discovered during the history department's orientation in the fall of 1986. There I was approached by a fellow graduate student who asked me coyly, "Weren't you Lyndon Johnson?" Indeed, I was, or more accurately, had been when I played Johnson during an in-class exercise in the America and Vietnam class. That simple question was the beginning of a truly wonderful relationship.

In working on this project for the past decade or so, I have received invaluable help from a number of people and organizations. The Richard Schlater Fund at Rutgers and the George Marshall Foundation provided me with financial assistance for research travel. The numerous librarians at the archives I visited were uniformly helpful, but special mention must go to Jean Holliday, now retired from the Seely G. Mudd Manuscript Library at Princeton University. Her enthusiasm and breadth of knowledge made working there a real joy. Martha Lund Smalley and Joan Duffy of the Yale Divinity School Library also deserve special thanks for their assistance in securing some wonderful visual materials. Clark Atlanta University provided financial assistance for reproducing the illustrations. Portions of Chapters 2 and 3 appeared in the *Journal of American–East Asian Relations* (Fall 1992).

Friends and former colleagues from Rutgers and elsewhere who read parts of this or provided inspiration during the process include Jonathan Nashel, Torun Willits, Roy Domenico, and George Sirgiovanni. As is his wont for excess, John Rossi did more, both then and later. Mark White, a magnificent chap in his own right, not only read the whole thing and made useful suggestions, he also assisted in the research. Warren Kimball, at Rutgers-Newark, proved to be as sharp an editor as he is boisterous a personality. Ralph Levering of Davidson College and Bob Schulzinger of the University of Colorado at Boulder provided helpful suggestions on earlier versions of chapters I presented at two conferences.

I spent three years as an adjunct assistant professor in the history department at the University of Arizona. In many respects, I was sorry to leave, mostly because of the many wonderful people I got to know there. Colleagues who commented on drafts include Kathy Morrissey, Patrick Miller, and Jim Millward, who also gave me useful pointers on Chinese history and names. Along with Alison Futrell, he plays a mean guitar and can sing, making them my first choice for a history department talent show. John Krueckeberg's power of Dale Carnegie-ism proved helpful as did his comments. Most importantly, however, I benefited from my association with Michael Schaller. He read the entire manuscript, read revised sections, and provided professional guidance and personal friendship, not to mention a heavy-duty child's backpack for hiking around the mountains and deserts of Arizona. Alexander has certainly enjoyed the rides, the view, and pulling on his dad's hair.

I have limited my acknowledgments to the people who directly affected this project, with three exceptions: my mother, Joan, who is a nice person, fine company, and a good grandmother to Alexander, and Tom and Eva Fox, who have provided great, good friendship along the way and essential help at critical times, most recently during the move to Atlanta. I cannot thank them enough for so many things.

Scott Kampmeier deserves special attention because he is a fine historian in his own right. More directly for my concerns, he has always been willing to put aside the time to read my work, make insightful comments, and cook and share a good meal.

At Stanford University Press, Muriel Bell, Barbara James, and John Feneron have all been helpful in assisting me in understanding the publishing process. Shirley Taylor deserves special mention for catching not only my phrasing infelicities but a few factual errors as well.

I should note that in using Chinese names, I have tried to follow the example set by Jonathan Spence in *The Search for Modern China*. That is, I have used the pinyin system for the most part with a few notable exceptions. Chiang Kai-shek remains in Cantonese rather than being switched to Jiang Jieshi, for convenience mostly since all the documents I quote spell his name that way. Canton is Canton in the 1930's but Guangzhou in the 1980's, reflecting the change in usage. Likewise, I use Beijing when discussing recent times, and Peking and Peiping when historical circumstances warrant. I follow the original spelling in quoted matter and have basically put everything else into pinyin.

Finally, there are three people without whom I could not have completed this project, at least not as it presently stands. Michael Adas proved to be a model researcher and teacher, not to mention good company. He helped guide this project in certain crucial respects while I was a graduate student at Rutgers and since that time has continued to offer me his comments and advice.

If I had not taken that class on America and Vietnam in the spring of 1985 with Lloyd C. Gardner, now the Charles and Mary Beard Professor of History, beyond avoiding the restaurant business, I do not know what direction my life would have taken. As an adviser, scholar, and teacher he is unique. His laissez-faire approach to what avenues of history his students explore is complemented by his keen personal interest in his students as people. His example, guidance, and friendship have been invaluable.

The usual caveat about responsibility for errors applies here except for anything really egregious. In that case, I want the opportunity to reassess these acknowledgments.

This book is the product of a specific time and two particular places: New Jersey and Arizona. From the very beginning, there has been someone special, someone extraordinary, with whom I have shared equally wonderful and trying experiences. It all started with a simple question and took off in a direction neither one of us anticipated. For so many times, for so many reasons, and for so much more to come, this book is for Theresa.

T. C. J.

Contents

Contents

(Illustrations follow page 44)

Preface

Upon assuming the office of president in 1989, George Bush brought with him the personal conviction that he understood China and that he had special insights into its people, their society, and the nature of the monumental innovations he was sure were imminent there. In fact, a little over a month after his inauguration, he traveled to China on his first official visit abroad as president. He told Chinese television journalists that their country was one of the first to experience the new "winds of change" sweeping the world toward the twenty-first century. These transformational gusts, "sometimes gentle, sometimes strong and powerful," had caused China, "like a tree in a winter wind . . . to bend and adapt to new ways and new ideas and reform." This fresh spirit of hope augured well for Sino-American relations; the American people and their Chinese counterparts, moreover, enjoyed a fundamental value in common: a dedication to family. Over the years, this was what had bound the two nations together in spite of some rather trying episodes. "The Americans and Chinese share many things," he observed, "but perhaps none is more important than our strong sense of family."[1]

A month later, speaking with Amish and Mennonite leaders in Lancaster, Pennsylvania, Bush, in a rather offhand intejection, recalled the years when he and his wife, Barbara, had lived in China during the mid-1970's while he served as the American emissary to the People's Republic. At the time, the two had wondered about the condition of the Chinese family, fearing that there might have "been an erosion" of it under Communist rule. They were relieved, deeply moved even, to discover that its importance had persevered: "The family has never been weakened in China," the president commented, "it's always been strong. A totalitarian state can't stamp that out, and that faith can't be crushed by a state doctrine." During their most recent visit, an emotional moment had come when some members of the audience at one of the president's speaking engagements had suddenly yelled, "How is our sister, Dorothy?" The memory of the Bushes' daughter, who had been christened at the age of sixteen while they lived in China, was simply overwhelming. "I was all choked up," the president admitted; "every family has experienced something that sticks in their hearts." For George Bush, it was China.[2]

The events of June 3, 1989, quickly challenged the president's sentimental recollections as Chinese authorities ordered a military crackdown on protestors in Tiananmen Square. The resulting loss of life, bloodshed, and imprisonment of thousands of mostly student demonstrators led Bush to confess a "certain sense of personal disappointment" over the actions taken by the Chinese government.[3] At a news conference two days after the massacre, he indicated that the United States' response would be informed by his knowledge of Chinese history, his "keen personal interest in China," and his broader understanding of the Chinese people, which he asserted was rather substantial.[4] In the end, although the president condemned Beijing's actions publicly, he pursued a policy that was thought of as constructive engagement; this included sending a secret team consisting of National Security Adviser Brent Scowcroft and Deputy Secretary of State Lawrence Eagleburger to China a month after Tiananmen. The former, upon meeting with Deng Xiaoping, toasted the Chinese leader as "*A friend forever.*"[5] Further evidence of this policy came the following year when the Assistant Secretary for East Asian and Pacific Affairs, Richard Solomon, outlined the administration's thinking during congressional hearings on whether to renew China's most-favored-nation status. "I, for one, have faith in the dynamism of the marketplace, in the inexorable effect of economic modernization on social and political reform." He concluded by reminding the senators that they "should not underestimate the power of international commerce as a force for change. So long as China is engaged economically, the very forces for reform that erupted at Tiananmen will still be in play. China cannot sail against the winds of change."[6]

George Bush clearly wanted to be the one to steer those "winds of change"; he yearned to be there when that magical moment arrived, when China became the land of his dreams. His hopes were nothing new, however; in fact, the history of Sino-American relations contains a range of varied and long-standing cultural constructions on the American side, ranging from racism and xenophobia to naïveté, paternalism, and awe. That Bush subscribed to a combination of the last three is obvious, but understanding why he did so involves considering the ideas Americans have acquired about their role in world affairs.

Because images of China have largely come from Americans' assumptions about themselves and not from the reality of Chinese linguistic, historical, or cultural similarities, an intensive look at Chinese history cannot explain this phenomenon in and of itself. Instead, the history of China can best function as the background to this story. But just as with any painting, the background is an important part of the whole in how it serves to offset and highlight the events and characters in the foreground. Likewise, traditional diplomatic history cannot provide all the answers, though it can address some of the major issues relevant to this discussion. More germane is the observation made by the historian Amy Kaplan, "A political or economic process abroad is inseparable from the social relations and cultural discourses of race, gender, ethnicity, and class at home."[7] By bringing together cultural and diplomatic histories and by focusing on the mass media and popular culture within the United States as well as on the work of certain Chinese relief agencies, which depended on the help of domestic contributors, it becomes clear how and in what way the cultural and political context coincided with specific administrations' goals in certain episodes, and, in other instances, limited the options open to foreign policy makers, but in either case had a significant impact upon the policies desired versus those actually pursued.[8]

Almost fifty years before President Bush spoke about his aspirations for China, another influential American expressed many of the same ideas. Best known as the founder and chief editor of *Time*, *Life*, and *Fortune* magazines, Henry R. Luce is also remembered for articulating and encouraging much of the prevailing sentiment toward China during the 1930's and 1940's. Bush talked about "winds of change"; Luce saw a wave of western Christianity, political democracy, and economic capitalism about to surge through China. Bush called for a "New World Order" at the end of the Cold War; Luce, in a 1941 essay in *Life*, anticipated an "American Century," during which the American people would have to accept their broader obligations. Luce's essay outlined an overall structure for international affairs that had as its foundation a world in which the United States was the new Middle Kingdom: "America as the dynamic center of ever-widening spheres of enterprise, America as the training center of skilled servants of mankind, America as the Good Samaritan, really believing again that it is more blessed to give than to receive, and America as the powerhouse of the ideals of Freedom and Justice."[9] America would function as benevolent hegemon, or paternal authority, acting under the presumption that it alone knew what was best for other nations.

Luce occupied a crucial position in twentieth-century American society by virtue of the media power he wielded in the age before television. Important as he was for journalism and the mass media, however, he has been largely neglected in studies of the nation's foreign policy.[10] By 1939, Luce's multimedia empire reached millions of Americans every week. Later, when Time Inc. launched overseas editions of *Time* and *Life*, his message was received by millions more outside the United States. With publishing success and the subsequent ventures into radio and newsreel production came the tremendous power of determining what information people received. This was particularly true of *Life*. Its revolutionary format, using photographs to convey impressions, tell stories, and provide simplistic analyses of complicated events, served Luce's purposes well. As a result, his journalistic itinerary often influenced the opinions and attitudes people developed about the subjects covered by his media. Like most politicians, Luce had an agenda; more importantly, he had the substantial means with which to promote it.

Luce was not the only person to have such optimism about China's future. Missionaries, writers, politicians, as well as many ordinary citizens, became enthralled by the same image of a China that reflected American ideals. Pearl Buck, Franklin D. Roosevelt, Wendell Willkie, Walter Judd, Joseph Stilwell, Claire Chennault, Albert Wedemeyer, among many other prominent literary, political, military, and business leaders, plus the thousands who worked for the various philanthropic, political, educational, and cultural organizations, sought to bring about that same China. Thus, regardless of how important he was for the creation and perpetuation of this manner of thinking, Luce is only a convenient lens through which it can be discerned.

The earlier notion of an American Century for China came about through the intersection of two developments. The first was the liberal internationalism embodied in the Open Door principle enunciated by Secretary of State John Hay at the turn of the century. The historian Emily Rosenberg, in her outline of the nature of America's expansion from the 1890's until the end of World War II, applies the

term "liberal-developmentalism" to the extension of American commerce and culture abroad, part of which involved the "belief that
other nations could and should replicate America's own develop-
mental experience": America's economic and social history could
serve as a universal model for the rest of the world, as could its popular culture and political ideology, making the entire national experience an appropriate model for other countries. Even William Appleman Williams, in his revisionist study of American foreign policy,
lists this phenomenon as one of the guiding principles of America's
approach to international relations: namely, "the idea . . . that other
people cannot *really* solve their problems and improve their lives unless they go about it in the same way as the United States."[11]

The second, as James Guimond observes in his study American
photography, was the conservative populism of the 1930's and 1940's,
when the conventional sentiment was expressed in a "willingness to
see ordinary Americans and their middle-class institutions and culture in such a positive way." Guimond notes, in discussing a *Life* article on a typical Saturday night in Franklin, Indiana, "What *Life's*
readers wanted, it seemed, was a stereotyped village that confirmed
their nostalgic beliefs about small towns in which no one is bored,
poor, or lonely."[12] Not only did the coverage of domestic issues reflect
this kind of thinking, but the attention accorded international stories
did too, especially those relating to China.

The writer Graham Peck once commented on the nature of American projections onto other peoples by warning: "American anthro-
pomorphism . . . is one of our gravest handicaps in foreign affairs. As
a nation we seem over-eager to attribute our own character to other
nations."[13] What he described can be termed "America-morphism" as
much as anything else, and from an analytical standpoint, better still
are the fundamental assumptions inherent in a paternalistic outlook.
Paternalism, and all it implies about treating adults as children, lies
at the root of the American attitude toward not only China but a good
many other nations, particularly in Asia. Regarding nations as less-
than-sovereign entities and looking upon other peoples as childlike
often provides a convenient rationale for policies that necessitate involvement or interference in the affairs of another nation. Ostensibly,
under the guise of "benevolent" intentions, these actions are taken
for the good of the recipient.[14] Paternalism, evoking as it does familial
relations, most notably those between father and child, is especially
suitable when applied to an earlier era in the twentieth century, when
the United States tried to assume the role of a father, implicitly, and
sometimes explicitly, casting China as a child. Although not unfa-

miliar in United States national attitudes toward other Asian nations, this thinking toward China has been unique in its longevity
and pervasiveness.[15]

Growing out of the varied circumstances, exigencies, and necessi-
ties of the 1930's and 1940's, a paternalistic outlook brought a
missionary-conversion ethos together with a secular sense of national benevolence. Americans came to profess faith in a China developing along the path blazed by their nation. The Chinese people
appeared willing and eager to adopt Protestant religion and democratic political ideology, especially under the guidance of their nominal leader, Chiang Kai-shek. After 1931, Chiang's popularly accepted
image in the United States became one of a valiant, heroic Christian
ready to lead his people into an American-style future. An economic
angle to the relationship promised an enormously profitable trading
connection, one guaranteed by China's massive population. These
ideas further reinforced what Americans wanted to believe about
themselves; thus they endured. The idea that China could be changed
also carried with it the assumption that China should be changed
(and vice versa).[16]

But rather than simply being foisted onto an unsuspecting public
by a manipulative media in collusion with vested interests, these notions were offered, received, and more commonly accepted as a partial solution to existing problems. In seeking to change China
through the application of social and political structures abroad,
Americans tried to reassure themselves of their uniqueness and special place in history—assumptions that were brought under question
by the Great Depression and World War II. To see China with the eye
of paternalism was to see the United States as the developmentally
more advanced nation, offering its knowledge and experience to a
grateful recipient, all supposedly in a spirit of genuine altruism.

The effort to categorize the Chinese people as enthusiastically
malleable reinforced the domestic trend toward conservative populism in a number of other important respects. The hierarchical clas-
sification of races played a role in this development, and so did constructions of gender roles, in that both strengthened the status quo
instead of promoting social change. Amy Kaplan has argued that placing imperialism in the foreground of American culture "shows how
putatively domestic conflicts are not simply contained at home but
how they both emerge in response to international struggles and spill
over national boundaries to be reenacted, challenged, or trans-
formed."[17] The broader cultural constructions of China were part of
the process Kaplan describes. In attempting to see themselves in a fa-

vorable light through the projection of idealized images about their own characteristics, attributes, and habits onto the Chinese, Americans were gazing at China as if it were a mirror, "an occasion for striking self-adoring poses," as one commentator later put it.[18]

Images, conceptions, and cultural constructions here involve the public discourse over United States' relations with China; they include the beliefs, emotions, stereotypes, opinions, mental pictures, and perhaps most importantly, the hopes that were all a part of the intracultural dynamics of the popular thinking about China. This phenomenon also entailed the use of facile comparisons to understand China, its people, and their history through the prism of American examples and experiences. To encourage this perception, media accounts of foreign events used simplistic analogies and distorted imagery, something that persists to this day. On the relevance of this for policymaking, one sociologist has argued, "Publicly available meanings facilitate certain patterns of action, making them readily available, while discouraging others."[19]

Many cultural historians contend that the relationship between consciously promoted public images and their impact remains elusive. In his extensive study of advertising and American society from 1920 to 1940, for example, Roland Marchand concedes, "I cannot prove conclusively that the American people absorbed the values and ideas of the ads, nor that consumers wielded the power to ensure that the ads would mirror their lives," but he insists that the advertisements reflected not reality, but rather a distortion of it.[20] Much the same holds true here. There is no one-to-one relationship whereby the propagation of a specific image produced a set of quantifiable results. The correlation between culture and policymaking is not that simple. But any examination of Sino-American relations must take the media into account, for it is there that much of the public debate has unfolded. Two sociologists have even argued that "media discourse dominates the larger issue culture, both reflecting it *and* contributing to its creation."[21]

In that respect, it is fair to say that not only did Henry Luce, through his media empire, influence the way in which many Americans came to view China, but his consistent efforts, combined with those of others, certainly reflected many of the ideas Americans wanted to hold about China, regardless of their accuracy. In speaking to the idea of public discourse, one historian has indicated that "interests, power and values play themselves out on a single, level field of reality, the conceptual field of language."[22] Public language, both printed and spoken, whether attributable to government officials, missionaries, business executives, newspaper reporters, or ordinary citizens, constitutes an important realm for determining the various assumptions that shaped Americans' thinking about China. And for that rhetoric to strike a responsive chord, the historian Michael Hunt has written that it "must draw on values and concerns widely shared and easily understood by its audience."[23]

Henry Luce knew that as well as anyone. His efforts were directed to the larger hope of a friendly China intent on adopting American ways. This message found resonance within the general population because of what it said about the American people and how it reflected what they wanted to believe about themselves. At its most intense, this phenomenon spanned only eighteen years. It began with three events in 1931—Chiang Kai-shek's conversion to Christianity, the publication of Pearl Buck's novel *The Good Earth*, and the Japanese invasion of Manchuria—and ended rather abruptly in 1949 when the Chinese Communists came to power. Still, it can be considered an American Century of sorts because it was a period distinctly marked by a particular way of looking at China, Asia—the entire world for that matter—that asked Americans to accept their global, paternal responsibilities. When that reflexive image was shattered by events in China over which the United States had no control, the reaction was highly emotional, and seriously damaging both professionally and personally for those caught in the cross-currents of American national myths and Chinese historical realities. The United States took nearly thirty years to reestablish official relations with China after the 1949 revolution. To understand the depth of the emotions that made that lengthy denial possible, to comprehend the manner in which normalization came about, and to gauge the present direction Sino-American relations are apparently taking, it is first necessary to look at the images that once dominated the American way of thinking about China and have now, it appears, gained currency once again.

AMERICAN IMAGES

OF CHINA

1931-1949

Missionaries and the Creation of American Perceptions of China, 1890-1931

Missionaries are the pioneers of trade and commerce. Civilization, learning, instruction breed new wants which commerce supplies.
— Charles Denby to Secretary of State Gresham, 1895

Religion is the most fundamental thing in civilization.
— John R. Mott, "Urgency and Crisis in the Far East," 1908

One would be justified in concluding that apparently China exists for the missionary, rather than the missionary for China.
— Walter Judd to William Strong, 1927

From the last decade of the nineteenth century until 1931, American national attitudes toward China were based upon two powerful but contradictory impulses. The first centered around what J. A. Hobson called God and Mammon: "The cooperation of economics and religion." China appealed to America's evangelical sense of enlightenment and regeneration, that "holy kind of violence," as the Puritan Thomas Hooker called it in referring to the point where God's infinite perfection intersected with man's manifest imperfection and, in the process, lifted the individual from a degraded condition to one of exaltation. A similar but secular variation of this phenomenon was at work with respect to national attitudes toward China. Americans, so it was assumed, would bring their infinite national goodness and virtue—their Christian dedication and sense of national mission—to the imperfect lives of the millions of Chinese. One Presbyterian missionary wrote, "Christian Civilization will bring to China a truer conception of the nature of man, a better understanding of his relations and duties, of his dignity and destiny."[1] The American Minister in Peking, Charles Denby, articulated much the same notion, in a cruder fashion, in 1895: "The educated Chinaman, who speaks English, becomes a new man; he commences to think."[2] However expressed, the sentiment was the same: the United States would give China the opportunity to remake itself in America's spiritual, political, and cultural image. This determined strand of Protestant Christianity, the God Hobson mentioned, moved many missionaries to travel to China.

The same idea also excited enormous economic prospects of the China market. China was a distant, mysterious but ultimately enticing land, beckoning to Americans with the potential wealth of Asia, the Mammon part of Hobson's dichotomy. American industrialists, manufacturers, and investors saw a vast opportunity to absorb the nation's rapidly increasing productive capacity of the late nineteenth century. And government leaders, fearful that the prolonged economic woes of the 1890's might foment a social revolution at home, saw at least a partial solution to their economic, and ultimately political, problems.[3] Here the forces of Mammon evidenced themselves most obviously in Secretary of State John Hay's Open Door notes. Hay's fear that the Europeans were carving up the China pie before the United States could get a slice led him to issue his notes in 1899 and 1900. Although America did not have the military power to enforce his diplomatic caveat, he understood that the nation's new industrial base gave it the means to compete favorably with the Europeans if given the chance.[4]

On a much different level, but one no less important, the second impulse in American conceptions of China was a direct contradiction to the previous enticement of spiritual and economic salvation. This impulse centered around the virulent racism that led to exclusionary legislation and kept most Chinese from entering the United States after 1882. Many Americans looked upon the Chinese, especially the laboring class, as members of a subhuman race that threatened to undermine their way of life. The fear of a Yellow Peril gripped them with a nebulous, but powerful, dread of uncontrolled Asian expansion. Labor leaders who favored developing trade with China to protect American jobs were opposed to having Chinese emigrate to the United States and threaten to take away those same jobs.[5] Pressures upon western state governments, especially in California, finally led to the passage of a series of Chinese exclusion laws, which remained in effect until 1943.[6] American perceptions of China thus ran the gamut from Christian paternalism, to economic aspirations, and finally to racist preconceptions, in short, a mélange of often contradictory attitudes, expectations, and hopes. Entreating China on the one hand and keeping the Chinese out of the United States on the other underscored the marked contrasts between the pressures for international expansion versus the domestic forces of racism and xenophobia. In the end, the two extremes were not necessarily exclusive; rather, they tended to reinforce each other.

The conspicuous incongruity between these two perspectives essentially derived from the American sense of national and cultural paternalism, which centered around the simple but fundamental assumption that the Chinese people wanted (or at least should have aspired) to become more like Americans. Starting with Christianity, Americans sought to bring the light of heaven to the heathens of Asia; from there, democracy quite naturally followed. "The missionary movement," one historian has commented, "was democracy at work."[7] From a religious conversion to Christ came the ability to comprehend and enjoy the democratic way of life. That, in turn, invariably led to a demand for American agricultural, industrial, and manufactured products, until the Chinese were destined to become just like Americans. Charles Denby, writing Secretary of State Gresham in 1895, observed that missionaries played a crucial role in the development of overseas trade, but humanity had not "devised any better . . . engine or means for civilizing savage peoples as proselytism to Christianity."[8] He was not alone in his assessment. Enthusiastic American missionaries saw China as a land replete with a population ready for conversion to Christianity and Western ideals. Because that vision meant that the Chinese people would become active consumers of American products, business leaders and politicians could join missionaries in looking upon the Asian nation with the same sense of promise.

Part of the initial evangelical enthusiasm for China developed from the religious revivals held by Dwight L. Moody during the latter half of the 1880's. One meeting in Northfield, Massachusetts, became famous for the group that came out of it. The Student Volunteer Movement for Foreign Missions (SVM), an offshoot of the Young Men's Christian Association, devoted itself to spreading the Christian gospel to the less fortunate peoples around the world. The members went forth brimming with the confidence and optimism that they could evangelize the entire world in one generation—and certainly China, where, as one missionary noted, a million Chinese died every month without the benefit of Christ. One member of the SVM, Horace Pitkin, remarked, "China was the goal, the lodestar, the great magnet that drew us all in those days."[9] Many of the volunteers were women who felt an obligation to serve.[10] This kind of dedication led Pitkin and his missionary friends Sherwood Eddy and Henry W. Luce to jog an additional mile, exhorting themselves to go the extra distance

with the chant, "This will carry us another mile in China." These
three American Protestant missionaries epitomized the zeal of those
who set out with the idea of creating a new China based upon the
Western, Christian model. Although Pitkin, Eddy, and Luce never accomplished their ambitious goal of evangelizing the entire world,
they, along with others like them, did succeed in creating lasting
impressions of China in the United States.

The Presbyterianism of Henry Winters Luce, in particular, invig-
orated him with a sense of national and religious purpose. These two
forces—his love for his country and his religious mission—came together and formed the core of his outlook on the world. In a letter he
wrote to a friend while traveling through Texas in 1895, he exclaimed,
"This is a great country out here—one feels like renewing his grip on
God about every five minutes."[11]

The elder Luce passed along these ideas to his son, Henry Robinson
Luce, and continued to do so even after Henry R. had left China to
attend Hotchkiss at the age of fourteen. In one letter dated November
1914, the father wrote to his son that the recent outbreak of war in
Europe signaled not that Christianity had failed Europe, "only [that]
Europe has failed to be Christian." He later indicated that Jesus was
a man "ahead of his own time . . . ahead of our time." Christ's teachings were best understood not within the context of an era long past
but instead for what they truly were: "permanent, fundamental, re-
alizable."[12]

Missionaries like Henry W. Luce brought with them a number of
preconceptions and expectations that shaped the manner in which
they viewed not only the Chinese but also their own mission. The historian Frederick Jackson Turner expressed much of the growing national sentiment in 1893 by observing that the American frontier was
closed. But many American missionaries saw themselves as a natural
part of the nation's continued westward expansion, beyond the Pacific. China was part of the new frontier.[13] One missionary to China,
in an attempt to transmit some of his nation's frontier heritage to his
children, constructed a log cabin made out of bamboo so that they
could experience their nation's dynamic past in spite of being raised
thousands of miles away from America.[14]

At the same time, however, many missionaries to China recognized its history as a great civilization. Its huge population offered
enormous potential. One woman expressed her aspirations in a pamphlet in which she argued that of all the heathen nations of the world,
China stood first in line because of the immense need of its people

and because of its "leading position in the scale of nations." The writer, Geraldine Guiness, added that recent developments as of 1890—namely, the distribution of over half a million Bibles, Testaments, and Scriptures in the last six months—appeared to augur well for the promise of a Christian tidal wave sweeping over China.[15]

Eighteen years later, John R. Mott, one of the original leaders of the Student Volunteer Movement and subsequently a high-ranking member of the YMCA, observed to his peers who were meeting in Liverpool, England, that China was "in the midst of an intellectual revolution." The opportunity this profound change presented for Christian missionaries was astounding. The existing fluid conditions, he suggested, allowed Christianity the chance to set the course for China for centuries to come: "May God help us to infuse China with Christian thought, Christian spirit, Christian influence?" The possibilities were there, and a Christian education promised to be one of the keys toward realizing their goals.[16]

In addition to the change missionaries tried to bring about within China, their experiences had a significant impact upon their own children. Many "mishkids," as they were often called, remembered their days growing up in China with fondness. Pearl Buck, whose fiction played an important role in boosting Americans' romantic notions about China during the 1930's, remembered her days growing up there with a great deal of tenderness and affection.[17] Henry R. Luce, who grew up in Qingdao, recalled of that city, "There was one department store, wonderfully cool in summer, full of many of the wondrous things Americans could read about in the Sears Roebuck catalogue, and rich with the smell of newly opened boxes." It was "a perfectly extraordinary city," he wrote; "There is just nothing to compare it with . . . [where] the delicately curving waves kissed the silken shore. This was Tsingtao until 1914."[18] Another missionary daughter, equally nostalgic, described the Chinese countryside of her childhood: "There is no place more peaceful than a Chinese valley on a summer's evening. . . . When each mountain like a shaggy animal lies with outstretched head on the flank of the next, and when the softest of sunset light slants down to the light green of the valley floor, one is charmed into tranquillity."[19]

But for both Luce and Buck, the way in which they developed ideas about the United States was important. Buck recounted how her parents told her wonderful stories about an idealized America, a "dreamworld, fantastically beautiful, inhabited by a people . . . entirely good, a land indeed from which all blessings followed":

While I was a child my [parents] regaled me with memories of quiet village streets, large houses set far back in trees and lawns, decent folk walking to church on Sundays to worship God in beautiful old churches, law-abiding men and women, children who obeyed their parents and learned their lessons in school. Doctors cured the few sick folk, or sent them to wonderfully clean hospitals, and certainly no one had cholera or dysentery or typhus or died of bubonic plague. Neither were there lepers to be seen lounging along the streets intimidating the pedestrians and shopkeepers, and beggars there were none.[20]

Henry R. Luce's mother read to him from the Bible and from a children's history of the United States, and his father told him stories about his own favorite Americans, particularly Theodore Roosevelt.[21] Indeed, Luce later came to espouse the same kind of muscular Christianity usually associated with TR. One historian has asserted that Luce's love of America was "one of the many signs of his father's influence."[22] But Luce, like Pearl Buck, grew up with an idealized view of a perfect America: "I had no experience of evil in terms of Americans. . . . Put along with that [the] idea that America was a wonderful country, with opportunity and freedom and justice for all, and you not only get an idealistic, but a romantic view—a profoundly false romantic view."[23] This Christianized, idealized notion of America apparently inspired the missionaries and others caught up in this way of thinking to see in the crowded and often desperate circumstances of China only boundless opportunity. Even in the face of rapidly changing conditions there, they persisted in their belief that China would be able to fulfill their dreams of success on a scale unmatched anywhere else in the world.

Of the enormous changes that occurred in China between the 1890's and the 1920's, the most important was the final collapse of the Qing dynasty in 1911. During the 1920's and out of the conditions of the internecine politics of the warlord era in Chinese history, two parties arose to struggle for the control of the nation for the next thirty years: the Guomindang (National People's Party) and the Chinese Communist Party (CCP). For American missionaries, the rise of Chinese nationalism during the 1920's generally took an anti-Christian tone. Christianity was associated with Western domination through such devices as the unequal treaties and foreign concessions. The missionary movement in the United States felt the impact of events not only abroad but also at home. Fewer Americans responded to the evangelical call. In 1920, some 1,731 new missionaries set sail for foreign nations in an attempt to bring Christianity to the heathens, and 2,783 members of the Student Volunteer Movement signed the organization's pledge. By 1927 the number of missionaries leaving the country had dropped to 558, and a year later, only 252 members signed the Student Volunteer Pledge. Moreover, by 1927, evangelizing the world had in one generation fallen to one of the three least important reasons for becoming a missionary.[24]

There was still the call of social progress, however, and if converting Chinese to Christ now seemed less important than before, at least bringing improved agricultural methods, medical techniques, and education could stimulate the same kind of missionary interest.[25] But the switch had its costs. As one of the principal organizations involved in this change from evangelizing to improving living conditions, the YMCA found negotiating this hazardous path very tricky. One historian has noted, "As long as the Y spread American ways, it thrived because of donor contributions." When the organization changed its focus, it found Americans unwilling to fund the new programs.[26] The late 1920's therefore constituted a difficult period for American missionaries, and a transitional one too, domestically as well as in China.

In spite of these apparent setbacks, many missionaries were still optimistic. The hostile environment created by nascent Chinese nationalism, and an increasing harassment of the missionary community, failed to discourage the Reverend William R. Johnson, for example. Johnson, a Methodist missionary who lived in China from 1906 until 1942, found cause for hope in the Chinese Nationalists. Writing to a friend late in 1927, he insisted that Protestantism remained "favorable to the chief ideals of the Nationalists—freedom of conscience, democracy and national aspirations viz-a-viz the Powers." He added confidently, "China sees more clearly than ever who her friends are." The Nationalists were much more promising than the news reports had indicated, he insisted; moreover, Chinese public opinion had never been so unified. Because Protestant missionaries had served as such a positive force for independence, he predicted they would soon profit handsomely from their past efforts.[27]

Not all missionaries agreed, although their reasons did not reflect on the Chinese people. These missionaries criticized Johnson's sort of optimism by saying that certain brethren were not developing themselves to making conditions better for the sake of the Chinese but were more concerned with their own comfort and safety than with carrying out the higher mission ordained to them by God. Walter H. Judd, a medical missionary and one-time chairman of the National Student Council of the SVM—and a man later described by one historian as the American most responsible for building an American constituency for Chiang Kai-shek through his activities as a member of Congress—said that he had traveled to China with the intention of helping the Middle Kingdom turn toward the "direction of cooperation and peace."[28] But in 1927, in a nineteen-page single-spaced letter to the Reverend William Strong in Boston, Judd offered a scathing critique on the state of American Protestant missionary activity.

Judd expressed his severe disappointment over the "smug complacency" that had infected the missionary community. He enumerated the serious mistakes that its members had been making for decades, among them the proclivity to live in elaborate brick compounds, which he thought not only was inconsistent with the missionary purpose but also had the effect of severing ties with the Chinese community. Too many American missionaries were satisfied with preaching the Christian gospel during "office hours," and instead of living among the people they were supposedly saving, they constructed "a miniature home land," a "little America" in which their immediate and overriding loyalties were only to themselves and to those of their "own blood, language, flag, and culture."[29]

Judd believed that the recent harassment of missionaries had been carefully planned to scare as many Americans as possible into leaving the country. He deplored the cowardice and rationalizations that accompanied the exodus, and he had no patience with missionaries who felt betrayed by the Chinese, for whom, they argued, they had selflessly served for so long. How, he asked, could anyone reasonably expect the Chinese to possess any sense of loyalty toward a group of people who, more than anything else, had tried to "sow superiority complexes, special privileges, patronizing philanthropy, foreign concessions, gunboats, foreign flags on missions and Chinese churches, etc. over a period of thirty-five years?"[30] Judd concluded that Protestant missionaries had fallen well short of their professed reasons for traveling to and remaining in China. They had succumbed to preserving their comfortable life, and the moment any discomfort appeared, either mental or physical, they immediately packed up in a rush and fled for protection under a foreign flag.

Even though some missionaries were staying on in China, Judd insisted that they were doing so more for themselves than for the Chinese. Holed up in their brick compounds, refusing to delegate any authority to their Chinese disciples, intent on living the sort of life they had left behind in the United States, American Protestant missionaries had failed. Their Catholic counterparts, Judd argued, had achieved a far greater degree of success, partly because the Catholic priests' vow of celibacy prepared them for the rigors of China's rural life and also prevented them from worrying about the safety and comfort of their families. Although Judd himself understood how the pull of providing for one's family could compromise the missionary's program—he had experienced it too, he conceded—the Protestant missionaries would continue to fail to make greater progress without the same sense of commitment as the Catholics. Judd's later assessment of the Guomindang's collapse in the 1940's reflected the same critical view of the Americans' lack of commitment. Only when Americans—and Protestant missionaries especially—dedicated themselves more vigorously to the cause of China could the situation be reversed.

Essentially, Judd was disappointed that the Americans had not made the most of their opportunities: there was too big a gap between the missionaries' intentions and what they had actually done to bring changes in China. Ironically, the missionaries were most effective at home. In fact, two secretaries of state provide some evidence to support the idea that the activities of the missionaries fostered the original American sense of sentimentality and romanticism about China.

Dean Acheson, secretary of state under President Harry Truman, described the enthusiasm with which Americans in the early part of the century sought to help China. "Hardly a town in our land was without its society to collect funds and clothing for Chinese missions, to worry about those who labored in distant, dangerous, and exotic vineyards of the Lord, and to hear the missionaries' inspiring reports." Acheson explicitly made the connection between America's economic interests in China, the clipper ships "racing to the Orient . . . intent upon the profits of the China trade," and the pattern of missionary intentions "to educate the minds and heal the bodies as well as save the souls of the heathen Chinese."[31] And Acheson's successor, John Foster Dulles, in a speech at the twenty-fifth anniversary dinner of the China Institute in America in 1951, observed that sentiment "rather than materialism [had been] . . . the essence of the relationship of the American people with the Chinese people." Contacts between Americans and Chinese had been largely "cultural and spiritual, notably through missionaries."[32]

God and Mammon, then, under paternalistic language and as part of a liberal-developmentalist ideology, forged the basic premise for American attitudes toward China. America would help China by bringing it into the modern world, which, of course, would be an "American Century." Whether or not Acheson and Dulles were in full sympathy with the pattern of missionary intentions "to educate minds" and the simultaneous zeal of businessmen intent upon the China trade, they recognized the strength of the God-Mammon dichotomy. And as public figures, they seemed to verify the long-standing American view of China as a country that needed America's help.

But if neither Acheson nor Dulles believed in the simplicity of the China-American relationship, there were many others, not just missionaries, who did, and they made it their set task to impress a new generation of Americans with their views. One of the most successful in this endeavor was the son of Henry W. Luce. Henry R. Luce, like his father, whose primary success as a missionary came through his ability to raise money, found that he, too, had a talent for business. But unlike his father, the younger Luce's accomplishments came on a much grander scale in the secular world: instead of religion, journalism became his missionary work.[33] His importance in the Christian conception of China came about because he achieved such notoriety as a businessman in the field of mass media. And Luce did more than make money. As one of his employees said of him, "he was the towering editorial genius" of the twentieth century, an arguable assessment to be sure, but one not without considerable support.[34]

Protestant missionaries had reached out to Americans through the slow process of preaching at Sunday gatherings over and over in their efforts to raise money for the cause of China. But with one issue of *Life* in the 1940's, Henry R. Luce reached more Americans than missionaries had spoken to in the previous half-century. And it was Henry R. Luce's steadfast belief in the eventual creation of a Christian, democratic China that combined with his business acumen and journalistic savvy to forge a focused and ultimately influential conception of what China represented to the United States.

Henry Luce and the Rise of Time Inc.

I have read and listened and listened and read and nothing has helped me as much as Mr. Luce's words.
— Allen Alderson to President Franklin Roosevelt, February 1941

Henry Luce took his responsibility as a journalist and publisher seriously, but he also championed a decidedly pro-American perspective. From his point of view, what was best for the United States was more important than any sort of traditional journalistic impartiality. A frequent quip made about Luce was that he believed in God, the United States, and the Republican Party, though not necessarily in that order. More to the point, Luce believed that God had chosen the United States, of all nations of the world, for a special mission because Americans were inherently a deeply religious and virtuous people who were supremely positioned to carry out God's work on earth. He believed that his duty as a publisher was to further those ends that naturally resulted from America's unique moral and religious qualifications. He was a Republican because, naturally, God favored a capitalist, free enterprise system. He even went so far as to suggest, in a vein reminiscent of Alexander Hamilton, that America needed a ruling aristocracy. Since the country did not have the natural hierarchy of a European class society, America should look to its business leaders to fill the position. Coming immediately after the stock market crash of 1929, Luce's proposal failed to arouse much popular support.

At the same time, however, Luce understood what the majority of Americans wanted to read. His persistent curiosity about every subject imaginable served him well as a publisher. And along with his shrewd sense of mass taste he had an evangelical sense of mission. Instead of simply reporting events, he wanted to shape public opinion. Like the preacher who seeks to save the unrepentant, Luce tried

to fulfill his personal destiny of converting Americans to his understanding of the United States. Part of that conception included viewing foreign relations through the glass of American exceptionalism.
The United States had a mission, and Henry Luce was determined to
use his capabilities to bring about the realization of that national purpose.

In his ideas of how this sense of mission related to China, Luce
picked up where others, like his father, had left off. He took their message and propagated it to more people, more consistently, and over a
longer period than Horace Pitkin, Sherwood Eddy, or John Mott could
have ever dreamed possible. As the most vocal salesman of an Americanized China, Henry Luce occupied a key position in the unfolding
story during the 1930's and 1940's. But another aspect to this devel-
opmental process was the willingness displayed by Americans to accept a sentimental and paternalistic rendering of China. As two sociologists have observed, "Packages succeed in media discourse
through a combination of cultural resonances, sponsor activities, and
a successful fit with media norms and practices." As the principal
champion of a romanticized China, Luce managed to tap into long-
standing cultural and historical symbols, apply them to China, and
project them to millions of Americans. The relationship between the
media and their audience is a symbiotic one, further complicated by
the fact that many "journalists straddle the boundary between producers and consumers of meaning."[1] Luce straddled that and many
other fences in his vigorous efforts to make available public meanings
and constructions of China. Their impact became increasingly obvious as he enjoyed phenomenal success in the field of corporate journalism.

The success that Time Inc. achieved in presenting its ideas about
China paralleled the company's remarkable growth during the latter
half of the 1930's. In 1937, despite the continuing economic depression, Luce's adventures in journalism—print, radio, and newsreel—
continued to expand and earn enormous profits. The circulation of
Time (founded in 1923) had risen from 450,000 in 1935 to over
600,000 in 1937. *Fortune*, directed to a more specialized readership,
passed the 100,000 mark in 1937. It was Luce's new photo-
journalistic magazine, *Life*, however, that catapulted his corporation
into a media empire. The first issue appeared late in 1936, and by
1941, the three magazines had a staggering 3.8 million subscribers.
Life's immediate success—so huge and unexpected that Time Inc.

initially lost a substantial sum of money—propelled Luce into the dominant position in American journalism for the next two decades.[2]

Henry Luce, Harry to almost everyone who knew him, once said that since he had invented the newsmagazine, he could dictate its form. For *Time*, his concept was a magazine that appeared to be composed by one person, "Not any one man," he remarked in a letter to *Fortune* editor Dwight Macdonald in 1934, "but a sort of superman—the sum total of the very few men . . . who really 'make it.'"[3] Longtime editor Thomas Matthews observed, "Every press undertaking has a personality."[4] At Time Inc., Luce's personality overshadowed all else and gave the journalistic endeavor cohesion and direction. Luce himself once said, "Most of what I know . . . and much of what I think has been expressed in some millions of words in Time, Life, [and] Fortune."[5] Not that individuality, independence, and imagination could not contribute to the collective superman. On the contrary, Luce insisted that these very characteristics were central to the success of *Time* and to the same extent *Fortune*. Strong, independent thinking was virtually a prerequisite to working at Time Inc. because of the strains and demands of group journalism. I. Van Meter, an editor's assistant, echoed those thoughts in his reply to some questions sent in by a *Time* reader in 1937: "We think the jobs *Time* and *Fortune* do are best done by a group with all the checks and balances that group journalism implies." He added that the group journalism approach enabled *Time* and *Fortune* to present "as nearly as possible a completely objective picture of the world in which we life."[6] Time Inc. repeatedly stressed its commitment to accuracy, fairness, and objectivity: the company's primary purpose was to achieve with each issue of *Time* and *Fortune* (and later *Life*) a precise and reliable picture of international and domestic news. One letter to subscribers stated that, in ninety minutes, *Time* "gives you all of the news—curt, clear, complete."[7]

For its fifteenth anniversary in 1938, *Time* heralded its latest effort to expand its news coverage and to refine its already demanding standards of excellence in the collection of facts: "*Time* now undertakes to perfect the newsmagazine service so minutely, so jealously, *that every single department of Time can stand inspection under the expert's microscope.*" In addition to a superb news-gathering organization, *Time*, the letter said, now possessed one of the world's great "news-verifying systems."[8] The company rededicated itself to achieving unprecedented accuracy with a rigorous set of new standards.

When it expanded into radio and newsreel production in the 1930's,

Time Inc. set itself even more ambitious goals. *"We hope to take you on stage for some of the greatest moments of history,"* "The March of Time" radio program announced in 1941, and *"let you feel the news as an unforgettable experience in your own life."* The radio program allowed Americans to "live the great events of the year as a memorable personal experience," and it promised to place its listeners at the scene, so that every one of them had *"a personal* sense" of what it was like to be on Crete during the Nazi invasion, for example, "amid the terrific uproar of falling bombs and chattering archies."[9]

With assurances of accuracy and objectivity, not to mention drama, Time Inc. gave the impression that its magazines, its radio program, and its newsreel provided a complete, unbiased picture of the important developments in the United States and around the world. How could anybody question this professed goal of reporting the facts so accurately and objectively?

For all this apparent concern and dedication to reporting the facts, Luce himself freely admitted that his magazines carried biases, obviously reflecting his own opinions. But in his way of thinking, the bias was there for the benefit of the readers. "Impartiality," he once said, was "often an impediment to the truth." Thus *Time's* responsibility lay not so much in assembling the facts as in conveying "the truth as [*Time* saw] it."[10] Simply collecting and arranging facts would be meaningless without the proper moral framework. In other words, the important thing was "having correct value judgments."[11] But Luce's pronouncements about the importance of partiality, as derived through proper moral training, were not echoed in advertisements for his magazines. On the contrary, *Time, Life,* and *Fortune* continued to insist upon their dedication to reporting the facts objectively.

Luce's approach to the world of journalism was not universally acclaimed, not even by staff members and certainly not by many of those who were the subjects of articles in *Time, Life,* and *Fortune.* Many of the latter complained of biases, especially when something written about them ran against their interests or portrayed them in a less than favorable light. Some *Time* staff writers raised issues of fairness and accuracy while they still worked for the company, or else they waited until after they had left. Former *Fortune* editor Dwight Macdonald's three-part series on Time Inc.'s news coverage, published in the *Nation* in May 1937, detailed what he considered the obvious biases of Luce's magazines and the way in which they served to mislead readers.

Macdonald had tried to bring to Luce's attention the problems he saw in *Time's* slanted coverage of the news in 1936, while he was still an editor of *Fortune* and a respected longtime employee of Time Inc. "For some time," he began his letter to Luce in 1936, "I have felt that *Time* was not as journalistically impartial as it might be, that it has a bias toward the right." His own political leanings tilted toward the left, he admitted, but he did not suggest that *Time* should switch to suit his affiliation; he only wanted *Time* to strive to be "a truly objective and impartial magazine." The magazine's reputation, its "greatest journalistic asset for fairly reporting both sides of a question," would be jeopardized should such a bias become institutionalized. He was not alone in his concerns. Three other Time Inc. editors, Eric Hodgins, Wilder Hobson, and Archibald MacLeish, wrote in support of the letter.[12]

To prove his point, Macdonald included three articles from recent issues of *Time*, which he analyzed in detail, pointing out where and how he thought there was partiality. "*Time*," he concluded, "has developed a technique of implying things by shrewdly chosen adjectives and neatly turned phrases." He had had a brief tenure at *Time* and knew the technique that a writer was trained in "to put a prejudiced twist on his story without having to back it up with documentation."[13] By that sort of writing *Time* was able to perpetuate a subtle political message—especially when the writers were decidedly prejudiced—and raise implications not justified by the material, all the while seeming to report events with the "objective" facts. Luce's response to Macdonald's concerns was a simple statement: "This is the kind of 'steering' criticism which is most valuable to *Time* at this stage in its career."[14]

Dissatisfied with what he considered Time Inc.'s growing political slant, especially as it manifested itself in a series of *Fortune* articles on the United States Steel Corporation, Macdonald resigned. His three-part series in the *Nation* followed soon after. The first article, in the issue of May 1, 1937, described Luce as an "impassioned idealist, impatient of fact and ever conscious of a 'mission' to improve his fellow-men." He was a man who was fascinated with "outstanding ('potent') individuals." Although *Time* always featured a portrait or photograph of an individual on its cover, Macdonald pointed out that Luce could even salute "radicals, once they achieved power," so that Joseph Stalin received better treatment than the Soviet Union as a whole, because Stalin was a person who could be slotted into the poor-boy-makes-good story. In the same way, Benito Mussolini could be celebrated as someone who had achieved success, with no mention necessarily of working conditions in fascist Italy, the political health of the nation, the various economic and social costs of Mussolini's policies, or Italy's foreign policy. The air of objectivity assumed by Luce's magazines, Macdonald said, especially in the way that such an attitude was developed through a constant emphasis upon facts, really hid the sophisticated manner in which opinions were quietly passed on to the readers of *Time, Life,* and *Fortune.* "No opinions are expressed directly," he noted. Rather, the editors and writers of Time Inc.'s magazines had "developed certain methods of editorializing, all the more effective because the reader—and often the author—doesn't realize what is going on." Although the ostensible foundation of the articles published in Time Inc.'s periodicals was fact, facts could be used selectively to put a slant on a story: "Obviously much depends on just which facts are selected to tell the story."[15]

Many readers of both *Time* and the *Nation* found these charges astonishing, but also revealing. In a letter to a friend after the article appeared, one reader, R. D. Miller, wrote, "I shall not defend the Editors and less, the publishers of [*Time* and *Fortune*] anymore, though they are an entertaining and clever lot of rascals."[16] His reconsideration of his earlier attitudes about *Time* and *Fortune* was not based solely upon Macdonald's assertions. Miller himself wrote to *Time* about the charges made in the series. In responding, editorial assistant I. Van Meter repeated Luce's earlier idea that Time Inc.'s magazines were written by a superman, representing the collective efforts of the various staffs. "Nobody is ever 'author' of any article in *Fortune*," Van Meter commented. But Macdonald had not claimed authorship of the articles on U.S. Steel. Instead, he had discussed at some length Time Inc.'s group journalism process and the way in which articles at *Fortune* were researched, written, and edited, and the number of different people who took part in the operation. What Macdonald objected to about the U.S. Steel articles was that the conclusions reached by the editorial staff were not consistent with the facts collected by the researchers. Having been an editor for many years, and not simply a staff writer, Macdonald had not "chafed under [the] group journalism system" of Time Inc. as Van Meter suggested. Even Luce had made note of Macdonald's importance to the company. A few years earlier, Luce had written to him, "You are quite clearly one of the most talented individuals who have developed in this organization."[17] Van Meter, however, ignoring such considerations, closed his letter to Miller by ducking behind a cloak of journalistic dignity, a tactic Luce himself fell back on when necessary. Macdonald's *Nation* articles contained "many inaccuracies," Van Meter declared, and to rebut them point by point would only involve *Time* "in a controversy in which [it] had no proper part."[18] Miller's friend who had brought *Time*'s bias to his attention remarked of Van Meter's condescension, "Any one under indictment who loftily attempts to retire from the scene on their dignity, stands convicted unless the judge and jury are completely non compos mentis," but he allowed that "his smooth facile power of deception would arouse the envy of Machiavelli."[19]

Macdonald's articles had the authority of a journalist who knew about Time Inc. at first hand, but they were not the only challenge Luce's media empire received. Luce's self-righteousness and determination to promulgate his views brought him into conflicts not only with his own employees but with various business and political leaders, including Franklin D. Roosevelt.

Roosevelt and Luce could not have been more opposite when it came to ideology on domestic programs. Although the two would find some common ground in foreign affairs, neither was willing to recognize as much. Luce's disagreement with the New Deal would not allow him to credit FDR with implementing plans very much like what he himself proposed. Similarly, the president disliked Time Inc.'s criticisms of his programs and Luce's refusal to be won over by the Roosevelt charm and popularity.[20] In one illustrative example, the two collided in late 1940 over *Time*'s coverage of the election.

Roosevelt insisted that *Time* had seriously deceived its readers. He argued that the newsweekly's masterful way of implying that which it could not state openly or legitimately did not stop it from leaving hints, which, though not explicit, certainly left no doubt as to the magazine's intentions. In one article, *Time* had suggested that a somber air of stifled fear had pervaded the house at Hyde Park during the recent election returns. The president could not let such insinuations go unchallenged, because he knew they were patently untrue. In a memo to his press secretary, Stephen Early, Roosevelt wrote in reference to *Time*'s coverage of the election, "There are some things in life that one should not let certain people get away with."[21] He felt so strongly about the inaccuracies that he personally wrote a letter to Luce explaining his objections and expressing his feelings about the article in *Time*. He passed the letter on to Early with the request that he either revise the letter and send it along to Luce or write a new one himself. Whatever his decision, Roosevelt wanted to see a copy of the final draft.

Early forwarded FDR's letter and request to the president's administrative assistant, Lowell Mellet, who reworked the president's draft and, in his own terms, expanded it from three pages single-spaced to almost four. Mellet began by analyzing the first fourteen sentences of the *Time* article one by one, carefully dissecting the impressions suggested in each sentence. He then explained why, as a longtime newspaper man himself, he felt the impressions were wrong or misleading. He also pointed out numerous erroneous assumptions and factual errors. For example, he noted that the house at Hyde Park usually had the shutters closed in the evening, and therefore *Time's* suggestion that something was unusual in closed shutters was deceptive. *Time* had also made mistakes in the number of people who were present and the clothing they were wearing. "It may be argued that there is no harm done to anybody by a single one of these sentences," Mellet said, but "great harm is done when a weekly publication such as yours, to which a great body of readers looks for information, furnishes its readers fairy tales and fiction with the pretension that it is furnishing fact." With that, Mellet struck at the heart of the matter: Luce had an uncanny ability to walk the tightrope between fact and fiction. *Time* had added an adjective here and an adverb there—all seemingly innocent enough when taken alone—to convey a distinct, and false, impression of the proceedings at Hyde Park on election night, the overall effect of which was definitely anti-Roosevelt.[22]

After carefully laying out what he saw as *Time's* factual errors and tendentious insinuations, Mellet established the larger problem of *Time's* approach. Luce, he said, expected "a degree of divine discrimination on the part of men who make your publication that they do not and can not possess." When facts become facts simply because they are printed, Mellet observed, larger troubles lay ahead. "I believe *Time* is on a dangerous road," he warned. "Some of us, and you are one, are working and fighting to preserve democracy. A democracy fed on fairy tales by an irresponsible press will not be competent to stand up against the forces now loose in the world." He finished his letter with a recommendation that Luce's publication pursue the truth. Although sometimes harder to obtain, it was just as interesting as "a reporter's or a rewrite man's imagination." In a final sarcastic jab, Mellet added that a general policy of writing the truth "might enable the publisher to sleep better, in the knowledge that he had ceased to attempt a function on which God long ago took a prior claim."[23]

Luce's reply to Mellet's letter was a perfect example of Luce's mastery of circumlocution and prevarication. He merely ignored the issues Mellet had raised about the *Time* article. Confessing that he was uncertain how to handle the accusations, he wrote, "Simply to rebut your objections to the one story seems to be beside the point since what really concerns you is the entire theory and practice of *Time*." He insisted that he would love "to argue the case right down to the fundamentals," but he avoided that by saying, "You evidently don't like *Time*," as if that made any discussion impossible. With the accusation that Mellet harbored ill feelings toward *Time*, Luce redirected the focus, and retreated with his dignity presumably intact. Mellet did not like *Time*, but, Luce declared, "Many people not only like it but consider it to be the major advance in journalism in our time."[24]

Roosevelt's remark in a note to Mellet about Luce's letter was that it was indeed "a slippery reply": "I said on Sunday night that you cannot make an agreement with an incendiary bomb." It was true that "*Time* makes false reporting extremely attractive," and that, of course, was the problem. The more Luce packaged his version of events in an appealing manner, the more people were willing to believe them, in spite of the distortions or inaccuracies. "George Washington had the courage to admit a sin," Roosevelt added tartly, "Henry Luce lacks that ability!"[25]

If Henry Luce lacked the ability to confess his sins, then so did his magazines. Conceived of as being written by a "superman" and reflecting Luce's biases, *Time*, *Life*, and *Fortune* could not be expected to admit that which their founder and editor could not. The magazines therefore made it a practice not to answer directly any letters or charges of inaccuracy.

The print medium was not the only way through which Luce promulgated his ideas to American people. In 1931, Time Inc. moved onto the radio waves with a Friday-evening program called "The March of Time." This program was originally created as a way of advertising *Time*, and it was offered free to radio stations around the country in exchange for promotional considerations. The format was simple in that it was meant only to bring the pages of *Time* to the airwaves in a dramatic form; each program corresponded closely to articles in that week's issue of the magazine. "The March of Time" was supposed to represent "a new kind of reporting—the re-enacting as clearly and dramatically as the medium of radio will permit of some memorable scenes from the news of the week."[26]

"The March of Time" proved to be a popular success. It was skillfully produced, and it employed a group of capable actors to impersonate the voices of important and well-known personages around the world. At various times, Art Carney, Bill Adams, and Stats Cotsworth all portrayed President Roosevelt.[27] When it became known that many listeners thought it was the president himself who was speaking, the White House intervened. Cognizant of the power of Roosevelt's voice and fearful that it might soon saturate the airwaves,

White House press secretary Stephen Early requested that the radio program cease impersonating the president.[28] The administration could not play favorites, Early contended, and if the White House allowed "The March of Time" to imitate FDR's voice, then it would have to allow other stations and programs the same right. If overused, the president's smooth timbre and reassuring delivery would quickly lose their impact.

"The March of Time" complied with Early's request, but many listeners objected to the ban, and in letters to the press secretary and the president, they expressed their dissatisfaction. One republican (Harmon Butler) wrote that initially he had been skeptical of Roosevelt's plans, but hearing the president's voice on "The March of Time" every week, even if simulated, reassured him that America finally had a leader who could guide the nation. He did not get to hear enough of the president: "Each Friday night I listened eagerly for a new message of hope and encouragement."[29] Another listener who wrote to the White House said much the same: "My conversion to the support of this administration resulted largely from an appreciation of the leadership and high-mindedness of our President, made apparent to me through the excellent broadcasts of the March of Time."[30]

Although many people who wrote to the White House understood the reasoning for the ban, they felt an exception should be made for "The March of Time." Most of them argued that this program should be treated differently because it consistently reported the news with a commitment to high standards and a devotion to the truth. "I understand the statement that all broadcasters must be treated alike," Butler admitted, "and that not all have the good taste and ability of the editors of *Time Magazine*," but he felt that because "The March of Time" radio program was so "outstanding" an exception should be made.[31] "*The March of Time* can be depended upon" to present the news and the president fairly, another writer stated. He felt it provided "a real public service" and should be allowed to continue simulating the president's voice.[32] Other listeners concurred. One wrote that the radio program's "presentation was so careful and skillful," that he—and others like him he was certain—"was being granted an insight into and understanding of the personality and spirit of [the] President."[33] One woman called it "the best news program on the air" and said the ban of Roosevelt's voice "smack[s] too loudly of Mussolini and Hitler."[34]

The radio program quickly became so popular that when Luce decided to cancel it because of high production costs, over 22,000 listeners wrote in protesting the decision.[35] After securing some financial assistance from the Columbia Broadcasting System, he relented and the program ran until 1939. It was brought back in the fall of 1941 and continued until the end of the war.

In addition to radio, Time Inc. moved into the motion picture business in 1935 with a monthly "The March of Time" newsreel. Unlike the radio program, which was designed simply to provide advertising for Luce's magazines, the newsreel was supposed to make money. Within one year, it appeared in more than 5,000 theaters in the United States and more than 700 in Great Britain. In 1936, a year after the newsreel was launched, 12 million Americans were regular viewers.[36] "The March of Time" combined newsreel film, documentary footage, and the recreation of certain scenes, often with the cooperation of the original participants, with spoken text, to create, in the words of official Time Inc. historian Robert T. Elson, "a new form of compelling journalism."[37] Although to many this new kind of journalism was indeed compelling, "The March of Time" newsreel never became the profitable venture it was originally envisioned to be. High production costs and a relatively limited number of outlets left no room for expansion and the sort of huge profits earned by the magazines.[38] Nonetheless, it came close to breaking even, and, not the least, it served as a magnificent promotional tool for Time Inc.'s magazines. "The March of Time" newsreel continued to play in theaters until 1951.

Both the radio program and the newsreel tried to convey through their respective mediums what *Time* did in print. Both covered the same important people, issues, and events that dominated the news. Luce himself had little interest in the motion picture medium. His main concern remained with his magazines, and for the most part he had little to do with the production of the programs. But he did not have to; with the stories coming directly from the most recent issue of *Time* or *Fortune*, there was little need for such direct control. As *Time* editor Thomas Matthews noted, with regard to certain issues, specifically China, Luce did direct the policy of the magazine. Each newspaper and magazine has its own personality, Matthews pointed out, or, at least, tries to establish one, for that is part of how a readership is created and sustained; but at *Time*, and also at *Fortune* and *Life*, Matthews felt that Luce heavily influenced the essence of that personality. Overt manipulation could be kept to a minimum, for after a magazine achieves its own identity, "that is the thumb everyone is under." In the end, certain types of stories were always inappropriate given the "personality" of the magazine.[39]

The temperament of Luce's publications was determined by more than just the articles. In fact, the articles published in the pages of

Luce's magazines constituted only one way in which Time Inc. as a whole influenced American popular thinking and fostered certain ideas about China. Andrew Kopkind once remarked that what Time Inc. really signified was the rise of corporate journalism, not only for America but for the entire world. The implication of such a development was staggering, he argued, because with such a massive corporation behind its enterprises, Time Inc. could "produce mass ideological manipulation, create worthless demand, and impose a whole range of values which are important to the interests of the corporation, but destructive to the individual."[40] Kopkind specifically targeted the advertising copy, more than the articles, for creating this artificial necessity. "Over the weeks and years," he noted, "it is the ads which tell readers how to dress, what to buy, and what to value in life." In sum, "the whole *feel* of *Time* . . . its design, its audience, its marketing methods, and its trans-verbal tones give it a cultural position—and by extension, a political one—which mere articles could never establish."[41]

Although Kopkind directed his attack at Luce's entire empire, especially the advertising copy, the content of the articles cannot be ignored. And more directly, his comments are especially pertinent for Time Inc.'s coverage of China during the 1930's and 1940's. With China, Luce created the kind of "worthless demand" Kopkind mentioned by pandering to the American predisposition to see American traits in other peoples. He managed to foster dangerous and harmful illusions about China, ones that ultimately backfired.

In his overall approach to business, Luce brought a keen sense of what the American public was interested in reading. But his influence cannot be measured simply by adding up the number of magazines he sold. Although often overlooked in discussions of American foreign policy, Luce, as much as any member of the Roosevelt or Truman administrations, helped set the public agenda. The resonance his ideas had within America can be seen in the continually rising circulation figures his magazines achieved year after year. By reaching millions of Americans every week, those magazines could, and did, play a part in forming national opinions on various events, ideas, and people. From roughly 340,000 subscribers in 1931 to over 7.3 million readers of his three major magazines less than twenty years later, Henry Luce commanded a central position in American society.

In his speeches, Luce celebrated a vigorous America that acted benevolently and altruistically in the realm of international affairs. Devoted to certain fundamental propositions, his America operated with the best interests of all nations in mind. He dedicated himself to ensuring that his country did not turn its back on the historical, and providentially ordained, mission that beckoned. His unyielding faith in America's future stimulated the way in which he saw the rest of the world.

With China, he felt the twin emotional pulls of the United States and of the land where he had spent his childhood. He held steadfastly to the idea that the United States and China formed the perfect union: America with its political, moral, and economic strength and China with its unique position to allow the United States to fulfill its destiny. China was an opportunity for the United States as well as an opportunity for him to achieve whatever he wished on an enormous scale. This view, obviously paternalistic, clouded Luce's thoughts on Sino-American relations. Like a devoted parent, he could not let go of the notion that China would one day develop in America's image. He believed that America's success depended on the Chinese adopting American ways. When later events did not follow that path, he tried to force a change upon American policy. The primary way in which he did that was to misrepresent China to the American people. By equating China and everything Chinese so closely with ideals and events familiar to most Americans, Luce sought to foster illusions about Sino-American harmony that Americans would then insist must be preserved. In this endeavor, however, he needed some assistance.

CHAPTER TWO

Time Inc. and Its Stake in China

You and I know that America is capable of great idealistic movements, the primary motive power of which is the unselfish betterment of humanity.

—James Linen, Jr., to Henry Luce, March 1941

You know the remarkable thing about China is that everyone who comes here becomes enchanted with the tremendous possibilities for achieving whatever it is they want to achieve.

—Henry Luce, quoting a young Swedish woman, June 1941

China beckoned to Henry Luce in much the same way as it had to his father's generation of missionaries. Sherwood Eddy had once called China "the lodestar, the goal," and so it was for the younger Luce too. It represented the opportunity for the United States to act benevolently in world affairs and to affect the environment in which it lived—both principal components outlined in his essay "The American Century." China became a symbol of American success—in a sense, a younger, Asian equivalent of America. Within the exceptionalist ideology that stimulated Luce's thinking lay the fundamental tenet that the United States had the obligation to expand, to extend its influence; and many events and currents came together to make China one of the most attractive places for spreading that American dream.

Before Luce began his concerted effort to propagate the idea of an Americanized China, however, three important events unfolded during the period 1927–31 that made his endeavor more likely to succeed. The first involved the nominal unification of China under Generalissimo Chiang Kai-shek and his conversion to Christianity. The second concerned the publication of a novel written by an American raised in China, and the third dealt with the Japanese military's decision to make part of northeastern China a sphere of influence.

Chiang's political position arose from his successful military exploits after the death of Sun Yat-sen in 1925. Beginning in July 1926, Chiang launched the Northern Expedition. From a secure position in Canton, he led his National Revolutionary Army north, and within a year he was in control of the territory south of the Chang river, including the important cities of Shanghai, the tri-cities of Wuhan, Hankou, and Hanyang, and Nanjing, where he established the seat of the new Nationalist government. Just as importantly for his American supporters, in the spring of 1927 he initiated the first of his many anti-Communist campaigns, moving his forces against the left wing of the Guomindang and the Chinese Communist Party in a series of bloody incidents in Shanghai and Wuhan. This ended the united front between the Guomindang and the Chinese Communists, a political coalition that had been in existence since 1923; this also began two decades of repeated efforts by Chiang to eliminate the Communists by means of military force.[1]

Equally vital for Chiang's subsequent reception in the United States was his religious acceptance of Christ. The process began in 1927, when he agreed to study Christianity at the request of his new family, specifically his mother-in-law.[2] His bride, Soong Meiling, like her parents, was a devout Christian. She took him for walks and read from the Bible for four years until he finally decided to adopt her Methodist beliefs. Chiang's conversion seemed to be an auspicious harbinger for the entire missionary community, Catholic and Protestant alike. Of further importance for Chiang's personal fortunes, his marriage to the middle Soong daughter made him a member of one of the richest and most powerful families in all China.

These two developments had a great deal to do with Luce's conviction that the United States could fulfill its historic mission in China. Stimulating the national—and in Luce's case personal—impulse to convert the unregenerate, Chiang's growing strength combined with his newfound Christianity to foster the strong sense of optimism about future Sino-American relations. Along with other American pro-Chinese sentimentalists, Luce latched on to the generalissimo and his wife and promoted them as clear examples of China's movement toward becoming more like America.

Chiang's apparent unification of China and his religious conversion combined with two other events, which together created the framework for American interest later in the decade. The first was the publication of Pearl Buck's novel *The Good Earth*, in 1931. This novel, translated into thirty languages, was awarded the Pulitzer prize for fiction, was made into a Broadway play in 1933, and in 1937 appeared as an Academy Award–winning Hollywood film, produced at an estimated cost of $3 million. *The Good Earth*, in all its forms, introduced millions of Americans to China through the trials and tribulations of Wang Lung, his wife O-lan (played by Luise Rainer in an Oscar-winning performance), their family, and the characters who came in and out of their lives.

Buck's novel managed to ride the crest of what the historian Jonathan Spence has called an "extraordinary upsurge of works either about China or inspired by it" in the West.[3] The exoticism of Asia came home to Americans in the form of a central character whose attachment to the land closely resembled Jeffersonian ideas about a virtuous class of yeoman farmers. Buck did not write from her understanding of American history so much as from her own experiences, but the great popularity of her work was clearly tied to its cultural and historical resonance with Americans' ideas about themselves and their heritage as settlers, pioneers, farmers, and frontiersmen—all characters intimately associated with the land in some respect. One reviewer of the film described the story as that of "Wang's devotion to the land and the tragedy that threatened to overwhelm him when he neglected it."[4] At the time of *The Good Earth*'s publication, many Americans were experiencing the shock of seeing how years of neglect, overcultivation, and natural calamity had ruined their own land, a devastation that literally saw the creation of dust bowls in certain parts of the country. Wang Lung's persistence and his subsequent ability to overcome the obstacles that his family faced by returning to his land offered at least some hope to disillusioned Americans. Thus, of all the fictional portraits of the Chinese during the 1920's and 1930's, Spence says, "it was Pearl Buck's Chinese peasants, with their stoic dignity, their endurance, their innate realism, and their ceaseless battles with an unrelenting nature, who reached deepest into American hearts."[5]

Finally, in 1931, the Japanese invaded Manchuria. The Hoover administration, overwhelmed by the problems of the domestic economy, was not prepared to go beyond rhetorical condemnations. It did not recognize Japan's aggression, but it, and the country as a whole, was disinclined to translate moral outrage into concrete action. The beginnings of Japan's military encroachment did not cause an immediate and overwhelming response in the United States to do something. Instead, together with the Chiangs' Christianity and the images of *The Good Earth*, they laid the foundation to which Americans would later return in an effort to build their dream of China.

As the United States grappled with the sudden and drastic effects of the depression after 1929, China faced a number of its own problems, many of which were even more daunting. After establishing control over the southern half of China with his military expedition,

Chiang continued his quest to subdue the remaining warlords. He saw the Chinese Communists as the chief threat to his rule, and after turning against them in 1927, he initiated a series of campaigns designed to eliminate their influence, the most systematic of which began in 1931 and continued over the next five years.

Much of Chiang's military program relied upon the advice given by German advisers, especially General Hans Von Seeckt, who visited China in 1933 and again in 1934–35. Seeckt's ideas and recommendations struck a responsive chord in Chiang because they paralleled what he wanted to do in the first place. Following the Prussian concept that a singular individual, a "leading personality," needed to steer the nation's direction, Seeckt's counsel neatly allowed Chiang to place himself in such a position. Moreover, the general's theoretical discussion of the relationship between the state and the army called for the creation of an elite military force of manageable proportions, which, in turn, could be used to bring about the internal solidarity Chiang wanted to fashion.[6]

Coexistent with the Nationalist government's solicitation of German advice was the rise of a fascist organization called the Blueshirts. Led by Dai Li, a graduate of the Whampoa Military Academy, and a man who later served as head of the Bureau of Investigation and Statistics (an internal security organization), the Blueshirts sought to bring social order through the application of fascist principles. In the words of historian William Kirby, members of the society "opposed capitalism, materialism, individualism, democracy, and communism. They sought a unanimity of national beliefs and activities, forged by the 'leadership principle' from top to bottom, the 'militarization' of education, the nationalization of industry, and (interestingly enough) the collectivization of agriculture."[7] Chiang further attempted to bring some sense of control to Chinese society by embarking upon a curious hybrid of traditional Confucian principles and Christian ideals in an effort called the New Life Movement. This movement, begun in 1934, eventually came under the direction of Madame Chiang and included a series of prescriptions relating to the proper conduct of the people in an effort to instill a sense of unity and purpose.[8]

The reasons for molding national identity became all the more important after the Japanese army precipitated a skirmish with Chinese forces in the city of Mukden in September 1931. Using this incident as a pretext, the Japanese army then invaded Manchuria; by the end of the year it had gained complete control, and in March 1932 it announced the creation of the puppet state of Manchukuo, with the former emperor Puyi as chief of state. During the next two years, Japanese forces expanded the extent of their control south to the Great Wall.

Rather than fight the Japanese aggressively, Chiang continued to concentrate his efforts on the Chinese Communists. In 1934, after a number of failed attempts to dislodge them from their soviet along the Fujian-Jiangxi border, he finally began an extermination campaign that combined the military tactics of slow and careful strangulation with political indoctrination of the local population. Recognizing their untenable situation, members of the CCP, numbering some 80,000 at the beginning, broke out of the Guomindang encirclement in October and embarked on the famous Long March, of roughly 6,000 miles to the northern province of Shaanxi, which they reached a year later.

Throughout the decade, Time Inc. consistently showed its approval of Chiang's efforts to eliminate the Communists. Although Chiang's first *Time* cover appearance in 1931 stressed his resolve to resist the Japanese encroachment into Manchuria, his second one in 1933 focused on his attempt to bring about internal unity, namely, by putting down the only "really serious threat to his authority": the Chinese Communists.[9] By the end of 1936, all Luce's publications had clearly evidenced their support for Chiang and his policies. When Chiang made his second *Time* cover appearance of the year in November, in the post–election week issue, he sat alone, smartly dressed in his military uniform, thoughtfully gazing to the right with his left hand appropriately gripping his officer's sword.[10] The legend beneath the picture captured the essence of the article: "Good roads, good morals, good bombs are his answer to Japan." Luce's political sympathies were obvious: Roosevelt had just won a second term in a landslide victory over Republican Alf Landon, but *Time* hit newsstands around the nation with a handsome picture of China's nominal leader on its cover instead of a picture of America's overwhelmingly reelected president.

The article on the generalissimo appeared to justify the editorial choice by pointing out that Chiang Kai-shek "was unquestionably the greatest man in the Far East." Events in China were quickly beginning to change, and *Time* hailed Chiang as representing the spark for a new China. He had begun to implement a coherent plan of overall resistance to the Japanese. Through his policies, which included slowly unifying his nation, drawing up a strategic plan for resisting Japanese aggression, effectively eliminating the Chinese Communists, and instilling proper moral values into China's soldiers and citizens, he

would return China to the community of great nations. Luce's newsweekly provided a valuable service to Americans by reporting on this
transformation, since it had received little attention outside Asia; as
Time phrased it, Chiang's "brain and will have driven the Chinese
people to extraordinary achievements, few of which have made world
headlines."[11]

Chiang's recent demonstration of resolve represented an important
change from past actions, though *Time* was not criticizing his former
inactivity; on the contrary, it rationalized his seeming lack of resistance to the Japanese by explaining that he had pursued an attitude
of "turning the Christian other cheek" to their insults and military
advances. But change was coming. The "small-boned, slender-
waisted" Chiang, also known as the "Ningpo Napoleon," had recently
overseen the construction of concrete pillboxes, trenches, and other
fortified defensive works.[12] Moreover, the "Southern Methodist"
Chiang had instilled "some rudiments of Christian conduct and morality" into his two and a quarter million troops. The results, *Time*
observed, were evident in a new national fighting spirit.

In developing its overall picture of China's leader, *Time* paid particular attention to Chiang's handling of the Chinese Communists.
In what became its standard line on the subject, *Time* argued that the
extermination campaigns should be viewed not as precipitating civil
war but rather as allowing the Nationalist troops to engage in military
practice sessions before they fought the Japanese in the real game of
war. Chiang, *Time* said, "had waged innumerable practice wars upon
the Chinese Communist forces."[13] In constructing its scenario for
China, the magazine insisted that the Nationalist troops would soon
offer substantial and unified resistance to the Japanese with their
finely tuned fighting abilities honed through years of rehearsals with
the Communists.

Although Chiang's initiatives had not received their proper attention internationally, his actions had not gone unnoticed domesti-
cally. In return for all that he had done for his nation, the people of
China gave him fifty American-made warplanes as a birthday gift.[14]
Time remarked, "The Christian birthday cake . . . carried not 50 can-
dles but replicas of 50 foreign-built bombing planes."[15] "The March of
Time" newsreel took note of the gift in one of its releases, and the Associated Press used the story in its 1941 biographical sketch of
Chiang, observing that the planes served as a "significant symbol of
China's growing modernization."[16] The birthday cake was an apt
symbol of Chiang's baptism. Not only was the cake a Christian one,
but Chiang's primary reason for adopting Christianity was his "need

of a God such as Jesus Christ." *Time* called Madame Chiang the "Christian Miss Soong" and lauded her role as China's Christian dynamo in the nation's spiritual transformation.

The November 9, 1936, *Time* cover article was the start of Luce's long and consistent campaign to foster an image of Chiang Kai-shek as the popular leader of his people, dedicated to bringing Christian morality, political democracy, and modern industry to China. Time Inc.'s efforts alone did not catapult the generalissimo to instantaneous international prominence, but they did anticipate the growing American interest in China, so that the next episode in the Chinese drama had a ready audience. In December 1936, barely a month after Chiang's *Time* cover appearance, the Chinese warlord Zhang Xueliang kidnapped the generalissimo during his visit to the city of Xi'an, in Shaanxi province, to which Chiang had flown to outline his military plans for yet another "final" extermination campaign against the Communists. Zhang Xueliang was a loyal subordinate who had eradicated Communists from the Hubei-Henan-Anhui region in central China west of Nanjing, but he was unhappy with Chiang's insistence on prosecuting a civil war against the Chinese Communists instead of organizing national resistance against the Japanese.[17] Zhang and his troops therefore detained—"kidnapped"—Chiang for thirteen days. During that time, the importance of whether Chiang lived or died combined with the inherent drama of the kidnapping to create not only a sensation within China but an international story as well, one reported by Time Inc. at great length.

Time's initial coverage on December 21, 1936, made two points very clear at the outset: Chiang was "the most powerful man in Eastern Asia," and his kidnapping had been arranged by a former opium addict who apparently had fallen victim to Communist, or pro-Communist ideas. Evidently, Zhang wanted China's leader to stop his military campaigns against the Communists and concentrate his resources upon actively resisting the Japanese. *Time* insisted that Chiang had intended to fight the Japanese all along, but it again stressed that Nationalist troops needed more practice fighting the Communists. Zhang's precipitous actions had done nothing to promote Chinese unity or harmony, and his decision to hold China's great leader only confirmed earlier judgments of him as a drug-crazed, Communist sympathizer.[18] *Time* reiterated these two themes in its next issue: Chiang was still the greatest man in Asia and his death would threaten to undermine "the enormous progress China has made . . . during the past decade"; and Zhang Xueliang had a drug habit, for which he had been treated but not cured: "Young [Zhang] was NOT cured of drug addiction in Peiping, for the reason that his concubines kept smuggling the stuff to him in the hospital."[19] The December 28 article did admit that Zhang's reason for the kidnapping—to force the generalissimo to fight the Japanese actively—was extremely popular, even if it was "an ex-dope's not too bright idea." But it repeated *Time*'s excuse for Chiang, that his army needed a little more practice fighting the Communists before taking on the Japanese. Battling the Communists would promote harmony within China, because, *Time* said without elaborating, they were "un-Chinese in important respects." It added that if the Chinese Communists ever got hold of Chiang, they would see to his swift execution.

Time's summary of the situation in China was not altogether accurate. At the time of his kidnapping, Chiang was not universally heralded as the leader of China, and indeed his insistence on waging "practice wars" against the Communists had led to increased dissatisfaction with his leadership.[20] Two days after his arrival in Xi'an, a few thousand students there organized a march to protest Japanese activities. They also tried to present a petition, the thrust of which was that Chinese should not be fighting Chinese, at a time when the country faced a Japanese invasion. The students met armed resistance and two were wounded when the local police, supported by members of Chiang's personal force, opened fire. Zhang Xueliang worked to ease tensions from the shooting, and as part of that effort he presented the students' demands to the generalissimo only to be chastised for trying "to represent *both* sides."[21]

Chiang was not interested in the students' concerns. The Chinese Communists represented a much greater threat in his mind than did the Japanese, and he was determined to secure his position before turning on the foreign enemy. He wrote in his diary that he told the commanders of certain troops in Shaanxi "that the bandit-suppression campaign had been prosecuted to such a stage that it would require only the last five minutes to achieve the final success."[22]

Chiang's refusal to listen to advice caused considerable friction within certain groups. In particular, the Dongbei troops, which had been stationed in Shaanxi since losing their Manchurian homeland in 1931, wanted to fight the Japanese, not other Chinese, and they now refused to continue the campaign against the CCP, which was urging national unity to resist the Japanese. Chiang had flown to Shaanxi in an effort to placate the Dongbei troops, and when once there he pressed his plan to attack the Communists, he found himself on the morning of December 12 in the embarrassing position of being held captive. He was immediately presented with an eight-point program that called for the reorganization of the Nationalist government to include all political parties, a prompt end to the civil war, and the commencement of organized resistance against the Japanese. Many of the troops demanded Chiang's death but only after he had been humiliated in a public trial.[23] Chiang was saved from this fate by the Chinese Communists, who, instead of lusting for blood as *Time* had said they would, quickly arrived on the scene to calm matters down. Headed by Zhou Enlai and supported from Moscow by Joseph Stalin, who feared an increase in Japan's power if China disintegrated into political chaos, the Chinese Communist delegation submitted its proposals to Chiang, and in so doing acknowledged his position as commander-in-chief.[24] The Communists recognized that a united front against Japan required a living Chiang with his position and prestige intact. Far from advocating his execution, therefore, they convinced the Dongbei troops that he must not be killed. Thus all parties reached a tenuous understanding, and on Christmas Day Chiang Kai-shek left Xi'an.

Very little of the details or outcome of this episode ever appeared in Time Inc.'s coverage. Propelled by Luce's romanticized notions, *Time*'s euphemisms about "practice sessions" clouded the truth of growing discontent with Chiang's insistence on conducting civil war while faced with a foreign invasion, and thus Chiang emerged from the kidnapping with greater recognition and prestige than ever before. And Americans, misled by the inaccurate, incomplete reporting, continued for the most part to have wholly erroneous ideas about the political and social conditions in China.

Richard de Rochemont, a prominent staff member of "The March of Time" newsreel, commented of this period, "We felt we were on the side of the angels in most cases, with the possible exception of Chiang Kai-shek, whom we regarded as a protégé of Mr. Luce, and who was the only sacred cow we admitted."[25] Luce could not resist the temptation to intervene to guarantee the appropriate type of coverage for his beloved symbol of China. "The March of Time" produced a special newsreel called "The Far East," about Chiang's kidnapping by the "one-time drug addict" Zhang Xueliang, whose irresponsible action had brought China's progress to an abrupt halt. Like *Time*, the newsreel coverage was clearly not in sympathy with Zhang's insistence on war with Japan. On the contrary, Chiang's policy of ignoring the Japanese insults "until strengthened and unified" seemed the best course of action. The bulk of the newsreel was devoted to illustrating how Chiang's policies had brought progress to China. The modernization of key cities gave an indication of the country's headway toward achieving an industrial economy on a par with that of Western nations. "Booming her way through the world depression," "The March of Time" asserted, "Shanghai is a symbol of the progress Chiang Kai-shek plans for all China." It is not surprising that Shanghai would stand as the mark of advancement. Shanghai had become the "capital of big business," and according to Luce, big business was the engine of progress.[26]

"Today, Shanghai's skyline towers with the tallest buildings ever erected outside the United States." The newsreel shots of Shanghai's skyscrapers were in fact very like those of New York City—indeed, they appeared to have been part of an earlier piece on the same newsreel about young American women seeking jobs there. That aside, not only had industry promoted the construction of tall buildings just as it had in the United States, it had also compelled China to move into the modern world and discard such outmoded practices as ancestor worship. With the Chinese abandoning their outdated past and moving rapidly forward in their national evolution, "The March of Time" predicted an attractive future for the majority of the people: "As money circulates freely among natives, great masses of workers throng into new Chinese-owned department stores to buy modern merchandise." The footage accompanying the text showed department stores that looked like Macy's or Gimbel's, filled with Chinese consumers enduring the rigors of shopping. The Americanization of China even included the manufacturing of Eskimo Pies "for Chinese consumption." More text and footage showed that skyscraper construction and production lines were only part of China's modernization. There was footage of Shanghai's social life, with its "new clubs where gay, young Chinese enjoy European entertainment." Ancient teahouses had recently given way to soda fountains, and the popularity of the "sophisticated cinema shown in deluxe first-run movie houses" also served as examples of China's ongoing transformation.

The overall message was: "China needs a Chiang Kai-shek to lead her if she would successfully fight off Japan." The "slim, young brother-in-law of sainted Sun Yat-sen" was the only person who could forge the nation's unity and continue the progress toward creating a modern society. With so much already having been accomplished under his brief rule, the future appeared to hold unlimited promise. In this conception of Sino-American relations, the vast geographical distance separating the two nations could no longer hinder the converging trends between them in religion, politics, business, and culture.

To Chiang's Christian supporters, Zhang Xueliang's release of the generalissimo on Christmas Day had obvious significance. *Time's* coverage repeated the familiar themes: "the most powerful man in Eastern Asia" being freed by the poorly dressed, "one-time dope fiend," Zhang Xueliang.[27] It highlighted the Christian angle, noting that Chiang had "insisted upon reading the Bible during most of his" captivity. Later, Chiang would speak publicly of how his religious faith had sustained him during the period, comparing his own ordeal with the many trials faced by Jesus. Clearly, the timing of his release provided a coincidence too great for Christian supporters to ignore. In effect, Chiang and China were spiritually reborn.

Chiang himself played no small part in publicizing the Christian aspect of his character. It was something he continually stressed in his public addresses. His Good Friday message in 1937 is a notable example. This sermon, given at the Central Conference of Eastern Asia of the Methodist Episcopal Church in Nanjing, was entitled "My Spiritual Conception of Good Friday."[28] Chiang began the sermon by observing, "Without religious faith there can be no real understanding of life." He then went on to expound on his thoughts during the preceding December when he was held captive by Marshal Zhang. He had been a "constant reader of the Bible" for ten years, he said, and while in captivity, he had requested only one thing: a Bible. Although his travails were meaningless compared with Christ's, he felt that his two weeks of detention in Xi'an had instilled in him an even greater sense of mission and purpose: in the same way that Christ had entered Jerusalem knowing what dangers awaited him, he had traveled to Xi'an fully dedicated to serving his country "without any consideration of personal safety." While he was held captive, his thoughts had turned to "the forty days and nights Christ passed in the wilderness withstanding temptation." And as he pondered the hardships Christ had endured, he redoubled his will to resist the evil forces that had set upon him. "With the spirit of Christ on the Cross I was preparing to make the final sacrifice at the trial of the so-called 'People's Front.'" As Christ had died for mankind, so he would sacrifice himself for the Chinese people. He had, as he noted later, extended himself into an instrument of Christ in "his plan for saving the world."[29]

A year later, Chiang insisted that the plight of the Jews nearly two thousand years before and the present situation facing the Chinese were more than coincidental. Like Jesus, he too had "been promoting a social revolution" with his New Life Movement. And as Jesus had led a religious revolution against considerable odds, Chiang's efforts to bring Christianity to China could be viewed in the same light.[30] Chiang also linked himself and his Christian charity to the celebrated founder of the Chinese Republic, Sun Yat-sen. He insisted that Sun had taught him a great deal and that although his original trust in Sun had not been religiously oriented, "it was similar to a religious faith." He discussed Sun's Christianity and indicated that Sun had displayed many Christian characteristics, the principal one being "love—love for the emancipation of the weaker races, and for the welfare of the oppressed people." As Chiang became attached to those ideals, he came to see the beauty of Christ's teachings.[31]

With speeches like these, Chiang bolstered his supporters at home and abroad. In the words of one American admirer, Chiang was "introspective, patient, tolerant, full of wisdom, ascetic and almost saintly."[32] For Luce, such public confirmation was no longer necessary. By early 1937, he had firmly established his support for Chiang and the Nationalist government. The generalissimo's religious conversion had provided the foundation for Luce's attachment, and his chimerical political and economic progress solidified Luce's confidence in his ability to march China down the road toward Christian salvation, political democracy, and economic modernization.

For many of the American missionaries who traveled to China, democracy was "a way of life as well as a political system, and it was the Christian way of life."[33] Those words apply equally well to Luce's thinking. According to his general conception of the link between religion and politics, Jesus Christ equaled democracy. Like the Protestant missionaries of his father's generation, Luce believed that if Christianity could be brought to China, democracy would certainly follow, and from there, the development of trade would rapidly ensue. Although it was a nineteenth-century United States minister to China who had said that missionaries were the pioneers of trade and economic development, it was Henry R. Luce who attempted to bring that idea to fruition in the twentieth century.

Luce's central focus upon an American-dominated international system stemmed from his unyielding faith in an ideal United States that used its power benevolently to further the spread of freedom around the world. It followed that the United States was uniquely appointed to handle the world's problems. "The challenge of the circumstances of our age is, above all, a challenge to America," Luce told a graduating class at Stanford University. The pressing moral imperatives challenging the world were particularly important for Americans, because of their unique moral sensitivity—"an American kind of feeling": "Nothing is more American than to feel what ought to be done can be done and what can be done ought to be done."[34]

One of the things that Luce was sure "ought to be done," before, during, and even after World War II, was for the country to throw its full support behind the Nationalist government of China. In a letter to the president of the National War Fund one month before the Allied invasion of Normandy in 1944, he emphasized specifically what he believed "ought to be done by American generosity": namely, the National War Fund should increase its financial support to China.[35] "The very simple fact," he wrote, was that the Chinese people were the most numerous of America's allies, and yet the United States had done very little to assist them. China's enormous size, in addition to its important contribution to prosecuting the war effort, dictated that it should receive greater assistance.

China's vast geographical territory and its tremendous population combined with Luce's faith in the overall historical mission of the United States to create the unique position China came to occupy within a much grander concept. The two nations were destined to form a perfect and complete union, in which the United States was the provider and China the recipient. And with its hundreds of millions of people, China promised to be a fabulous recipient, or the most prodigal of sons. First, however, Luce had to explain China to his fellow Americans, so that through a better understanding of their Asian counterparts they could help in the journey toward world harmony.

A year after the Japanese attack on Pearl Harbor, Luce was the principal speaker at a pro-China service held at Saint Thomas Church in New York City. His main theme was the similarity between the United States and China and the benefits that would derive from their cooperation: Chinese-American understanding would "in no small part" soon provide America's spiritual, economic, and political salvation. The Chinese had readily accepted Christianity into their society because it was so close to their more familiar beliefs: "When the Christian prayer first came to China the humblest farmer instantly understood it, so like it was to his: 'Our father who art in heaven.'" Indeed, China's religion was directed toward the brotherhood of man—of all mankind, in fact. With their emphasis upon helping all nations and through the selfless continuation of their struggle against the Japanese, the people of China challenged Americans to provide the kind of military and spiritual assistance the nation prided itself upon. China looked to the United States to live up to its spiritual and moral ideals: "China challenges our Christian faith . . . and if we fail there, we fail totally."[36]

Luce emphasized that this challenge to the United States was especially important because China had "embarked upon a vast reformation—partly inspired by the Christian gospel." For the United States to keep pace with this progress, Americans would have to raise "with new devotion, the banners of our faith." The effort promised to be considerable, but the results would more than make up for it: "When America's victory of faith meets China's victory in the grand confluence of history, we shall fear no more the decline and fall of civilization." And the only way for the United States to respond was as a Christian nation. "The United States cannot meet this challenge . . . except as it is a Christian nation, moved, in this matter, by the prayer of those who truly pray: 'Thy Kingdom come, thy will be done—on earth.'"

Luce's pro-Chiang stance was clear, and his insistence that China was engaged not in a revolution or a repudiation of the past, but rather in a reformation, a reconsideration of China's traditional strengths, allowed him to borrow liberally and loosely from Chinese history to support his statements. The one person who epitomized all that America hoped China would achieve was Chiang Kai-shek, the "sword and symbol of this mighty reformation." Whether Luce was following Chiang's own personal assessment or really believed it to be true, he alluded to Chiang in terms that explicitly drew a connection to Jesus Christ. Just as Christianity revolved around the actions and words of one man, so too had China come to be represented by one man. The Chinese were not known as the sort of people who became attached to a single figure, he said, "But in their great crisis they found the man they needed": "the greatest soldier in Asia, the greatest statesman in Asia, America's friend: Chiang Kai-shek."

Luce's speech went from superlative to more superlative, in an evangelical fervor of impassioned praise for China, Chiang, and the union with the United States of America. Chiang was China's savior: "For a hundred years the Chinese have been waiting for him." They had been waiting ever since the "dissolution of old China" began in the middle of the nineteenth century, and just as Moses had come to rescue the Jews, so Chiang had come to rescue his people. Indeed, since the Taiping Rebellion in the middle of the nineteenth century, "the Chinese have understood that the signs portended vast upheaval and out of the anguish would come the man to lead them. He has come." Wherever Chiang traveled, Luce declared, there went the government of China. Regardless of his military titles and despite the problems caused by Japanese actions, Chiang "carried with him, like a holy grail, the invincible purpose that China shall be united and that China shall be free."

Luce's Christian conception of the relationship between the United States and China led perhaps inevitably to his attempt to influence the direction of Sino-American relations. In his 1941 essay, "The American Century," Luce had offered a general prescription for the kind of American internationalism he envisioned, one that predated the nation's overt involvement in the war. But within his broader plan there lay plenty of room to include the special relationship he had in mind with China. He began by exhorting his countrymen to look beyond the geographical boundaries of the nation, to see the interrelationship between world events and America's national security. The country was at war, he declared, even if Americans did not realize or admit it. The United States had failed in 1919 to provide for a healthy international community, one free from the sickness of aggression. Because of that failure, the nation now faced another crisis, but that predicament provided for another opportunity as well. This conception of history presented Americans not so much with an opportunity as a duty to face up to their global obligations. America was "the most powerful and the most vital nation in the world." With such a position came tremendous responsibilities, and Luce implored his fellow citizens "to accept wholeheartedly our duty and our opportunity . . . and in consequence to exert upon the world the full impact of our influence, for such purposes as we see fit and by such means as we see fit."

Whether or not the United States chose to accept this obligation carried with it important and far-reaching consequences not just for the nation but for the structure of the entire world. Isolationism, Luce said, constituted a morally and, from a practical standpoint, a bankrupt policy, and he inveighed against returning to the traditional but no longer useful foreign policy views of the Republican Party. But President Roosevelt was also at fault for not guiding the country more vigorously toward accepting its manifest duty in international affairs. America's new policy, Luce declared, must be "an internationalism of the people, by the people, and for the people." Economic enterprise, technical and artistic skills, altruism, and ideals—all had to be exported in order to guarantee the creation of an American-inspired world. With regard to China, *Fortune* magazine stated that American commitments there were "too long-standing, too deeply derivative from basic Protestant Christian attitudes" to be abandoned during these difficult times.[37]

Disseminating the American spirit within Asia appeared to be an especially well-founded idea given the region's potential economic opportunities. The area would be worth nothing if the United States repudiated its responsibilities. A more promising alternative, however, showed China to be worth "four, five, ten billion dollars a year" if the United States undertook to fulfill its obligations. Three months after "The American Century" essay appeared, *Fortune* advanced the same ideas about the potential of the China trade, and again the figures mentioned were in the billions.[38] The "New China" presented the United States with an historic opportunity and the nation should seize it without delay. Through Time Inc., Luce urged Americans to recognize that events in China had a direct impact on their lives. Because of the connection between the two nations' fortunes, American foreign policy in Asia had to encourage the development of a strong China. "China is bent upon the creation of a new world," *Fortune* proclaimed, and the United States, "in considering the problem of foreign trade," should assist this construction, because China, "the biggest potential market on earth," was eager for the United States to exert its influence in the area. *Fortune* had earlier noted that a failure to help "would do violence not only to China but to U.S. pride, to the feeling that we are a great democratic Christian nation with ideals to uphold in all circumstances."[39]

In order for *Time, Fortune,* and, after November 1936, *Life* to reinforce these notions about China's potential, the three magazines had for several years purposely shown the "Middle Kingdom" in the most favorable light possible. One of the three points always emphasized was the close resemblance between China and the United States geographically and even in some sense historically. Geographically, the two nations were presented as virtually indistinguishable. In one issue, *Time* declared that, having captured "China's Boston (Peking), New York (Shanghai) and Washington (Nanking)," the Japanese were advancing on "China's Chicago (Hankow)."[40] Canton was described as "the teeming, sultry New Orleans of China."[41] China also had areas similar to American regions and states. Outer Mongolia could be equated to America's Pacific Northwest and the Shaanxi province held promise as "China's potential Pennsylvania."[42] (China's Pittsburgh, however, did not lie in Shaanxi province, for one *Fortune* article noted that China's Pittsburgh was the wartime capital of Chongqing, which is located in Sichuan province.)[43] Referring to

China's western region, *Time* commented, "Coastal Chinese . . . know more about Western China than George Washington knew about [America's] Wild West." When Japanese victories in the eastern region forced the Chinese to retreat westward, *Time*'s story on the massive movement of people and equipment again inserted a comparison with American history: Chinese government officials, soldiers, and students had embarked upon a "covered wagon trek to their Wild West."[44]

The second consistent editorial policy was to show Chinese government officials and the Nationalist army in a favorable light. Almost without hesitation, Time Inc.'s magazines saluted their abilities and their accomplishments. *Time* lauded two Guomindang officials as Asia's "greatest, suavest diplomats." Chiang's brothers-in-law, always highly regarded in the pages of Time Inc.'s publications, were "the solid, wistful Yale-trained, Dr. H. H. Kong, and the glossy, competent Harvardian, T. V. Soong."[45] A *Fortune* article described the two in equally flattering terms.[46]

A *Time* cover story in June 1941 praised Chiang's military adviser, Chen Cheng, whom *Time* called "brilliant" in his command of the approach to the wartime capital of Chongqing. Although the Chinese army was unknown to the world at large, the article said, and was short on the important tools of modern warfare, it made up for its lack of equipment in "numbers, know-how and morale." The troops were hardened and "campaign-wise" after so many years of fighting. Countering what it felt was the common American misperception of Chinese troops, *Time* noted, "China's best troops belie all the old saws about Chinese cowardice and indifference." As proof of their fighting spirit, it offered a description of them as "husky, shaven-pated sons of the soil who . . . like better than anything else to close with the Japanese hand to hand." Recently, they had added to their courage an ability to fight for long periods of time under difficult conditions and with few rations. The young but promising officer corps that led these troops made the defeat of the Japanese that much more likely. Chen himself was only forty-one, and the entire corps constituted the "youngest officer class in the world," but they were tough and intelligent. Physically large by Chinese standards, "hearty and jolly at rest and brutally energetic in action," these young officers displayed a strong devotion to the democratic ideals espoused by Sun Yat-sen, "China's George Washington."[47] *Fortune*, too, described the top officers as strong, intelligent, youthful, and enthusiastic: "probably the most colorful group . . . since Napoleon fished the marshals of the Grande Armée out of the regimental barracks."[48] More importantly, they loved the United States, because they felt America would send them the military equipment they desperately needed to fight the Japanese. "If & when someone delivers China's soldiers the goods," *Time* predicted, "they will be able to finish the job."[49]

Earlier, *Time* had extended its praise of China's soldiers to the Communists, even as Chiang was struggling to assert his dominance. "Some of Chiang's best troops," *Time* noted in an issue in December 1938, "are the Chinese Communist armies."[50] The guerrilla fighters damaged railroad lines, harassed Japanese troop and supply convoys, and swarmed over isolated garrisons. Wherever the Chinese Communists could achieve favorable odds, they attacked. *Time*'s coverage even highlighted Zhu De, commander of the Communist troops, as "China's No. 1 Guerrilla Fighter." The "modest, crinkly-eyed" Zhu and his guerrillas were part of what *Time* called the "New China." *Fortune* joined in with praise of its own. "The Communist guerrillas," it noted, were "men of an unparalleled efficiency."[51] And in the most surprising instance, in June 1939, *Time* even asserted that the communism espoused by Mao Zedong and Zhu De amounted "to little more than a Populist desire to give land to the tax-gutted and landlord-ridden Chinese peasant."[52]

Time Inc.'s dalliance with the Chinese Communists was not allowed to go too far, however. It was apparent that the military actions of Mao's guerrilla fighters helped tie down Japanese forces, but the Communists nonetheless represented the biggest political threat to Chiang's rule. *Time* warned that the generalissimo could not relinquish too much political authority or proffer too many military supplies to the Communists. Rather, he had to follow a policy *Time* called "flexuous." By 1941, writing about Chiang's difficulties generally, the newsweekly sided with the Nationalist government wholeheartedly and defended its partial destruction of the Chinese Communist New Fourth Army as a necessary move to prevent internal disruptions "by disarming and disbanding the Communist[s] . . . for insubordination."[53]

The third editorial policy in regard to China was, of course, the consistently favorable treatment of Chiang Kai-shek begun in the 1930's. *Time* lauded Chiang in cover stories and even named him and Madame Chiang as man and wife of the year for 1937. Similarly, *Fortune* showed excessive bias toward the generalissimo, especially in an issue in the fall of 1941. The *Time* cover article of January 3, 1938, celebrated Chiang because he had brought unity to the Chinese people.[54] In revitalizing the economy, raising, training, and equipping a capable military force, and providing an impetus for the moral rejuvenation of the nation, Chiang had taken the "traditionally disunited Chinese people" and given them the rudiments of a "national consciousness." The progress China had made under Chiang was "phenomenal." The creation of a sound currency, the construction of an infrastructure, the development of flood control and famine relief—all constituted "revolutionary" fundamental changes. Chiang's effective and modern military force was attacking the Communists in the way "a football coach uses a scrub team to train the regular army of New China." The article defended Chiang's slowness in moving against Japan: "New China was not ready to use her War Machine" when the Japanese attacked in the summer of 1937, and this policy was the best one for China. Only the weight of "Chinese public opinion" had forced Chiang to reconsider his "practice sessions" against the Communists. A later article echoed the same theme: Chiang "was determined to resist the Japanese," but first he had to "organize his nation, strengthen his army, build roads, prepare for the inevitable retreat into the interior."[55] Thus, his refusal to fight the Japanese in 1937 was for the good of the entire nation.

Not the least, *Time* observed in its January 1938 cover story, Chiang had strengthened the moral fabric of his nation. *Time* described Chiang's New Life Movement as a "big dose of the castor oil of Puritanism," as if exaggeration placed Chiang's social retrenchment in the context of American religious history. But Chiang's program was far more rigid than anything imagined by John Winthrop, Thomas Hooker, or John Cotton, especially in its call for the thorough militarization of Chinese life.[56]

Time Inc.'s other major piece celebrating Chiang was the September 1941 issue of *Fortune*, which was entirely devoted to "China the Ally." The content and general tenor of the four long articles were much the same as *Time*'s January 1938 man-and-wife-of-the-year portrait. *Fortune* characterized Chiang as "still virile, . . . [the] bitter, hardened, soldier of the camps."[57] His glory in creating one China had not been dulled by the fact that he had defeated the warlords with "an astuteness less military than human and political." His retreats in the face of Japanese attacks are described as "great" retreats, just as his future offensives would undoubtedly be equally "great." The future of China lay with Chiang: "and he has so far discharged his responsibility with superb skill." In *Fortune*'s portrait, Chiang was a politically shrewd, militarily astute, and morally upright leader who seemed to symbolize everything America could want in a foreign head of state. He was intent upon bringing China into the Christian, democratic community of nations, and he also—to *Fortune*'s satisfaction—offered to assist the United States in finally realizing its dogged belief in the China market. From there, the two nations could march toward their mutual goal of creating a Christian capitalist world order.

The period immediately preceding the American entry into World War II saw a dramatic shift in the quantity and type of information Americans received about China. Time Inc. saw its circulation figures rise to unprecedented heights, and it further expanded its reach by venturing into radio broadcasting and newsreel production. In the process, it became the first multimedia empire in the world. Along with this growth came the development, propagation, and reinforcement of certain conceptions about China. Ideas about Chinese democracy, its importance as a potential market for American trade, the fighting integrity of the Nationalist troops, and most of all, the strength, wisdom, and Christian convictions of Chiang Kai-shek— all became mainstays in articles. Whatever was really happening in Asia was somewhat beside the point. Contradictory information was either ignored or rationalized so that the larger image of an Americanized China remained viable. In his account of life in provincial China, the journalist Graham Peck wrote that he had returned there from the United States in 1940 filled with ideas "acquired from the American press: the gallant losing battles, the brave and clever guerrillas, the millions of determined refugees fleeing west . . . a new country a-building. . . . And looming over the whole united land [was] the massive figure of the Generalissimo, his attractive wife only slightly in the background."[58] Of the American media, none was as large as Time Inc., nor any as consistent in propagating that message.

During the last half of the 1930's, the coverage of events in China offered by Luce's media outlets reflected his personal biases more than it accurately reported the developments there. But for Luce, that was the point. Of his approach to journalism, one commentator noted, Luce "was the missionary, the believer, a man whose beliefs and visions and knowledge of Truth contradicted and thus outweighed the facts of his reporters."[59] He took it as his duty not simply to relate world events but to educate Americans on their responsibilities. He was not a reporter; he was a preacher, and he sermonized on behalf of China.

The five years before the United States entered World War II proved to be pivotal for American conceptions of Chiang, especially as they were shaped and publicized by Time Inc. From 1936 until 1941, Chiang was portrayed as China's political and spiritual savior. During the same period, as Luce's personal convictions about China intensified, his media conglomeration grew at a dazzling pace. These two developments reflected and reinforced the larger assumptions circulating in American society about China. In that respect alone, they are important for understanding the fundamental hopes of the "American Century" there.

Uncle Sam feeding a Chinese child, by Ed Hunter. From "Cheer China," for the benefit of United China Relief, Incorporated. B. A. Garside Collection, Hoover Institution Archives.

China Fights On, by John Gaydos. UCR's 1945 poster. George C. Marshall Research Foundation.

How Organized Labor Can Aid the People of China. Indusco Papers, Butler Library, Columbia University.

⟶ten reasons why

Organized labor in America, it is believed, will wish to give its support to United China Relief for ten major reasons:-

1. Because China is aiding in the world struggle against Fascism. The war in China is just another phase of the fight against Hitlerism and what it stands for.

2. Because China, in keeping the Japanese aggressor occupied, is acting as a battlefront for our own country in the Far East. China means America's defense.

3. Because China is waging a War of Independence such as we fought back in 1776-1783. Japan is seeking to destroy the national existence of the Chinese nation.

4. Because, if the Chinese are beaten, they will be organized on a slave-labor basis by a dictatorship. Chinese labor will thus bring down our own labor standards.

5. Because if, with our help the Chinese are victorious, they will develop their nation as a free people, who believe in democratic rights and principles.

6. Because as a result of the continued resistance of the Chinese people, their needs constitute one of the greatest needs of all time. It is almost impossible to measure the degree of human suffering involved.

7. Because the Chinese have generously contributed in times of need in our country. Back in 1918 they gave to the American Red Cross in behalf of flood victims $1,400,000—14 times the amount asked.

8. Because in addition to the superb Chinese army, the Chinese people, organized into heroic bands of guerrilla fighters, have been an important factor in stopping an aggressor in his tracks.

9. Because China has fought to *help herself*, organizing a great system of cooperative industrial enterprises and vest-pocket workshops which play a vital part in enabling the people to carry on.

10. Because Labor officially endorses this effort and has formed a representative National Committee to aid it and because many leading labor groups have already generously contributed to it.

How Organized Labor Can Aid the People of China. Indusco Papers, Butler Library, Columbia University.

China Shall Have Our Help, by Martha Sawyers. United China
Relief's 1942 poster. George C. Marshall Research Foundation.

China—First to Fight, by Martha Sawyers. UCR's 1943 poster.
George C. Marshall Research Foundation.

"The Madonna and Child," by Madame Lo-Chang. Special
Collections, Yale Divinity School Library, Records of United China
Relief, Inc., Missions Pamphlet Collection.

"The Nativity in a Cave"

"The Nativity in a Cave." by Lu Hung-Nien, presents the Holy Family with a charming little angel standing by with his lantern. In the cave the flowers are in bloom; outside the cave one sees the little shepherds in the snow. The artist is on the art faculty of the Catholic University in Peking. When a boy he loved the picture cards in the mission Sunday School. But one thing grieved him. No Chinese children were ever seen with Jesus. So his first Christian painting was "Jesus and the Little Children" and he put his own face on one of the children.

Original painting lent by Dr. William B. Pettus

Printed in U.S.A.

These cards sold for benefit of

United China Relief

Representing

Church Committee for China Relief

105 EAST 22ND STREET, NEW YORK, N. Y.

"The Nativity in a Cave," by Lu Hung-Nien. Special Collections, Yale Divinity School Library, Records of United China Relief, Inc., Missions Pamphlet Collection.

How to Spot a Jap, by Milton Caniff. United Service to China Archives, Seely G. Mudd Manuscript Library, Princeton University.

Madame Chiang Kai-shek before Congress, February 18, 1943.
National Archives.

RE AMMUNITION FO

Parade in San Francisco for Madame Chiang, March 25, 1943.
National Archives.

Chiang, Roosevelt, Churchill, and Madame Chiang at the Cairo
Conference, November 28—December 1, 1943. National Archives.

Miss Lace for United Service to China, by Milton Caniff. United
Service to China Archives, Seely G. Mudd Manuscript Library,
Princeton University.

Formosa—Free China's Valley Forge, by Marguerite Atterbury of
the Committee to Defend America by Aiding Anti-Communist
China. Right Wing Pamphlet Collection, Sterling Memorial
Library, Yale University.

The Last Stand (Freedom for China), by Burris Jenkins, Jr.
H. Alexander Smith Papers, Seely G. Mudd Manuscript Library,
Princeton University.

If China Goes. *Time*, March 29, 1948.

CHAPTER THREE

United China Relief and the Creation of American Images of China

The fate and the future of democracy in the Orient depend upon the
outcome of what is now taking place here in China.
— Mrs. Henry H. Meyer in a United China Relief broadcast, May 1941

In the four and a half years before Pearl Harbor, while Henry
Luce pushed his special interpretation of Sino-American relations,
events in China unfolded in such a manner as to draw the attention
of an increasing number of Americans. The ambivalence evident in
the earlier part of the decade gave way to what historian Akira Iriye
has described as the "revulsion at the idea of sacrificing China in order to arrive at a deal with Japan."[1] Ultimately, Americans went from
reading about Japanese aggression and viewing newsreel footage of
the fighting to finding themselves at war. Developing alongside these
obviously negative images of the Japanese were the increasingly favorable impressions of the Chinese, the net effect of which was to
heighten national interest in the region and bolster the sense of Sino-
American affinity long proclaimed by sentimentalists.

Beginning on July 7, 1937, Japan expanded its aggressive and brutal
policies, moving south from Manchuria and into central China.
Chiang's forces made a valiant stand in Shanghai, suffering terrible
casualties in the process, but the Japanese were only temporarily
checked. By the end of the year, they had driven Nationalist troops
west of Nanjing. Upon occupying the city in December, Japanese soldiers embarked upon a horrific reign of terror and destruction, including the mass raping of tens of thousands of Chinese women. The
next year saw the Japanese push their military advance farther westward, whereupon Chiang relocated the Nationalist capital to the city
of Chongqing in Sichuan province.

Accounts of Japanese atrocities reached Americans and China's heroic resistance became a major story for the year. In a Gallup poll con-

ducted late in 1937 on what events had interested Americans most during the year, the Ohio floods topped the list, but just below them came the Sino-Japanese War, above Roosevelt's Supreme Court battle and Amelia Earhart's dramatic disappearance over the Pacific.[2] Moreover, Americans' sympathy clearly lay with the Chinese, rising from 43 percent in August 1937 to 74 percent by May 1939.[3] *Fortune* magazine reported in a 1938 survey that more Americans were disturbed by Japan's invasion of China than by the German movement into Austria in March of 1938.[4] Concern and sympathy did not necessarily translate into tangible assistance, however. As historian Michael Schaller has observed, "China remained an abstract concept in the minds of most Americans, a largely disorganized and unimportant foreign state."[5] But it was out of this very abstractness that the idea emerged of a malleable China ready to adopt American ways. Regional circumstances in Asia along with fascist aggression in Africa and Europe combined with the persistent stagnation of the domestic economy to create a climate that made such a view of China more likely. Henry Luce was certainly committed to that perspective, and now he began to find others who were similarly inclined.

In combination with Luce's media corporation, another important influence on American perceptions of China came into play before the nation's entrance into World War II, and, like the coverage offered by Time Inc., it had a substantial effect on shaping American attitudes toward China. A group of relief agencies, heretofore separate in their fund-raising activities and in their allocation of monies yet united in their dedication to providing humanitarian aid to China's war victims, combined their operations under one coordinating agency with the name United China Relief (UCR). Because of his keen interest in China and his vast financial resources, Luce played a major role in the creation and success of the organization. Not only was he instrumental in its construction, but through the people he lent from Time Inc. and others whom he recruited from the ranks of business, he had a considerable hand in the fundamentally pro-Chiang attitude the agency adopted.

The overall goal of UCR was to educate Americans about the wartime conditions in China and to raise money to alleviate the suffering there. The image of China that it promoted in its publicity and informational material was remarkably similar to the one envisioned and advanced by Luce through Time Inc. Although it never operated from overtly political motives as Time Inc. did, the agency nonetheless furthered the same false impressions about China as a land very much like the United States; that is, the Chinese people held the same ide-

als as Americans, and they sought to replace their ancient and outmoded past with a more workable future closely based upon the
American example. United China Relief worked to translate the com-
passion engendered by the war into something useful and concrete for
the Chinese people.

Since the late 1930's, certain Americans had been organizing relief
efforts with the hope of tapping into the latent American sympathy
for China. Prior to the creation of United China Relief in 1941, American humanitarian initiatives had for the most part been scattered
among eight agencies: the American Bureau for Medical Aid to
China, the American Committee for Chinese War Orphans, the
American Committee in aid of Chinese Industrial Cooperatives (Indusco), the American Friends Service Committee, the Associated
Boards for Christian Colleges in China, the China Aid Council, the
China Emergency Relief Committee, and the Church Committee for
China Relief. Each had its own separate concern: the American Bureau for Medical Aid to China, for example, raised money to provide
for modern medical treatment of wounded and sick soldiers as well
as the civilian victims of the war, and the American Committee for
Chinese War Orphans directed its efforts toward providing housing,
food, and care for the rising population of refugee children. The
uncoordinated efforts of these various agencies provided some hu-
mane support for China's destitute, but their achievements remained
dwarfed by the enormous problems and needs.

A group of dedicated people decided that a more centralized effort
would help the beleaguered nation. Thus began the endeavor to create
United China Relief.[6] Early attempts at coordinating the fund-raising
and distribution activities of the existing organizations failed for a
number of reasons. The eight committees, jealous and concerned
about preserving their separate identities, were reluctant to give up
their autonomy. Compounding the competition and occasional bick-
ering was the inability to find a strong leader to oversee the transformation. But persistent efforts paid off, and by late 1940, a tentative
agreement was reached. The eight committees merged the following
February to form United China Relief, in what was initially designed
as a temporary organization. The final success came about in large
part because of the considerable efforts of Henry Luce.

From the outset of the negotiations, Luce pledged to use his influence toward building a board of directors composed of an "outstanding group of Americans." Toward that end, he succeeded wonderfully.
Aside from himself, United China Relief's board included such no-

table persons as Pearl S. Buck, John D. Rockefeller III, movie producer David O. Selznick, Republican presidential candidate Wendell Willkie, former ambassador to the Soviet Union William C. Bullitt, president of the Marine Midland Trust Company James G. Blaine, Morgan House banker Thomas W. Lamont, and chairman of the Studebaker Corporation and future Marshall Plan administrator Paul G. Hoffman.[7] Moreover, Luce saw to it that the new superagency would have "a very substantial initial operating fund" if the separate bureaus would put aside their differences, renounce some, but not all, of their autonomy, and form a united organization. The tentative plans completed at the end of 1940 led to final negotiations in January 1941 and the incorporation of United China Relief one month later.[8]

The plan was simple. The board of directors developed a comprehensive, fourfold approach. First, UCR obviously intended to coordinate and unify fund-raising efforts. This meant conducting drives and canvassing funds through mass mailings and other forms of large-scale solicitation. Second, UCR planned to distribute this money for humanitarian relief and rehabilitation within China. The general outline for the distribution went along five lines: medical and health needs; child welfare, which dealt primarily with Madame Chiang Kai-shek's orphanages for refugee children, also called "warphanages"; educational needs, including the construction of schools and the training of teachers; disaster relief; and economic reconstruction. Third, UCR wanted to implement programs that would educate Americans on the conditions in China. Although this was accomplished to some extent in the fund-raising drives, UCR specifically targeted young Americans still in school. It printed and distributed pamphlets, books, and films dealing with aspects of Chinese society including history, geography, and culture. Finally, through its activities, UCR hoped to reassure the Chinese people that the traditional American feelings of friendship and goodwill toward them persisted.[9]

Initial plans called for raising $5 million in 1941, with the first $1,175,000 to be distributed to the agencies in an effort to allow them to continue their existing programs without interruption. The amount equaled the total collected by the eight separately during 1940. Although UCR was to raise the money, the eight agencies retained individual control of distribution. The next $1,175,000 was to be similarly disbursed except that UCR would have some say in the use of this sum. All other funds exceeding $2.35 million were to be allocated solely by UCR. In the end, United China Relief raised approximately $3.25 million, short of its goal, but significantly more than was collected in the preceding year when the eight agencies had not coordinated their efforts. More importantly, according to one UCR staff member who summarized the activities for 1941, the agency had begun "to arouse the American people to an awareness of the situation in China and the importance of China's war of resistance to the rest of the world."[10]

In addition to helping in the creation of the board of directors, Luce lent a number of Time Inc. employees to UCR for key jobs. Otis P. Swift, for example, a Time Inc. publicity man, became the organization's publicity director. Theodore White, Time Inc.'s correspondent in China, served in the same capacity for UCR, and *Life's* internationally renowned photographer Margaret Bourke-White forwarded material from China that the agency used in its promotional campaigns in the United States. Luce also contributed a substantial sum of money from his own personal fortune. Between 1939 and the end of 1941, he donated nearly $60,000, most of it in the form of Time Inc. stock. He also solicited money from other wealthy Americans, including Doris Duke, the tobacco heiress, and Bernard Baruch, the multimillionaire financier who had been head of the War Industries Board during World War I. Baruch contributed a total of $6,000 for China relief before the end of 1941, and in 1942 he made the single largest individual contribution to United China Relief during its entire history when he donated $102,340.[11] With considerable assistance from Luce, then, UCR got off the ground with a number of important successes in the composition of its board of directors and in its initial fund-raising efforts.[12]

Luce applied himself in other ways as well. In an attempt to receive some recognition from the federal government, he requested a public endorsement from the Roosevelt administration. He wrote Secretary of State Cordell Hull, suggesting that official encouragement from Washington would erase any lingering doubts potential contributors might have about UCR's activities. He even went so far as to include a reply for Hull. In a draft for the secretary to use in responding to UCR's treasurer James G. Blaine, Luce had Hull writing, "The effort of the Chinese people to emerge from the present conflict as a progressive and democratic nation is one on which the sympathies of our own nation are deeply involved."[13] Hull in reply said that as a matter of policy the State Department did not endorse the efforts of private fund-raising organizations, but he added that the entire United States government was "favorably disposed toward every properly conducted [relief] effort, not in conflict with sound essential or accepted economic policies, to minimize or alleviate human suffering." Ironically, despite denying his request, Hull took Luce up on the draft offer and used some of Luce's own words in writing back.[14]

The secretary of state's response, although lukewarm, was somewhat encouraging but United China Relief still faced the formidable task of convincing Americans that the money they gave to the organization would indeed help the Chinese people. The Chinese exclusion law was still in effect, and in many parts of the United States people were not inclined to look upon the Chinese people favorably or even with interest; UCR faced the daunting task of persuading Americans that events in China were important to them. To this end, one agency memorandum indicated that the first structural requirement was a suborganization "designed to condition and influence public opinion"; second, UCR needed a separate bureau "to capitalize on that public opinion by converting it into cash for the relief of China."[15] In short, the organization had to convey a greater sense of how China's interests closely paralleled America's. To do this, it followed a three-pronged strategy that ultimately focused on projecting the fundamental notion that the Chinese people were very much like Americans.

Because many of its participating agencies were religiously affiliated, United China Relief functioned, at least in part, as a missionary organization. That, of course, meant that the Chinese people's acceptance of Christianity needed to receive repeated emphasis in UCR's promotional material. Furthermore, because UCR was a coalition of agencies that had been created with humanitarian goals in mind, it was imperative to convey an immediate sense of how American contributions could tangibly better living conditions in China. To accomplish all this, UCR had to make quick use of recent advancements in communications technology to promulgate its message to the largest possible audience.

Thus the organization had political, not just philanthropic, significance. One UCR memorandum indicated quite clearly that the organization's purpose was to sell "China to the American people."[16] The task required that China be portrayed as democratic—at least socially if not yet politically. Through the use of radio broadcasts, educational pamphlets, and public lectures given by UCR employees before civic, religious, and educational groups throughout the United States, the relief organization put forth a coordinated, multimedia program that presented China in a highly favorable light.

Throughout 1941, the radio broadcasts provided a dual avenue for disseminating the UCR message. From their point of origin in China, they could be heard by their primary audience, other Westerners, and printed transcripts of the broadcasts were distributed in the United States. Maud Russell, for example, of the National YWCA of China, gave a talk titled "Encouraging Democracy in China," which described the democratic reverberations created in China by women and the Chinese Industrial Cooperative Association. "Women, if properly educated," she asserted, "are one of the greatest forces of democracy," and Chinese women had made significant advancements participating in the "struggle for a democratic China" as more of them became educated, entered the work force, and assisted in the "process of nation-saving."[17]

The Chinese Industrial Cooperative Association also served as a transmitter of democratic waves inside China, Russell reported. This movement attempted to bolster the industrial output of the Nationalist government during the war by allowing localized units to produce such necessary items as shoes, blankets, cloth—"serviceable goods of the sort ordinary people needed, at prices they could afford."[18] In this way the Chinese Industrial Cooperatives (CIC) placed the initiative and impetus in the hands of the people. In raising money for UCR in the United States, Warner Brothers movie star John Garfield cited the cooperatives as an example of the constructive steps being taken in China: "Chinese Industrial Cooperatives signify positive Democracy on the march. Though the setting is China . . . the spirit behind this great movement strikingly resembles that of our own nation in the first century of its growth."[19]

Because the cooperatives also served a useful military function in that they proved to be difficult targets for the Japanese to bomb, the CIC appeared as patriotic units dedicated to promoting the development of light industry in the western region of China and at the same time a way in which many Chinese peasants could supplement their income.[20] Wartime necessity combined with the possibility of laying the democratic groundwork for the postwar world. *Time* concurred with the idea that the cooperatives provided a democratic stimulus. The success of Chinese democracy, the magazine declared, depended on "the crankshaft [being] turned over by democratic self-starters" like CIC.[21]

One of the biggest promoters of CIC was a New Zealander named Rewi Alley who had lived in China since shortly after World War I and now devoted his time, energy, and financial resources to making the cooperatives work. Although he was sure that the CIC could help people develop the individual and group skills necessary in a political democracy, his public comments often belied his growing sense of frustration with the program. Beset with peasants who proved either unable or reluctant to participate, hampered by corrupt persons who took advantage of the program for personal profit and gain, CIC never stimulated the mass economic and political changes that its ardent supporters envisioned. The Nationalist government was not in sympathy with the program because by teaching the tangible benefits of independent thought and action to Chinese peasants, it threatened to undermine the rule of Chiang's autocratic government. Through its control of CIC's central headquarters in Chongqing, the Nationalist government maintained a firm grip on the organization's progress in addition to keeping a tight reign over the financial appropriations by not increasing funding at the rate of inflation, which by 1940 had become a major economic problem.[22]

Despite these considerable hindrances placed upon CIC's activities, sympathetic Americans continued to report favorably on the changes being brought about. One missionary who agreed with Russell's and *Time's* assertions about the democratic currents circulating within Chinese society stated, "China is genuinely a democratic country, with democratic traditions extending back two thousand years." Evidently, the nation's democratic heritage was rooted in the daily experiences of life at the local level. It seemed as if almost every aspect of the human existence contributed to this centuries-long tradition. In the end, the assumption ran, China's schools, particularly the Christian colleges begun by the missionaries, would precipitate the jump from democracy at the local level to democracy on the national level. The Christian colleges, moreover, provided for a firm commitment to democracy and created a natural bulwark "against communism." Americans could help this democratic transformation to the national level and at the same time assist in thwarting the spread of communism by contributing money, thus allowing the Christian colleges to continue their work.[23] *Fortune* in its April 1941 article "The New China" noted that the "contributions of Western missionaries and of brilliant Chinese educated in Western universities" had finally begun to have an impact during the last two decades.[24]

Additional support for the cooperatives came in the form of a radio broadcast by Dr. Lewis S. C. Smythe, a professor of sociology at the University of Nanjing. The CIC instilled the fundamentals of democracy, he argued, with the end result being not only the production of blankets but also the creation of "better men." The key determinant was American money: $5 million to be precise. That sum would "put the cooperatives on their feet so they could make a real contribution toward winning the war and forming a bulwark of democracy in the countryside at the close of the war."[25]

Other testimonials abounded. In another broadcast titled "A Miniature Democracy," the speaker talked about the vocational school for Boy Scouts in Chongqing and how the school gave them a democratic setting.[26] Another broadcast mentioned the "seeds of democracy" inherent within the "many features of Chinese life"; the United States, the speaker said, needed to demonstrate "the benefit of America's own experience" and make it possible for the Chinese to gain "a fuller understanding of what the American dream has been."[27] The existence of democratic forces, another speech said, meant that Americans had an obligation to support them so that China would develop a "reasonable form of democracy."[28]

Many of UCR's efforts were directly tied in with Henry Luce and Time Inc., and many were fund-raising events. In one example, Clare Boothe Luce, Luce's second wife, successful playwright, and later congressional representative from Connecticut, spoke at a fund-raising dinner held at the Waldorf-Astoria Hotel in New York City in June 1941, shortly after she and Henry returned from a trip to China. The dinner was supposed to serve as a public demonstration to the Chinese people and their leaders of America's admiration for them. *Life* had carried an account of the Luces' trip with a text by Henry and photographs by Clare. The dinner was arranged to give the Luces the opportunity to share their recent experiences with a substantial group of well-connected Americans. The guest list included Pearl Buck, syndicated columnist Walter Lippmann, the president of CBS William Paley, Mr. and Mrs. John D. Rockefeller III, David O. Selznick, advertising executive Raymond Rubicam, and Wendell Willkie, who served as the toastmaster.[29] As part of the arrangement, NBC broadcast Clare Luce's twenty-five minute talk.

Luce lectured her audience on the recent events that had led to the bleak conditions in Europe and Asia. She insisted that under the direction of Chiang Kai-shek, China had been on the way toward "becoming a modern, healthy nation" when Japan expanded its aggressive activity in 1937, temporarily ending the impressive progress Chiang had achieved. Referring to "free and fighting China" a number of times in her address, she suggested that the United States and China were pilot and copilot in the world plane flying toward the future.[30] But the situation in 1941 proved to have more than its share of turbulence. The Chinese, "our spiritual allies and our fellow Christians," desperately needed American assistance and guidance to withstand the Japanese onslaught. The Chinese are indeed "fellow

Christians," she declared. "Over fifty percent of China's leaders, military, economic and political, beginning with the Generalissimo and Mme. Chiang are Christian, and are graduates of the thirteen Christian Colleges in China." With such a concentration of Christian leaders, China possessed a religious spirit much like that of the West. Missionaries had sowed spiritual seeds years ago that were now being harvested in abundance through "evangelical and dynamic Christianity." Just look at China's leadership, she said: "The saga of the Christian missions . . . in war torn China is one of the most gallant and beautiful stories of the modern world."[31]

Luce saved her ultimate praise of China's leading family for the conclusion: Chiang "and his lovely wife" were on the highest plateau of political and spiritual enlightenment because of their Christian beliefs and their actions as the leaders of China. They were "the greatest married team in the world, with the patriotic exception of President Roosevelt and his dynamic, bountiful and far ranging lady Eleanor," and they complemented each other with a separation of their tasks based upon traditional gender roles. His duties resided in the "military and political sphere" while hers consisted mostly of "morale, spirit and social service." Whereas the generalissimo was a "Chinese dynamo" with the energy of "any American dynamo in Grand Coulee Dam," his wife was a more subtle combination: "Mme. Chiang is part dreamy lotus flower, part sullen tiger lily, and part American rose . . . and though she carries no gun, if she did she would shoot as straight from the hip as any girl of the Golden West."[32] Luce closed her case for Madame Chiang by noting that she spoke "flawless, tumbling, forthright *American*."

Clare Boothe's speech contained myriad images, allusions, and references to political, historical, and cultural forces within America's past and present. But one of her themes—the role Christianity played in guiding China's modern leaders—echoed the public expressions made by many American supporters of Nationalist China. The Christianity of many of the Chinese people seemed to offer the most tangible evidence that China was on its way toward becoming more like the United States, and it was continually stressed in UCR propaganda material. In the process of designing and coordinating various dinners and rallies, like one at Madison Square Garden, UCR used techniques that incorporated and promoted many of the same assumptions held by more ardent and more politically motivated supporters of Chiang and his government. Fundamentally, UCR based its campaigns upon the assumption that the organization needed to sell China to the American people. The China that was to be sold, moreover, had to reflect American ideals and values. By invoking episodes and images from America's past and relating them to present conditions within China, UCR hoped to convince Americans that they had a significant stake in the outcome of events there.

One memorandum written by publicity director Otis P. Swift delineated the immediate needs for programs designed to raise money in 1941. A particular recommendation included auctioning off original copies of famous manuscripts; in response, Hollywood producer David O. Selznick offered the one from *Gone with the Wind*.[33] Other promotional activities included selling merchandise with a Chinese theme. United China Relief sent out brochures, rented retail space in cities around the nation, and sold merchandise ranging from tea and cookbooks to blouses, jewelry, stuffed pandas, and perfume—and Christmas cards. Of all the products designed, manufactured, and sold by UCR, the most representative of the people's aspirations for Sino-American relations were the Christmas cards, which of course tied together the two themes of Christianity and capitalism. These cards, often the work of Chinese artists, showed traditional Christmas scenes with Chinese persons instead of Caucasians, even, as in one card, "the Madonna and Child," with an Asian-featured baby Jesus and Virgin Mary. Another card titled "The Nativity in a Cave" showed an Asian-featured "Holy Family with a charming little angel standing by with his lantern."[34]

All the various cards sold by UCR pictured Chinese scenes of one sort or another. One postcard used the picture of a Chinese baby sitting amid the wreckage of Nanjing after the Japanese had destroyed the city in their offensive of 1937, more commonly and accurately known as the rape of Nanjing; the reverse side of the card bore a note of explanation: "This is Ping Mei—a child of China. . . . He is one of 50 million refugees who desperately need food, clothing, shelter, medical aid."[35] The powerful and moving picture of Ping Mei was reprinted in newspapers and magazines across the United States and was also used in newsreel footage.[36] As evidence of the power of the photographic image, when Madame Chiang arrived in the United States in November 1942, five years after the destruction of Nanjing, waiting for her at the White House was a letter from Cathleen Quinn of East Orange, New Jersey, with three dollars from her and her daughters with the intention, as she put it, of helping "the little guy on the railroad tracks somewhere in China."[37]

Although Mrs. Quinn was moved by the picture of Ping Mei sitting alone in the ruins of Nanjing, the UCR appeal that used his picture, like so many others, did not restrict itself to purely humanitarian rea-

sons for soliciting money. Aside from the deplorable conditions and
terrible suffering caused by the war, UCR insisted that China also offered hope for the future of the United States. Ping Mei, the message
continued, was "one of 450,000,000 friendly, democratic Chinese
who loved and helped America in the past—who need our help now
in order to survive and be a free, independent, friendly neighbor in the
future." In other words, his plight, as horrible as it was, apparently did
not justify aid in its own right; the democratic heritage of his people
and the promise for a brighter American future had to be added to
make the picture more appealing.

Other educational and inspirational activities of UCR included
speaking engagements by UCR officers and supporters. Executive Director B. A. Garside, a former missionary to China and later biogra-
pher of Luce's father, gave a speech in Richmond, Virginia, in the fall
of 1941. In his address, he spoke of the American responsibility to assist China in the gallant struggle against Japan. In fact, he argued,
America owed a debt to the Chinese for having continued for too long
a time to sell vital strategic materials that had allowed the Japanese
war machine to devastate the Chinese countryside. "China's friendship for us is one of the greatest tributes a nation ever had," he commented, especially since "often we have done far too little to deserve
it." Even more than the debt of friendship was the need to realize that
"help to China means that she can win a fight which is as much ours
as hers." China was fighting to preserve the same ideals and values
that America symbolized and the American people held so dearly:
"The Chinese people are holding the western ramparts for us and for
the democratic way of life in the world."[38]

In the same vein, Charles Corbett, the executive officer of the
Church Committee for China Relief, stressed the role of Christianity
in fostering democratic ideas and institutions. China had become
"the protagonist of democracy in the Far East": for the peoples of Asia,
China—not Great Britain and not the United States—was the new
beacon of democratic hope. "It is significant to say," he added in referring to Chiang Kai-shek, "that China . . . attained this position under a Christian leader who feeds his mind daily upon the Bible." "The
Kingdom of God," he went on, which American missionaries had
worked so long to bring about in China, was "a far grander conception
than democracy," far grander and much broader in its reach because
it "produces democracy as a by-product." The end result meant that
in Asia, there raged a battle between the forces of imperialism (Japan)
and democracy (China).[39]

Garside, in listing some of his reasons for advocating humanitarian aid to China, mentioned the economic potential future Sino-American relations promised. "In the years just ahead," he prophesied, "a free and independent China will turn to us for all the products that American industry and mechanical genius can produce." The connection between assisting China in 1941 and greater trade in the future was clear: "both America and China [would] climb to new heights of prosperity."[40]

Toward the end of 1941, Garside summed up the UCR's progress in a memorandum to Luce. He found the results encouraging. Although UCR had fallen short of its fund-raising goal, over the last seven or eight months it had created a "wide spread and effective publicity campaign on behalf of China."[41] He was especially pleased that most of the donations had been made by people who had given small amounts. The number of contributions was, in some ways, more important than the total raised. The more people who gave money to UCR, the more successful the campaign had been in spreading the word about China. In fact, the number of contributions UCR received late in 1941 was so large that the organization got behind in its acknowledgments. The reason for the flood of donations was due partly to an appeal Luce sent to subscribers of *Time* asking them for five dollars. He wrote of the common interests and goals shared by Chinese and Americans. The Chinese, he assured *Time* readers, held on to the same conceptions of liberty and humanity as Americans, and they yearned to include into the construction of their nation the same "hopes and aspirations" as Americans had built into theirs.[42]

The success of UCR's 1941 campaign led the organization to make a number of assessments toward the year's end. It had raised over $3 million, most of it between April and early December, but after serious study it decided that its future depended upon a more centralized organization with less power remaining with the participating agencies. Among the changes desired, UCR wanted a larger and stronger board of directors, a program committee to determine the allocation and distribution of funds, and a campaign committee to coordinate publicity and fund-raising activities.[43] Although some areas of responsibility and control remained in dispute between UCR and certain of the bureaus, the agency completed its reorganization and set new goals for the coming year. It announced a target of over $7 million for 1942; Paul G. Hoffman became the new chairman of the board; another prominent business executive, W. R. Herod, president of International General Electric, was elected president; and a new team of volunteer, unpaid business executives arrived with the intent of "selling China to the American people and organizing China committees throughout the United States."[44]

In less than twelve months, UCR had gone from an idea to a reality: a relief organization capable of raising millions of dollars for China. Unlike the earlier period in the decade 1931–37 when the Hearst chain of publications could insist that China's plight was "not OUR business . . . . We SYMPATHIZE. But it is NOT OUR CONCERN," the four and a half years before Pearl Harbor saw a dramatic increase in the attention paid by Americans to developments in Asia. As Akira Iriye put it, "Here was, as Americans saw it, a moral question."[45] The activities of UCR neatly coincided with and furthered that growing sentiment. And regardless of how intangible those emotions may have been, they still became crucial for American concerns in the early years of World War II.

Beginning in 1941 and continuing over the course of the decade, UCR worked to educate Americans about the benefits of an Americanized China. As an outgrowth of the earlier missionary activity, it naturally borrowed many of the missionary ideas, which it attempted to convey in images that would be immediately familiar to Americans. China still remained a symbol for national success, and the dedicated personnel of UCR encouraged a climate of investment in terms both of time and of money to help bring this triumph about.

By the time of Pearl Harbor, then, many Americans had developed a good deal of sympathy for China, which was struggling so desperately against the Japanese. Organizations like UCR attempted to translate that increased appreciation and understanding into tangible forms of assistance. Part of the program pushed by UCR and Time Inc. stressed the thought that China's fight was America's fight. It was not long before that was literally true.

CHAPTER FOUR

Crusading Together: The Glorious War Years

When China and the United States became allies after Pearl Harbor, it was like a marriage after an over-long engagement—a shotgun marriage, if you will, but still a happy union.

—A. T. Steele, *The American People and China*

The Japanese attack on Pearl Harbor did more to bolster the popular reputation of the Nationalist government in the United States than any other development or event in Sino-American relations between 1931 and 1949; suddenly, China and the United States were allies. Supporters of the Guomindang could not have been happier, for, as they had long claimed, China's fight was truly America's. When Henry W. Luce died on December 8, *Time*'s China correspondent, Theodore H. White, expressed his condolences to his boss; but the younger Luce was dry-eyed. At least, he said of his father, "He lived long enough to know that now China and America are both on the same side."[1]

Most Americans, of course, reacted to the Japanese attack with shock, anger, and outrage. The war in the Pacific, as John Dower has carefully detailed, had an immediate and drastic impact on American conceptions of the Japanese. During the 1930's, many Americans, military and civilians alike, had grown increasingly skeptical of the abilities of the Japanese armed forces, which had failed to force China, a presumably weak military opponent, into submission.[2] Pearl Harbor changed that image, but whereas the Japanese had formerly been looked upon as subhuman and decidedly inferior primates, now they were atavistic supermen. The apparent contradiction was not inconsistent in that both images were racist, as Dower explains: "Subhuman and superhuman were not mutually exclusive, as might be expected, but complementary."[3] Pearl Harbor, the sinking of the British ships *Prince of Wales* and *Repulse* in the South China Seas, the capture of Singapore, and finally, the defeat of the American forces in the

Philippines—in all these actions the Japanese proved themselves
well-trained and highly motivated fighters. This string of quick and
decisive victories at the beginning of the war created the need for a
new popular impression of Asia and Asians that would help explain
the early American setbacks.

The reassessment of the Japanese military allowed for a reconsideration of the Chinese too. American supporters of the Nationalist
government reasoned that if the Japanese were such capable fighters,
then the Chinese, who since 1937 had withstood the worst the Japanese could give, must be much better than was originally conceded.

The war thus served as a crucial impetus for revising America's
thinking about Asia generally and China specifically. The celebration
of the Chinese people as new military allies developed from the judgments that had been espoused as part of Protestant missionary rhetoric for the preceding half-century. The Christian conception of
China provided a convenient foundation upon which the United
States could build after December 7. In short, wartime circumstances
heavily influenced national attitudes. Fortunately, everyone, and not
just missionaries, could now look to an Americanized China in their
time of need. Through a series of tragic events, China and America
were indeed suddenly linked in military purpose; and the closer the
two appeared to be in their political and social make up, the better for
the overall war effort.

Although the news of America's entry into the war vindicated the
previous efforts of Time Inc. and United China Relief, the amount of
work that had to be done to accommodate the new situation was staggering. The most immediate task for UCR in 1942 was to create a
campaign for the year centering around a national China Week sometime in April. Publicity director Otis Swift outlined the initial needs:
UCR had to coordinate the various positions on the organizational
chart; the most important posts were in the radio, merchandising, and
speakers bureaus. As far as the promotion department went, Swift
listed publicity, direct mail, motion picture, field publicity, staff photographer, and booklet-pamphlet coordinator as the most crucial positions.[4] And all this must be coordinated at both national and local
levels. Swift looked to Time Inc. for publicity in its newsreel, radio
program, and magazines. He also expressed a desire to have Madame
Chiang visit the United States in order to generate publicity and enthusiasm for the cause. To foster a truly national celebration, he went
about building a publicity portfolio for UCR chairmen and women.

With the various educational and promotional tools at their disposal, these local leaders could then arrange matters at their level.[5]

During China Week, April 12–19, each day was set aside for a specific purpose.[6] Beginning with Sunday, April 12, China Relief Sunday, the UCR committee would distribute 1,600 pamphlets in the Greater New York area. On Monday, Cultural Relations day, educators and college presidents would release testimonials, and the New York Public Library and the Museum of Modern Art would open exhibits on Chinese art and culture. On Thursday, China Trade day, more than one hundred business leaders were to attend a luncheon given by 1942 chairman Wendell Willkie, Paul G. Hoffman, and Henry Luce to highlight the "importance of the potential of a Free China to post-war America." On Saturday, designated Festival day, there would be a picnic in Central Park. All the events of China Week were to be photographed, of course, especially kite-flying contests and ricksha races, and Joe DiMaggio's demonstration of batting techniques for Chinese children.

China Week would culminate with a day of thanks on Sunday, April 19. The final event for the New York City area was to be a parade with approximately 2,000 participants from Chinatown. Some of its special features, which were designed to increase the "novelty and attraction" and guarantee greater interest, included "comely Chinese girls in nurses uniforms," whose role was to dramatize China's medical needs. Four elephants (obtained through Pearl Buck's first husband), bearing gifts, were supposed to illustrate how China received supplies from the West along the "jungle trail" as of 1942.

Because China Week was to be the springboard for a year-long campaign that UCR hoped would raise the consciousness of every American on the subject of China, national coverage was necessary. The plan included working with Rotary International to reach the smaller cities and towns around the nation. W. R. Herod, UCR president, secured the support of his counterpart at Rotary, Tom J. Davis, by appealing to his business inclinations. As the last major area yet to experience industrialization, China would offer "the most stupendous opportunities for trade development" after the war, Herod wrote Davis, and he pointed out that with a population of 450,000,000, China still possessed "only a few thousand miles of railway and a highway structure far from adequate." China's natural resources would help raise the capital necessary to pay for American goods.[7]

Even before Herod's exhortations, Davis had sent a letter addressed to the president and secretary of all the local Rotary Club chapters in the United States, urging them to invite speakers on China in an effort to emphasize "the solidarity of the American and Chinese peoples."[8] In keeping with UCR's desire for maximum publicity, Davis suggested that when such meetings were held, local newspapers be contacted in order to spread the word about China more effectively. The promotion was very successful, he wrote Herod. Numerous programs had already been implemented and others were planned. In particular, he mentioned the example of Edwin G. Leipheimer, a "manager of seven or eight of the largest newspapers" in Montana, who had secured extensive coverage of China and had worked closely with the two major wire services, Associated Press and United Press International. Davis was very pleased: "So I would say to you, Mr. Herod, that Rotary International has done a rather effective job. In a few less than 3400 communities in the United States and Canada they have done this in the connection with China and our friendship with China."[9]

Rotary International's activity in early 1942 helped prepare the ground for UCR's more aggressive campaign that was launched with China Week in April. The main feature of the continuing campaign was to be an hour-long fund-raising radio program on Saturday evening, April 11. United China Relief had the help of highly professional media and film personnel. David O. Selznick, director of what was called the Hollywood Victory Committee, wired the New York office that he had obtained commitments from various well-known film stars—Cary Grant, Ginger Rogers, Loretta Young, and others—to donate commercial broadcasts to UCR during certain radio programs; UCR could then sell the commercials to corporations at regular rates. The money received from the advertising became part of the national fund-raising drive. One of the attractions to the film stars was, of course, that they could contribute to the cause without receiving income on which they would have had to pay income tax.[10]

The effort to use Hollywood actors became central to the success of the fund-raising broadcast. United China Relief wanted big names to fill the hour-long program: suggestions included Fred Allen, Jack Benny, Charlie Chaplin, Bing Crosby, Bette Davis, Walt Disney, Joan Fontaine, Cary Grant, Bob Hope, Paul Robeson, Babe Ruth, and Kate Smith.[11] The Hollywood Victory Committee also sought younger talent like Mickey Rooney and Judy Garland, both of whom also became part of an effort under the direction of Walt Disney that was called "Campaign for Young China."[12] Each star would be asked to perform in some manner consistent with his or her talents. Walt Disney, for example, might best promote the cause of China through a dialogue between Mickey Mouse and Donald Duck. In another instance, UCR wanted Babe Ruth, because of his tremendous appeal among sports fans, to talk about China's children. With such a star-studded docket, UCR intended to sell its message to Americans in the most appealing manner possible.

The New York segment of the program was produced by Charles Martin from the Biow agency. Tom Lewis from Young & Rubicam handled the twenty-minute segment from Hollywood. The program would include a letter from President Roosevelt read by Paul G. Hoffman, short radio plays by Maxwell Anderson and Pearl Buck, and a quiz show on UCR's activities with actors from the "Phil Baker Master Quiz Program."[13] A woman from Wyoming whose son had been killed in Southeast Asia was to speak on the importance of aiding China.

Publicity director Otis Swift made it clear that all material had to be checked with the Chinese consultants and the senior officers at UCR before airtime. He was especially concerned about the comedy material, fearing that an embarrassing skit would be placed immediately before a solemn statement by an official of the Chinese Nationalist government like Ambassador Hu Shih: "The nightly abominations that emanate from Hollywood simply must not precede the appearance of the Chinese Ambassador." He cited an example from the previous year as exactly the kind of inappropriate juxtaposition he would not allow.

Luce expressed his interest in the program and his excitement over the cooperation UCR had achieved with Hollywood in a letter to UCR's publicity director. "Daryl Zanuck is crazy to do a China picture," he wrote, and he reported that Sam Goldwyn would be the first of fifty Hollywood producers to contribute $1,000 to the China cause. He cautioned Swift, however, that there was a potential problem because of differences in the approach advocated by Selznick and the men from the Young & Rubicam agency. The latter would be satisfied with almost any program that contained a few big names, but Selznick wanted to stroke the emotional chords of the nation: "David wants to build a show which will send 40,000,000 Americans to bed weeping for China and emptying their pocketbooks." Selznick needed thirty days to "find the real rich material of China's emotion." Not one to miss a business opportunity for his media conglomerate, Luce mentioned that the entire Hollywood-UCR relationship ought to be discussed within Time Inc., because as he noted, "it means Hollywood relations with TIME, Inc. as well as with China Relief."[14]

Four days before the show went on the air, Russell Whelan, one of the chief producers, made a note about the basic assumptions that had served to guide its production. The use of Hollywood stars such as Mickey Rooney and Bob Hope, he observed, was intended to attract "the largest mass audience possible." With somewhere in the neighborhood of 400 to 500 radio stations carrying the program, he estimated the potential audience at larger than 20 million people. He explained how UCR planned to get its message across. The idea was "to sugarcoat [the] UCR plea and insert in the midst of the entertainment—the same technique that sells mountains of Jello and soap chips and dental cream each week."[15] In other words, China, like anything else, could be sold to the American people.

The radio program was widely publicized. There were full-page advertisements in *Variety, Broadcasting,* and *Radio Daily.* Four weeks before the show aired, plugs appeared on the Philip Morris radio programs and during the Bulova time signals on over 500 radio stations across the country.[16] United China Relief also coordinated periodical and newspaper coverage. A partial list of the magazines that agreed to run articles on UCR and China included *Vanity Fair, Vogue, Saturday Evening Post, Brides Magazine,* the *New Yorker, American Magazine,* and *Colliers;* another thirty-two signed on later.[17] In addition, various retail stores across the country, including Bonwit Teller, Bergdorf-Goodman, and J. D. Hudson, agreed to coordinate their window displays with UCR's activities during China Week. Later Elizabeth Arden, F. A. O. Schwartz, Lord & Taylor, and Strawbridge & Clothier in Philadelphia, among others, joined the effort.[18]

Wesley Bailey, on loan from Time Inc. and in charge of publicity for UCR, in assessing the situation said that the whole affair added up to "a pretty concentrated package labelled 'China.'" He predicted that the crowning moment would come with a "big red seal on that package in the form of a cover story in *Life.*"[19] But *Life* did not oblige, presumably because it had just run a flattering piece on the generalissimo in its March 2 issue, and even a Luce publication had to avoid saturating its reading public with too much of a good thing.

Nonetheless, Bailey and the other UCR executives were well satisfied with their efforts. Aside from the massive publicity generated over the event, UCR managed to persuade a number of leading newspapers to run pertinent editorials during China Week. Calling China "our sister republic," the *New York Times* mentioned UCR's activities and encouraged Americans, especially New Yorkers, to contribute to the organization. "United China Relief," it concluded, "will see that the American dollars go where they will do the most good."[20] The

Washington Post ran a story on UCR's efforts, complete with a picture of the women from the Chi Psi Upsilon sorority at National Park College in Forest Glen, Maryland, who had raised money by holding a sacrifice dinner; forgoing the usual salad and dessert, they contributed the savings to UCR.[21] Through these types of small fund-raising events and retail sales, UCR raised a considerable sum during World War II. Items like the Christmas cards netted sales of nearly $350,000 for the last three years of the war.[22]

In some ways, the money raised was not as important as the message conveyed. In promoting the various local and national programs that solicited funds, UCR used a well-coordinated approach that pushed the idea of China's similarity to the United States. "China's battle is ours," one sample letter declared; another said: "Every yard of China's front line is ours. The desperate problem facing China is ours." Despite the devastation wrought by the Japanese war machine, Chinese morale remained high. Not only that, but in emphasizing the similarities between the two nations, UCR noted that China's "love of freedom, so like ours," continued to motivate its people in their resistance. Educators had an especially compelling reason to give: "Probably no people hated the idea of military force as do the Chinese." The letter added, "With them, the scholar, the teacher, the philosopher have always come first—and will again."[23]

Educating young Americans in an effort to promote better relations between future generations of Chinese and Americans was always an important part of the UCR program. Such harmony could not be achieved "unless the elementary schools of the nation build a strong foundation of knowledge and respect for China."[24] Toward that end, UCR distributed, often without charge, articles, pamphlets, movies, and other educational materials for all levels, from the elementary schools to the high schools. One typical pamphlet, titled *China Primer*, shows the nature of the cultural forces at work in the construction of American images of China during the war.[25] This pamphlet was a revised, more readable version of a *Pocket Guide to China*, prepared by the United States Military Authorities for soldiers designated to serve there. The pamphlet started with the advice to the reader to forget all preconceptions about China, and then proceeded to a section called "The Chinese People are like Americans"—in fact, "Those who know both peoples often remark at the likeness." There were numerous reasons for this, including the enormous geographical size of the two countries, but Americans and Chinese were also alike in that "both love independence and individual freedom" and share similar political yearnings. It was true that the Chinese government was not the same as America's, but, the pamphlet said, "We are alike, also, because of our natural democratic tendencies."

Humor provided another tie between Americans and Chinese as jokes reflected a similar way of thinking between the two peoples. The Chinese loved slapstick humor, moreover, and the film masters of the genre, Charlie Chaplin, Harold Lloyd, and Laurel and Hardy, were as funny in China as in America. One UCR speaker discussed this dynamic from a psychological perspective, making a note of Americans' love of humor and how much this related to the Chinese, who were "a cheerful people" whose wit was much the same as Americans': "They have their clean jokes and their dirty jokes and their mother-in-law jokes."[26]

Part of UCR's educational effort included suggesting additional readings, and central to the organization's recommendations were articles from Time Inc.'s magazines. Another link came through UCR's production and distribution of films about China. Between 1942 and 1946, UCR produced four films: *Western Front* (1942), which told of "China's heroic defense," *China—First to Fight* (1943), *Here Is China* (1944), and *Report on China* (1945–46), which was edited by former "March of Time" employee Kenneth Cofod. These films concentrated on the same themes established in the organization's pamphlets, radio programs, and speeches. *Western Front* opened with a close-up of the Statue of Liberty, and the message, "With the United States as pattern and precedent," the new China had grown from America's example. The Chinese way of life now contained scenes "which might have been transplanted from Cincinnati, Detroit or South Bend." In China, "no less than in Chillicothe, Ohio," the American way of life predominated. The film also contained the obligatory celebration of Chiang Kai-shek, who, in bringing a sense of national purpose to China, had become the "undisputed leader and idol of four hundred millions of Chinese." His brilliant strategy against the Japanese and his ideas about "government, free enterprise and free labor taken from the United States" had led to the creation of a China that was "literally 'made in the U.S.A.'"[27] Through films like this, UCR promoted its vision of China in the same manner as Time Inc. Both organizations, moreover, while primarily focused upon the printed word, ventured into the new mediums of radio and motion pictures to reinforce the idea that the United States and China were remarkably alike.

While United China Relief organized its 1942 campaign, Time Inc. embarked upon its own instructional undertaking designed to bring

Americans positive news from the China-Burma-India theater. The news stories from the battlefront were very similar in tone to those *Time* had printed during the last half of the 1930's—that is, laudatory of Chiang Kai-shek's military prowess in the face of tremendous difficulties and also of his strong Christian convictions. The resulting celebration of his character took on many forms, but ultimately the message conveyed was one of complete support. In short, *Time* summed up its case by noting that he was "one of the half-dozen most important people in the world."[28]

The idolization of Chiang took on a heightened sense of urgency now that the two nations faced a common enemy. In yet another cover story, *Time* celebrated him as the "great Chiang." Reportedly known by his soldiers as a man who "sits like a mountain, moves like a dragon, and walks with the sure step of a tiger," he was portrayed as a popular military commander of his soldiers, most of whom were in awe of his abilities, and as the enlightened political leader of his people, bringing the best of Western ideas to his country. "China means Chiang," *Time* declared.[29] An article in *Fortune* at about the same time elaborated upon the loyalty he engendered among the Chinese by noting, "Chiang Kai-shek works as a man on men and commands an extraordinary devotion." Aside from what the writer called his "unanalyzable personal prestige," Chiang commanded such respect and loyalty because "he himself obeys, for he is one of the rare men of action who has been able to give a philosophic expression to his own foundations."[30]

If China did in fact mean Chiang, then *Time* clarified what the nation stood for by describing many of his important qualities. Not surprisingly, his Christianity came first. As a "practicing Christian," he rose every day at 5:30 A.M. to read the Bible. A *Life* portrait by correspondent Theodore H. White emphasized the sincerity of Chiang's conversion: "A man of Chiang's iron will" does not easily convert to a different religion, but his conversion was not brought about "for the sake of publicity." The article suggested that the apparent contradiction between the violence that surrounded his life and apparently "cut across the rather gentle faith which he professes" could be understood, as some missionaries explained, by thinking of Chiang in the biblical context as "an 'Old Testament Christian.'"[31]

More than a man of religious fortitude, Chiang intended to inculcate the fundamental tenets of political democracy and Christian morality into his troops. At least one *Time* reader was convinced; in writing to express her faith in Chiang's Christianity, she recounted a story in which, during a moment of prayer, he had beseeched God to look kindly upon the American people first, prayed for his own people second, and finally asked for the merciful treatment of the Japanese people. This proved that Chiang had a truly Christian heart, which he manifested by his willingness to forgive even those who brutalized his country.[32] Another reader wrote in to say that Chiang's "profound serenity and fortitude" made him a good candidate for Time's 1942 man-of-the-year.[33]

Time did not limit its coverage of the China theater to the present but often purposely drew historical analogies in an attempt to clarify Americans' presumably confused grasp of the situation. Chiang, the magazine remarked early in 1942, had managed to hold his people together despite the tremendous beating they had taken from the Japanese. "From Valley Forge through Valley Forge," he still continued to fight the enemy.[34] In another, somewhat muddled, attempt to compare China and revolutionary America, Time identified Dr. Sun Fo, president of the Chinese Legislative Yuan, as the son of "China's George Washington, Sun Yat-sen.[35]

All this historical analogy was part of Time Inc.'s fixed idea that Americans should learn to look upon the Chinese as much like themselves. In its big China issue of March 2, 1942, Life pounded the comparison with three photographs of Chiang Kai-shek looking very much like an American politician: first as an ordinary business executive, sitting working at his desk; second, with his wife at luncheon, seated in front of a framed picture of the generalissimo on the wall, the one that had appeared on the November 9, 1936, Time cover; and finally, in a typically American pose, seated with Madame Chiang on a plaid American-style sofa, laughing while they looked at a book and petted their Irish setter named Hami. This last photograph also had an important background detail, a picture of President Roosevelt on a shelf behind the Chiangs.[36] A variation of the same scene, with Hami sitting on the floor at the Chiangs' feet and the same picture of Roosevelt in the background, appeared in a pamphlet printed by American missionaries titled, "What Li Wen Saw."[37] The dog also received notice in at least one wartime article in the Saturday Evening Post.[38]

Although Time repeatedly commented on the Chinese soldiers' determination to carry on the war, it began to criticize official American military planners for their refusal to include a Chinese delegation in its discussions. This failure to consult with the Chinese seemed all the more deplorable because of the substantial experience they had purportedly accumulated in fighting the Japanese over the past ten years. Time called the generalissimo "one of the Allies' two greatest fighting leaders," and argued that China remained a potential base for future military operations.[39] In words that sounded vaguely like the veiled threats passed on by the Nationalist government to the Roosevelt administration, *Time* announced that certain experts thought of China as a "great military opportunity which the U.S. had neglected—an opportunity which if not grasped may not exist much longer."[40]

Fortune paid particular attention to this theme in its coverage of the Pacific theater. One editorial, in the August 1942 issue, outlined the reasons for the early military setbacks suffered by the United States, naming four parties: the Roosevelt administration, the U.S. Army, the State Department, and the American press.[41] The administration was culpable for its failure to ensure the delivery of promised military supplies, especially aircraft. The army was at fault for its inability to facilitate the shipment of military equipment and also for its refusal to include the Chinese in its planning sessions. China's success in inflicting casualties on the Japanese had already been proved, *Fortune* argued. (In a later issue it added, "In strategy and tactics, particularly those of defense, China is brilliant.")[42] The State Department bore its share of the responsibility for having earlier encouraged Japan while offering only lukewarm support to China. In fact, *Fortune* said, the State Department's policy lacked direction and coherency, both in the matter of extraterritoriality and in the Chinese immigration policy. The American press was quite as much to blame, for in failing to pay adequate attention to developments in China over the last fifteen years, it had misrepresented the horrible atrocities being committed against the Chinese. By reporting only the American government's promises of aid instead of focusing on the actual supplies sent—a far lower figure—the media gave the country a false impression of what American aid really amounted to.

After holding these groups accountable for their various shortcomings, *Fortune* cast its eye on the American people. The magazine reasoned that the entire nation was responsible for allowing the situation to deteriorate to such a level. "The Chinese," it asserted, "are to be approved, applauded, even beloved, but we do not take them seriously, nor do we think of them with any real concern." Ultimately, the only way to save the United States was to provide for the salvation of China. To do that, the Roosevelt administration had to allocate more military supplies for China; the army had to pay more attention to the experience the Chinese had acquired fighting the Japanese; and the nation's foreign policy had to provide for a "strong, free China closely and equally allied with the U.S."[43]

As the war progressed and the public grew more confident of an ultimate American victory in the Pacific, Time Inc.'s magazines began turning much of their attention to postwar planning for the region. *Fortune* was of course especially concerned with the business climate. China appeared ready to offer the United States numerous opportunities for investment, the magazine suggested, principally because Chinese plans could not be fulfilled without assistance from the United States. On the other side, American businesses would desperately need foreign markets like China to maintain full production. The Chinese had the dreams and the people; the United States had the technological know-how and the industrial capacity. The symbiotic relationship—spiritual, political, and economic in scope—meant that the differences between the two nations complemented each other perfectly. More directly for American businesses, postwar China had a tremendous potential for their products, especially heavy machinery. *Fortune* used one of Sun Yat-sen's writings to suggest that China would quickly move to build over 100,000 miles of railway. That task would require 20 million tons of steel, 25,000 locomotives, 300,000 freight cars, and 30,000 passenger cars. With China only capable of producing about two million tons of steel a year under present conditions, the rest of the nation's demand would have to be met through imports. *Fortune* believed that the future for American businesses there augured well, because the Chinese considered "American railway and heavy industrial equipment, American public-utility and communications equipment to be the finest in the world." More significantly, the Nationalist government was considering changes that would relax restrictions on foreign companies. The end result was "a grandeur of scope and promise that may set a new epoch in Asia."[44]

Just as Luce's publications promised a brighter future for Sino-American economic relations, United China Relief sought to capitalize on the myth of the China market. In 1944, in a radio speech commemorating the thirty-third anniversary of the overthrow of the Qing dynasty, B. A. Garside outlined the trade opportunities that awaited the United States after the war. China, he said, was "potentially . . . [the] largest and most accessible field for trade relationships," and commercial exchange would blossom under the imminent "democratic form of government." Because China possessed enough in the way of raw materials to guarantee a reciprocal relationship, the only things required to secure this enormous market were American "efficiency, fairness, and friendliness."[45]

The question of future economic development occupied the time and thought of a great many people concerned with Sino-American relations, but by no means did it constitute the only avenue through which they tried to convince Americans that China was fundamentally vital to the realization of America's dreams. Long-standing themes continued to receive repeated attention. The Chinese as a largely democratic people, their commitment to preserving freedom and liberty, their basic similarities with Americans—all were reiterated time and again as the war progressed. Pearl Buck expanded her activities on behalf of shaping American national attitudes toward China by setting up a nonprofit agency, called the East and West Association, for the purpose of promoting bilateral harmony and understanding. Similar to UCR in certain respects, this association tried to bring the two nations and their peoples closer together. In the process, Buck furthered many of the same assumptions held by UCR members: specifically, she repeated the notion that China was very much a democratic society. An appeal letter she sent to Mabel White Stimson, wife of Secretary of War Henry L. Stimson, asked her to become a charter member of the association with a contribution of one thousand dollars. Although the association itself was interested in American relations with Asia more broadly, Buck specifically mentioned that China deserved help, not simply because of the military situation in the Pacific but also because it was "the oldest democracy in the world."[46]

Like UCR, the East and West Association issued informational pamphlets that were supposed to explain China to Americans in terms they could understand. One publication discussed various figures from Chinese history, including "China's Joan of Arc," "Robin Hood," and of course, "George Washington." Here again, historical allusions got out of hand: when "China's George Washington," the pamphlet said, created his political philosophy, he was inspired by Abraham Lincoln's "Gettysburg Address."[47] The pamphlet called Chiang and Madame Chiang their country's Franklin and Eleanor Roosevelt, and it praised Madame Chiang for her "fine blending of East and West."

In proffering its conception of China, the East and West Association perpetuated other myths, including the one about the prevalence of democratic activities in Chinese daily life. China was said to have a classless society because most Chinese had known good as well as bad times during their families' history and therefore there had been no creation of a permanent aristocratic crust. Also working against a rigidly hierarchical society was the Chinese examination system. Its series of tests had created a heritage of "two thousand years of objec-

tive and competitive" exams, which ensured that the best candidates
would succeed, guaranteeing what the Association called "equality of
opportunity." This statement was pure fantasy. Rather than promoting any type of social egalitarianism or political democracy, the
Chinese system of examinations was explicitly designed to reinforce
the privileged position of the scholar-gentry elites. The exams themselves did not test practical knowledge but instead focused on the
memorization of ancient texts, requiring years of study usually with
the aid of a private tutor, something simply not feasible for members
of the lower class. Furthermore, women were barred from taking the
exams.[48] United China Relief was under the same misapprehensions
as the East and West Association. It found in the Chinese examination system a parallel with Horatio Alger's stories, and reported that
long before American youngsters began reading about the success of
Ragged Dick through his dedication to hard work, the Chinese had
seen countless youths rise through their system solely on their own
merits, leading to the conclusion that the majority of "China's great
leaders have been men of humble birth, but native ability."[49] Simply
through repetition, these popular misconceptions about Chinese society, in UCR, Time Inc., and publications of the East and West Association, seemed to bolster American supporters of the Nationalist
government. The unyielding insistence that these proclamations
were true allowed them to acquire a life of their own, and their popular acceptance grew accordingly.

   In 1944, UCR's new chairman, Charles Edison, son of the famous
inventor and former governor of New Jersey, obviously satisfied with
the theme of fostering Sino-American cooperation, suggested that
new programs should emphasize the "cathedral of friendship" being
constructed between the two nations. He urged the continued spread
of "the gospel of Chinese-American friendship" and played his part
during one NBC radio broadcast for the National War Fund by calling
China America's "sister democracy across the Pacific." He repeated
the oft-cited illusion that in their selection of a republican form of
government in 1911, the Chinese had been strongly influenced by the
American political example of 1776.[50]

   The lines between Americans and Chinese tended to blur even
more in some of UCR's other efforts to promote Sino-American unity.
The thesis was familiar: the Chinese people were a great deal like
Americans; but UCR extended the likeness beyond aspirations, ideals, and other intangibles to physical similarities. *China Primer* made
the case for a physical likeness between Americans and Chinese in
one particularly striking example of how racialistic paternalism to-

ward the Chinese has often been paired with racism directed at the Japanese (or vice versa). An illustration titled "How to Spot a Jap," taken from a U.S. army manual, compared the physical features of Japanese and Chinese, pointing out features that in a Chinese man resembled those of a European or American—size, eyes, feet, build. A Chinese man was "about the size of an average American," whereas a Japanese was shorter and "looks as if his eyes are joined directly to his chest!" A Chinese person's eyes were "set like any European's or American's." The pamphlet promoted the idea that, whereas the Chinese, and other Asiatics, were similar to Americans, the Japanese were a different, and inferior, race.[51] This supposedly educational comic strip also appeared in a March 1943 issue of *Life*.[52]

"How to Spot a Jap" is a clear example of how the twin forces of racism and paternalism formed a larger whole. In comparing the physical characteristics of white American males with their Chinese counterparts, and in stating that the two had more in common physically and racially than did the Chinese and Japanese, it suggested that the Chinese had apparently made physical progress toward becoming more like Americans in some bizarre form of Darwinian evolution. From such a perspective, racism and racialistic paternalism constituted opposite sides of the same coin. Throughout the war, long-standing and unfavorable preconceptions about Asian peoples were conveniently focused on the Japanese, while more positive ideas about the Chinese became handily incorporated into a paternalistic outlook that served a wartime purpose. By approaching Asians from the position of how readily they adopted American ways, China sentimentalists, regardless of their ultimate objectives, furthered a manner of thinking that depicted the Chinese in developmentally inferior terms.[53]

Dedicated workers for China did not see it that way, of course. "The Chinese are a good deal like us Americans," one speaker explained, because both peoples lived in similar geographical conditions: "It is a fact that people who grow up on continents are like each other, just as island peoples are like each other."[54] Even when differences were acknowledged, they were always placed in such a context as to suggest their relative unimportance within the overall picture. "Despite geographical, racial, and linguistic barriers," Chinese and Americans "think alike, react alike, and hold much the same ideals."[55] In assessing the future of Sino-American relations after the war, one commentator indicated that although Americans and Chinese did not look exactly alike, they felt the same: they have "the same sort of ideas [and] act in the same ways."[56]

The images conveyed in the pamphlets and speeches of UCR and the East and West Association and in the pages of Time Inc.'s publications manifested a high degree of faith in the ultimate unification of the two nations in the postwar world. It was a vision of Sino-American harmony very much like the missionary ideal. But neither it nor the insistence by supporters of the Nationalist government that the United States and China were two nations with similar traits demonstrated any accurate understanding of the circumstances inside China, and as the war progressed, in spite of the strength of their convictions, some members of United China Relief began to question whether or not they had oversold China. They worried that perhaps too beautiful a picture had been painted and that when the truth of the situation became known, and when that truth could not live up to the claims being heralded, there would be an inevitable backlash.

The impetus that sparked this debate was an article that appeared in the *New York Times Magazine* in November 1943. This article, written by Columbia University professor Nathaniel Peffer, was called "Our Distorted View of China." Peffer's thesis was that Americans had developed such fantastic notions about China that, in the end, more harm than good would come to Sino-American relations. He argued that after Pearl Harbor Americans engaged in what he called "penance" for the way in which they had continued to aid the Japanese during the latter half of the 1930's, and the sudden alliance with China against Japan allowed Americans to discover, or rather rediscover, a sentimental attachment to China based on a mixture of guilt and a desire to present a united front against a common foe. In assigning blame for the origins of this distorted view, Peffer specifically singled out missionaries and other Americans who had lived in China and had a predisposition to be sentimental about everything Chinese; their statements could "sometimes be extremely silly," he said. Their sentimentalities had led to the construction of an idealized China that was "a democracy pure and Jeffersonian, its leaders selfless, statesmanlike beings consecrated to the spread of liberty, every peasant guerrilla a boy on the burning deck."[57]

B. A. Garside responded to Peffer's article in an internal memorandum to UCR personnel. He admitted that UCR was "at least partly to blame," but he excused any excesses by noting that the organization generally had to rely on "second-hand reports." Without its own publicity representative in China, UCR had no way of confirming or denying the accuracy of the information coming out of there.[58]

Even when they did acknowledge certain problems in China, UCR officials sought to rationalize or justify them, however deplorable, without criticizing the Nationalist government in any way. In 1944, after UCR president James L. McConaughy visited China, he wrote a letter to UCR personnel in which he discussed how Americans had initially idealized the Chinese people; he conceded that many of the Nationalist soldiers were poorly fed, inadequately trained, and harshly conscripted even though weapons were unavailable. But rather than cast any blame on Chiang Kai-shek and Nationalist policies, he hinted that the blame fell on the United States, which, though finding equipment for Russian soldiers, could not seem to find anything for the Chinese. Indeed, he referred to Chiang Kai-shek as "poised and cordial," and he tried to counter recent American criticisms of Chiang's private life by invoking the virtual incantation, "I believe that he and his wife are active Christians of the highest character." He ended by urging Americans to continue their public support for the sake of China's morale, because the celebrations, parades, and other activities "heartened the people, as they learned of them over their radio and in their papers."[59]

Like President McConaughy, the executive members of UCR did not dwell too long on the implications of Peffer's article. A year later, Garside wrote a letter to Chairman Charles Edison in which he discussed the "radical changes" that had come about in American attitudes toward China over the last two years. He made mention of the initial sentiment toward "over-idealizing everything Chinese, and of crediting the leaders and people of China with superhuman traits of courage, tenacity, and heroism." Unlike his previous note on the subject, however, this time his memorandum refused to place any blame on UCR. "Here in United China Relief," he declared, "we have always tried to maintain a fairly even balance"; UCR had endeavored to stay above the partisan fray by concentrating on making constructive suggestions. Besides, he observed, UCR had avoided the "extremes of praise and adulation" specifically because the American people would not accept them.[60]

A more revealing example of how UCR more or less dismissed the notion that overidealized conceptions had developed came in December 1943, when Dr. T. F. Tsiang, China's delegate to the United Nations Relief and Rehabilitation Administration, spoke at a dinner organized in his honor by UCR. Tsiang mentioned the "iron determination" Chiang Kai-shek had shown in the face of much adversity; it was vital in understanding China, he said, to consider "the role which this man of destiny has played" in determining the course of Chinese history. In China's most dire time of need, "God sent a man of the hour to lead the nation."[61]

Certainly UCR had tried to get its message out, not only to Americans but to the people of China, and it continually stressed mutual benefits. In a phonograph recording made in Chinese for distribution in China, Chairman Edison spoke of how American aid had been given not out of sympathy, but rather out of national self-interest. "*We* need *China*," he declared, most immediately for its participation in defeating Japan. He complimented the Chinese people for their abilities, bravery, and devotion to the causes of freedom and peace. The Chinese "are our kind of people," he declared. (That same statement was also made by a character in the 1944 MGM motion picture *Thirty Seconds Over Tokyo*.) Edison concluded that, as much as China needs America, America needs China.[62]

Just what impact United China Relief's activities had on shaping American perceptions of China is difficult to gauge precisely, but the statistics on the numbers of materials shipped, speeches given, films shown, and meetings held show how widely UCR spread its message. Between 1942 and 1944, UCR expanded the number of local committees from 2,600 to a little over 3,500.[63] In 1944, UCR speakers addressed 558 meetings, including 147 schools, 108 women's clubs, and 62 church groups.[64] By March 1945, shipments of educational and publicity materials surpassed 27,000 and included more than one million items. Nearly 2,900 elementary schools around the country requested material; another 2,750 high schools received UCR packages, and 765 colleges and universities made use of UCR's services.[65] For 1945, UCR printed 100,000 copies of its new pamphlet, "Report on China," in anticipation of demand. Most significant of all was the amount of money UCR was able to solicit and spend. In the four-year period from Pearl Harbor until the end of 1945, UCR raised over $37 million for China.[66] Of that total, over $31 million was distributed by October 1945.[67]

These statistics speak to broader reception accorded UCR and its message about the future of United States–Chinese relations. In the words expressed by its various members, the promise of Sino-American harmony beckoned like the Holy Grail. This message was not new to Americans' concerns in Asia. Nearly a century earlier, Senator Thomas Hart Benton had talked about how civilizations had traveled west since the beginning of time, starting in Europe, moving to America, and now ready to leap across the Pacific. From its vantage point between Asia and the Old World, the United States was situated to reap enormous rewards. "The rich commerce of Asia will flow through our centre," he declared, and with that influx of commerce would come not only national wealth but also the "highest attain-

ments of letters, arts, and sciences."[68] In 1945, UCR's pronouncements about the future of Sino-American relations echoed the calls
of a "manifest destiny." Speaking of how in the past, Europe with "its
culture, its beauty and its opportunities" had meant so much to the
United States, UCR prophesied that for the next century, Asia would
mean all those things and much more.[69] The tremendous China market would finally be realized once peace was achieved.

The theme of China's future opportunities became more common-
place in periodicals and newspaper articles toward the end of the war.
To cite but two of many examples, the president of the United States
Chamber of Commerce, Eric Johnston, wrote a short piece for *Reader's Digest* in which he outlined the potential he saw for *"mutual
profit"* after the war. Sounding like Henry Luce, he declared, "The
future is ours," but to secure that promise, he called for a program
of vigorous, direct investment in other countries. Explaining that
American exports to China totaled $124 million in 1929, he sug-
gested that if the United States were more aggressive in assisting in
the process of Chinese industrialization, that figure could well ex-
ceed $8 billion.[70] Similarly, Donald M. Nelson, former chairman of
the War Production Board, who was sent along with Patrick Hurley in
1944 to smooth over certain diplomatic and military difficulties,
wrote an article for *Collier's* the following year in which he expressed
his confidence in the potential for profit offered by investments in
China.[71]

Meanwhile, the United States War Department painted its own
flattering portrait of China. One brush stroke came through the Office of War Information's Bureau of Motion Pictures, which advanced
ideas that reflected the wishful thinking of the Roosevelt administration in its attempt to elevate the Nationalist government, Chiang
Kai-shek, and China into a position as one of the Big Four. A government manual for the Motion Picture Industry recommended that
wartime pictures of China should take into account that "China is a
great nation, cultured and *liberal*, with whom, inevitably, [the United
States] will be closely bound in the world that is to come."[72] In an effort to promote these ideas generally, the War Department ordered a
"Why We Fight" series on America's wartime allies. This was a series
of seven documentary films designed for release in motion picture
theaters around the country. The director of the series was Frank Capra, who had won Academy Awards for his work on *It Happened One
Night, Mr. Smith Goes to Washington,* and *You Can't Take It with
You.* Capra's film on China's heroic struggle against the Japanese, *The
Battle of China,* employed the stock comparisons in an effort to

champion the notion that China and the United States were remarkably alike. In one sequence, the camera focuses on a book as its pages
turn. The first page shows a picture of Sun Yat-sen surrounded by a
text in Chinese characters; the next page has a picture of George
Washington, also surrounded by Chinese characters. Capra also developed the other conventional modes of viewing China. In emphasizing the applicability of Christianity there, he juxtaposed the words
of Confucius with those of Jesus Christ. The film also has scenes in
a Chinese Christian church, with a cloth poster of Jesus hanging from
the balcony. And to show China's modernization, Capra borrowed
footage from a "March of Time" newsreel showing Shanghai, where
"truly the East met the West."[73]

Capra's treatment of the Chinese displayed the strong sentimental
touch for which his films were well known, and in that respect *The
Battle of China* reflected the emotions and aspirations consistently
propagated not only by Time Inc. and United China Relief but by the
United States government. The film ultimately went too far, however, in its praise of China. Shortly after it was released in the fall of
1944, Chiang demanded that General Joseph W. Stilwell, the American commander of the China-Burma-India theater of operations, be
recalled, and the War Department temporarily withdrew the film.
Under the circumstances, the obvious contradiction between this
"epic paean to the resistance of the Chinese people against Japan's
aggression" and the serious problems in Sino-American relations was
all too apparent.[74] But the film was quickly returned to circulation,
and by the middle of 1945, nearly four million Americans had seen
it.[75]

The Office of War Information also prepared short films promoting Sino-American understanding. One such filmstrip, dating from
early in the war, focused on the jobs being performed by Chinese-
Americans working for firms like Ford Motor Company, General
Electric, and American Airlines as part of the overall theme of mutual
support and bilateral cooperation between Americans and Chinese in
the war against Japan. The film had footage of Chinese Boy Scouts
flying the Nationalist flag alongside the Stars and Stripes; other
frames celebrated Chiang Kai-shek, Sun Yat-sen, and the Chinese
children who saluted the American flag before they began school in
the morning.[76] A later OWI filmstrip comparing Danbury, Connecticut, with Pishan, China, insisted that cities, "like people, have much
in common even though they may be at opposite ends of the earth."[77]

Beyond what Frank Capra and OWI had to say to millions of Americans, Chiang also had his strident supporters in Congress. One of the

most vocal and influential was Congressman Walter H. Judd. As a former medical missionary, Judd had spent years trying to bring about
the realization of the same type of Christian, Western conception of
society that UCR and Time Inc. later insisted was becoming a reality.
And as a Republican congressman from Minnesota, he attempted to
steer American foreign policy toward supporting the Nationalist government without reservations. Judd's fervor manifested itself in the
numerous speeches he made defending Chiang's administration and
in his recommendations that the United States demonstrate its support with a substantial program of military and economic assistance.
In advocating a closer union between the two nations, he indulged in
the same type of rhetoric as that used by Time Inc. and United China
Relief, complete with American historical analogies and references
to Chiang's Christianity.

Near the end of World War II, when the defeat of Germany and Japan
was a foregone conclusion, Judd spoke to the House of Representatives on the situation in China. In his speech, "What Is the Truth
About China?" he outlined what he considered to be the principal
forces at work there.[78] He did this so Americans could better understand the situation and know how to formulate an effective foreign
policy in response. Americans had to think of the Chinese situation
not in terms of twentieth-century America, he said, but rather in relation to their own nation's past. Since China was still fighting its revolution for independence, it was unfair to compare conditions there
to those in the United States in 1945. In fact, he reminded his colleagues, the United States had required ninety years, "including a
Great Civil War," before it had fully straightened out the impact of its
revolution. Along those lines, he attempted to explain the internal
struggles between the Nationalist government and the Chinese Communists by invoking other episodes from America's past. "You will
remember that when our Revolution was older than China's is, conditions in this country . . . were so bad, the corruption and faction-
alism were so rampant in the Government . . . that representatives of
the people of New England . . . voted to secede." His reference to the
Hartford convention of 1814 never addressed the accuracy of the analogy, but for his purposes, such a consideration was never really important. Placing present-day China within the context of American
history was enough, apparently, to justify the existing policies of the
Nationalist government. Moreover, he could then assert, as he did,
that the Roosevelt administration needed to demonstrate its support
for America's ally—a nation so much like the United States—despite
the likelihood of civil war. He completed his comparison with the

comment that America's previous situation had been "child's play compared with China's." Not limited to one analogy, Judd drew from other periods in American history in order to understand the present abuses occurring in China. There was an American parallel to the unpopularity of Chiang's armies among the Chinese peasantry: "George Washington's men had to live off the land at times and they were royally hated and resisted by some of the Colonists because of that fact." In another comparison, he likened Japan's blockade of China to the North's blockage of the South in the Civil War and argued that inflation in China could be understood within the context of the same conditions that had existed below the Mason-Dixon line between 1861 and 1865.

Judd expounded a similar argument in a Town Meeting forum held in February 1945 on the subject of how unity could be achieved in China. Judd and the Chinese writer Dr. Lin Yutang debated the subject with Harrison Forman and Agnes Smedley, speaking for the liberals. In the debate, Judd tried to put Chiang's plight vis-à-vis the CCP into perspective by declaring that the generalissimo could no more accommodate the Communists' political and military demands than Abraham Lincoln could have compromised with the "Secessionists after they set up in the South a separate government with a separate currency, separate taxes and a separate army under a separate command."[79]

Judd was skillful at bringing contemporary analogies into any discussion of China. Of Chiang's political abuses, for example, he said, "If it is in some other country, we call it a Gestapo. If it is in our own country, we call it an F.B.I."[80] His clever way of arguing managed to reason, explain, rationalize, or justify just about every abuse committed by Chiang's government, all of which was interesting, because when it suited his purposes, Judd was the first one to proclaim that China had to be evaluated not according to American standards but within the context of developments in Asia. Anyone critical of Chiang or the Nationalist government, he insisted, "tended to judge China, not in terms of China's own past, but in terms of the West." And again, "We must judge China not in relation to conditions in America, but in terms of conditions as they were in China 20 years ago and 200 years ago."[81] He once wrote Henry Luce to the same effect, noting his concern with people who misunderstood conditions in China, all the while trying to bring about changes there: "I dread to see these innocents running around abroad judging an oriental country in terms of the West rather than in terms of what it was yesterday and of the direction in which it is now going."[82] Judd wanted to have it both ways: he freely substituted American analogies when it suited his purposes, but he shunned the same comparisons when they reflected poorly upon China.

Throughout his elaborate rationalizations, Judd expressed his absolute faith in the Chinese government under Chiang's direction. Despite criticisms leveled at the generalissimo from all sides, despite the inflation and corruption that continued to plague China, and despite the poor performance of Chiang's military forces during the war, he remarked, "Chiang Kai-shek, instead of being a heathen, barbarian, war lord, was a Christian." With that, he hit upon the key for many supporters of the Nationalist government: no matter what problems existed, no matter how desperate the situation appeared, Chiang was, in the end, a Christian. For someone like Walter Judd, as much as for Henry Luce, that alone made him eminently deserving of America's support.[83]

Under the circumstances of war, it was not surprising that many Americans should have accepted the idea that China was very much like the United States. The activities of literally thousands of local Rotary Clubs coincided with the much more focused efforts like the national radio program to create a virtual tidal wave of favorable, but illusory, images—of a gallant, determined Asian ally fighting shoulder to shoulder with the United States in its efforts to preserve a world in which the forces of freedom, democracy, and Christian morality prevailed.

From such an overall conception came the logical conclusion that China and the United States could work closely together in the postwar world. The political, social, and religious similarities that linked the two nations on the same side during the world war would also provide for a mutually beneficial relationship after the war was won. As China and America grew and expanded, so too, the argument went, would their cooperation. Together, they would foster a global renaissance unlike any the world had seen.

Despite the general celebration of China and the Chinese people proffered by Time Inc. and United China Relief, there was still something missing—a face, a person, or a personality who could epitomize all the mystery, wonder, and beauty of an Americanized China. Ultimately, it was Madame Chiang Kai-shek who proved to be the critical figure in Sino-American relations; she literally seduced the American people during World War II. In her, proponents of the Nationalist government could point to an example of the new China based on the American model, and that is exactly what they did.

CHAPTER FIVE

Madame Chiang and the Personality of Sino-American Relations

There was a saying . . . that Madame Chiang was worth ten divisions to the Generalissimo. In terms of her influence on American public opinion this was no exaggeration.
— A. T. Steele, *The American People and China*

The man who once said [Madame Chiang] was worth 10 army divisions to China was a piker.
— Edward T. Folliard, *Washington Post*

Equipped with all the finer feminine charms—beauty, poise, sartorial elegance, daintiness, sweetness—[Madame Chiang] also has a first-class masculine brain that many a ruling male might envy.
— Alma Whitaker, *Los Angeles Times*

Although the common goal of defeating Japan during World War II fostered the illusion of Sino-American harmony most trenchantly from 1931 to 1949, for a brief period of time, one person on her own had an impact nearly as great as the war itself. For a time, Soong Meiling—Madame Chiang Kai-shek—did as much to promote better relations between the United States and China, on the public level, as did Henry Luce. She advanced the notion that China and the United States had much in common by emphasizing the similar histories, mutual interests, and shared political and ideological aspirations that purportedly bound the two countries together.

Soong Meiling once said that the only thing Chinese about her was her face.[1] An American writer put the matter this way: "Madame's body was born in China but her mind was born in America."[2] Although both descriptions exaggerated the extent of her Americanization, Soong Meiling proved to be the perfect person for advancing the idea that China was on its way toward adopting the American model in all of its manifestations.

During the course of World War II, Madame Chiang Kai-shek attracted an extraordinarily high degree of favorable attention from

Americans. Through a tour she made of the United States in 1943, she cemented her position as the chief symbol of America's ally in Asia. Her public appearances drew large and enthusiastic crowds from New York to Los Angeles because she provided Americans with a real-life example of what they wanted to believe about China. As part of the new, Christian, and apparently popular Chinese leadership, she inspired sentimental and romanticized notions even in people who, before the war, had never really paid much attention to Asia.

Part of Madame Chiang's appeal stemmed from what can be called the prevailing "cultural constructions" of gender. The historian Joan Scott has argued that these assumptions basically derive from "the entirely social creation of ideas about appropriate roles for women and men."[3] During World War II, the popular acceptance of Madame Chiang in the United States located her within the existing model established by American society for women; this sudden embrace was also part of the larger effort to situate China within a liberal-developmentalist framework. She was defined, understood, and celebrated for her relationship with her husband, and, because she had no children of her own, for her role as the symbolic mother to the thousands of China's war orphans. A group of sociologists has indicated that the emphasis in British culture placed upon women as mothers has been part of a "positive categorisation," which leads to the conclusion that "for women the role of mother is paramount."[4] In discussing American culture and society during the 1940's, especially the war period, the efforts to portray women in a similarly conservative light—that is, as wives and mothers without, of course, overlooking the women who were entering the workforce in unprecedented numbers—can be seen as part of this phenomenon. Amy Kaplan's assertion that domestic debates often spread beyond the nation's boundaries, and, in the process, affect the cultural constructions of foreign policy, certainly applies to America's general understanding of China and the way in which the country came to view Madame Chiang Kai-shek. This understanding meant that aside from being celebrated as a good wife and mother, she also attracted the attention of many American women, who discovered that the war gave them the chance to change their status in the employment hierarchy. The traditional image of her as wife and mother therefore coincided with the popular conception of her as an important and influential figure in the Nationalist government.[5]

Not surprisingly, Time Inc. and United China Relief worked diligently with Madame Chiang, because her talent for bringing together China's long and complex history and the diverse culture of its people into a compact picture served their purposes. For her own part, Madame Chiang used both organizations to convey her message to the American people in an effort to reorient Allied strategy toward defeating Japan first and, in the process, to secure greater material support for China, for the present and in the future.

To understand the depth and duration of the impressions Soong Meiling made, it is necessary to keep in mind the larger context of wartime Sino-American relations. The main effort to show China to be America's heroic ally, properly aligned in its ideological and political ambitions—in short, America's good Asian friend—created the political and cultural context that made the enthusiastic reception of Madame Chiang possible. Although Madame Chiang's position as a public figure would undoubtedly have attracted widespread attention regardless of circumstances, the exigencies of the war and the search for cultural as well as military allies heightened the national fascination with her. For an organization like Time Inc., which delighted in personifying foreign nations by focusing on individuals, she presented an opportunity to emphasize such an approach to considerable effect. In similar fashion, United China Relief found her to be especially useful for advancing its own ideas about China. Within the dynamics of Sino-American relations, Madame Chiang symbolized the larger phenomenon itself, in all its complexities, nuances, hopes, and frustrations.

Soong Meiling was born in 1897 to a wealthy Chinese businessman who had made part of his vast fortune selling Bibles printed in English and Chinese. Having himself been educated in the United States, at Trinity College (later Duke University) and Vanderbilt University, Charles Soong decided that all his children would be educated in the United States too. Thus Meiling and her older sister Qingling arrived in Summit, New Jersey, in the fall of 1907, and the two girls spent one year at Miss Clara Potwin's school preparing for college study. The next year, when Qingling was old enough to attend Wesleyan College in Macon, Georgia—from which the oldest Soong daughter, Ailing, had graduated—she and Meiling traveled south. Although Meiling was still too young to enter the college, she quickly gained the affection of the faculty, administrators, and older students. In 1912, she enrolled as a freshman.[6]

After Qingling graduated from Wesleyan and returned to China, Meiling transferred to Wellesley College in Massachusetts in order to be closer to her older brother, T. V., who was attending Harvard. She remained at Wellesley until her graduation in 1917. When she returned to China the same year, she needed to reorient herself to China by relearning its language, history, and customs. It was at this time that she also assumed certain social responsibilities in Shanghai, including accepting a position with the local YWCA.[7]

In spite of the wealth her father had accumulated, Meiling's importance for Sino-American relations was not really settled until a decade later when she decided to marry Chiang Kai-shek. Chiang's association with the Chinese underworld, and his former wives and concubines, at first made him an unattractive suitor in the eyes of the Christian Soong family. Qingling was strongly opposed, and Meiling's mother also expressed serious misgivings about her daughter marrying a heathen. Whatever his blemishes, however, Chiang's position in the Chinese Nationalist party had steadily risen in the early 1920's, and after Sun Yat-sen's death in 1925 he had moved quickly to assume the position as his legitimate successor. Years after they had first met at a Shanghai social affair, Chiang finally managed to secure the consent of Soong Meiling's mother with the understanding that he would study Christianity.[8]

The two were married in Shanghai on December 1, 1927, in a ceremony that symbolized the long-standing aspirations of many American missionaries. The missionaries' excitement, one historian has commented, came about from the belief that Chiang's "marriage to an American-educated woman represented a rapid advance in the long struggle to convert China."[9] Missionaries viewed the Guomindang generally, and Chiang specifically, as the only legitimate Christian hope for China. One Methodist missionary importuned in a 1927 letter to the Reverend William Richard Johnson that members of the Guomindang were "distinctly Christian and therefore [they had to] prevail for China sooner or later."[10] Sympathetic to such thinking, Reverend Johnson was equally encouraged by the Chiangs' nuptials. He wrote approvingly that the two studied the Bible together for an hour each day, that Madame Chiang studied another two hours in the afternoon, and, most promisingly, that she advocated the Christian churches' involvement in assisting in the administration of the government's rural reconstruction programs.[11]

Of similar interest to the missionaries, Madame Chiang suggested that American culture needed to be introduced into Chinese society in order to bring about positive changes. In a letter she wrote on the subject of Yanjing University's part in reaching this goal, she said, "The importance of spreading American culture in China is almost as important at this period of moral, material, and political upheaval, as it is that we must speed up as fast as possible the education of leaders capable of exercising influence for constructive good upon the people in this new time."[12]

Although Soong Meiling's marriage to Chiang garnered a good deal of attention from the American missionary community, it was her reputed role in securing her husband's release at Xi'an in December 1936 that helped make her an international figure. That incident, one historian has noted, "was a turning point of preeminent significance for the career of Chiang Kai-shek . . . and [for] the outlook of the Christian community" in China.[13] It had a fortuitous effect upon Madame Chiang's reputation as well.

Rather than describing the importance of the Chinese Communists or Zhang Xueliang in bringing about the generalissimo's release, American press accounts focused upon Madame Chiang. And why not? It certainly made good copy, and the story of Madame Chiang's fearless actions greatly increased the favorable coverage of the Chiangs in the United States. Part of the reason for the rising concern over the Japanese war against China can be traced to the growing popularity of the generalissimo and Madame Chiang. The image of Madame Chiang as the intrepid savior became popularly accepted even though the reality was substantially different.[14]

The Xi'an incident, moreover, gave Madame Chiang an opportunity to promote herself, her husband, and the Nationalist government. Less than six months after her husband's release on Christmas Day 1936, the two Chiangs related their stories in a nine-part serialized account published in newspapers across the United States.[15] That paragon of Americanism, positive thinking, and individual initiative, Dale Carnegie, summed up the standard public line on Xi'an this way: "China trembled on the verge of another civil war—and one woman stopped it. One woman alone—Madame Chiang Kai-shek. . . . It was a turning point in history."[16]

In this story as in so many others, sentimentalism and sensationalism hid the truth: Madame Chiang apparently did manage to stall reactionary elements in the Guomindang armed forces that wanted to bomb Xi'an—and in the process probably kill Chiang rather than save him—but she was not crucial in negotiating an end to her husband's imprisonment, as nearly every American account suggested or even stated openly. That responsibility rested more with Zhang Xueliang and, to a lesser extent, Zhou Enlai and the Chinese Communists.[17]

Madame Chiang's account of the affair omitted these nuances and intricacies and glorified her part. She said that she had written to Zhang Xueliang and scolded him for his "impudent and impetuous action," almost as a mother would have done.[18] Her subsequent actions, too, took on a gender-related emphasis, for Madame Chiang noted that upon reaching her husband, she decided that she "would have to nurse him to secure some comfort for him." Part of her care included reading the Bible out loud. Madame Chiang's account went on to attribute the conversion of the Xi'an rebels to the side of the Nationalist government to their reading of her husband's diary and her letters to him. Chiang's diary, she said, gave the rebels evidence of Chiang's deep national convictions and his determination to do what was best for China, and her letters showed the strength of the Chiangs' Christian beliefs. Madame Chiang recorded the comment of one rebel leader who said to her, "'You know I have always had great faith in you, and my associates all admire you.'" After reading two of her letters, he observed that they caused everyone to hold her "'in even greater respect.'"[19]

The American media coverage of the Xi'an incident had a great part in creating an image of Madame Chiang that coincided with the well-developed myth of a special, decades-old Sino-American friendship. The Christian and American-educated Soong Meiling had returned to China to play a crucial role in saving the Chinese nation from chaos; additionally, she promoted the inculcation of American values into Chinese society. That powerful impression grew in importance when the United States and China became wartime allies.

The attack upon Pearl Harbor meant two things for American conceptions of Asia: first, ideas about Japan and the Japanese people became inextricably tied to racist notions that ultimately served a wartime function. Many Americans were quite satisfied with immigration restrictions on Asians, and the Japanese attack on the Pacific fleet confirmed anti-Japanese racist inclinations. At the same time, however, the equally long-standing attitudes toward the Chinese people became conveniently incorporated into the apparently more benevolent concept of ethnocentric paternalism. It was a switch that did not require any genuine rethinking on the part of most Americans. The Japanese were now the "evil" Asians bent on world domination—or at least an extension of Japanese power in the Pacific—and the Chinese were now in the category of aspiring Americans.

In her study of American women during the 1940's and the temporary circumstances that compelled a reconsideration of their traditional roles, Susan Hartmann has observed, "Even these new models were rooted in a context which sustained the centrality of women's domestic lives and their relationship with men."[20] Similarly, Elaine Tyler May has argued that domestic images of women during the war remained largely constrained by a "home and hearth" ideology despite the celebration of Rosie the Riveter: "The popular culture reflected the widespread admiration for the many thousands of female war workers but affirmed the primacy of domesticity for women."[21] As a woman who fitted squarely within domestic ideas about proper gender roles, Madame Chiang could be viewed as the foreign equivalent of an American woman. For men, she served as an attractive woman in need of assistance, the damsel in distress as it were, and her plea for American aid in 1943 can be seen within the larger context of fulfilling certain masculine assumptions about women on multiple levels. One historian has noted, "Gendered imagery abounds in popular portrayals of international relationships," and another historian has made specific reference to the way in which this phenomenon permeated popular depictions of Latin American nations as "fair maidens" in need of Uncle Sam's protection.[22] In standing as a symbol for China, Madame Chiang became a "fair maiden" of sorts, appealing to national ideas about a historical mission, chivalry, and machismo. Carl Crow's apotheosis to the mammon potential of Sino-American relations, *Four Hundred Million Customers* (1937), included a drawing showing China as a young, attractive woman being courted by both John Bull and Uncle Sam; another author (1942) wrote quite specifically, "China was like a coquette, breathing into you with all her charms, then leaving your roused excitement unrequited."[23]

There was another side to American conceptions of China, however, which related directly to wartime exigencies and to Madame Chiang's role as a person to be reckoned with in the traditionally male world of politics. With Madame Chiang's emergence as a very important person in a country that was now a U.S. ally in the war, American women, too, received a boost in recognition of their contribution to the war effort. By 1943 American women in great numbers were working in factories and serving in the women's armed forces, as nurses in combat zones, and in the Red Cross. But as Leila Rupp observed in her comparison of German and American propaganda aimed at, but also about, women during World War II, the standard picture of them as wives and mothers demanded some modifications in order to encourage their wholehearted contribution to the war effort. The changes in these popular images may have been temporary—even coexisting with the diametric forces that, particularly after the war was over, sought to restrain women's opportunities—but they nonetheless affected the manner in which many Americans came to view China through Madame Chiang Kai-shek.[24]

On more than one level, then, Madame Chiang was a compelling figure: first, as the appropriate image of the Americanized foreign woman, she confirmed the assumption that people of other countries could become more like Americans with salubrious effects; second, she projected a favorable national picture of China; finally, she communicated promising impressions of the United States to the Chinese as part of a larger reciprocal cultural exchange.

Examples of these various capacities abound. In its 1942 profile, the Associated Press Biographical Service described Madame Chiang in highly flattering terms that clearly focused upon her myriad roles as a woman. With subtitles like "A Thoughtful Wife," "Her American Education," "Romance and Marriage," and "'Mother' of Orphans," the AP made the standard references to her religious convictions, her role as China's "first lady" and her strong ties to the United States. In describing her personality, the sketch reinforced prevailing gender stereotypes about men and women by suggesting that her influence had brought about a softer, less aggressive touch to her husband's dealings with other warlords: "Much of his success in welding the warring factions of the nation together," it commented, could be "attributed to his religion and the influence of his wife." Her capabilities as a diplomat had led Chiang to send "her across the country by airplane to use her *captivating* talents of diplomacy" to ease tensions and bring about cooperation from various intransigent individuals. Furthermore, "She not only was the *charming* first lady of the land but a *homemaker*, shrewd watcher over her husband's delicate health." Another section recounted the story of how, when Madame Chiang arrived in Xi'an to rescue Chiang, she brought with her a copy of the Bible, his favorite meal, and a new set of false teeth with which to eat the food.[25]

Madame Chiang was herself interested in projecting her image, and in the immediate aftermath of the Japanese attack upon Pearl Harbor articles by her began appearing in American periodicals. In April 1942, the *New York Times Magazine* published an article by her that emphasized the need for mutual cooperation between the "Oriental" and "Occidental" worlds. Madame Chiang rebuked the Western nations for their past treatment of China and their arrogant demeanor; she hoped that the recent string of Western defeats at the hands of the Japanese would lead to a closer spirit of cooperation between the two worlds. Both, she insisted, had something to teach the other and in the present dire time of war, the need to recognize this was greater than ever.[26] Her accurate and forthright description of the history of foreign contact with China drew some criticism in the United States on account of its bluntness. Writing privately to presidential adviser Lauchlin Currie, Madame Chiang insisted that her purpose had not stemmed from any sense of "vindictiveness and bitterness" but arose "as a matter of conscience." China wanted to be treated as an equal partner by the Western powers "not patronizingly but willingly" and in reality, not just rhetorically.[27]

A month after the *New York Times Magazine* article, *Atlantic Monthly* published an article by Madame Chiang entitled "China Emergent." As the title indicated, this article was about the dominant position that China, "the Columbus of democracy," would shortly assume in Asia. China's new democracy, Madame Chiang declared, although certainly influenced by "the Jeffersonian views of equality of opportunity and the rights of the individual," would not be some "colorless imitation of . . . American democracy"; rather, China would develop its own brand of political and social democracy, one that represented "the steadfast and settled will of the people." China's democracy would guarantee representation of minority parties and would certainly "preserve the birthrights of the individual." The article also spoke of the need for assistance from fellow democracies throughout the world, most notably the United States; and it closed with Madame Chiang's hopes for everlasting peace and happiness, predicated upon achieving "a more Christlike ideal."[28]

Even before the war, Madame Chiang's popularity with certain American groups had elicited numerous invitations to visit the United States, including one from United Board for Christian Higher Education in Asia. Many of the same people involved in that group went to work for United China Relief, and in the spring of 1942 they invited Madame Chiang to come to the United States to help in the big China Week fund-raising campaign.[29] Pressing business demanded Madame Chiang's attention in China, so UCR had to wait. Her inability to travel in the late winter and early spring of 1942 met with approval in the White House. President Roosevelt told General Joseph Stilwell in February 1942, before he left to become adviser to Chiang Kai-shek and then commander of the China-Burma-India-theater, that such a visit would be "too much like a lecture tour of women's clubs." Stilwell agreed. The real reason for the president's concern had to do with his need to secure public acceptance of the Europe First strategy in the face of Pearl Harbor. An OWI report on public opinion for April 1942 observed that Americans generally believed that the nation's "strength should be concentrated first on defeating Japan." An appearance by Madame Chiang at that time might easily have complicated strategic matters.[30]

Madame Chiang did come to the United States quite soon, in November 1942, but not, it appeared, with the primary intention of promoting Sino-American harmony or of furthering the cause of United China Relief but rather for medical treatment. Injuries she had sustained a few years earlier while touring the battlefield were compounded by impacted wisdom teeth, sinusitis, and gastritis, and her condition required medical attention and rest, both of which the United States could provide. She was to be treated at the Harkness Pavilion of the Columbia-Presbyterian Medical Center in New York City, and the Roosevelts invited her to rest first at Hyde Park and then at the White House.[31]

Medical reasons aside, Madame Chiang's visit was an excellent opportunity for sympathetic Americans to promote their conception of China. Frank W. Price, a Presbyterian missionary in China who worked closely with the Chiangs while serving as an educator at Nanjing Theological and West China Union universities, wrote to her the month before she left for the United States. As clearly as anyone else, he outlined the reasons for her visit: "China's cause and China's needs and the importance of the China front must be *dramatized*. . . . We need not only sympathy and moral support, not only the promise of aid but a change of war strategy." All this led up to one point: "Some one now must go from China to Washington who can win the attention of policy-makers, compel them to listen to facts and secure a change in war strategy. . . . That person is yourself."[32] Madame Chiang, then, was to press the Nationalist government's case for greater economic and military support, specifically in the form of more planes, gasoline, and ammunition.[33] Immediately upon landing in the United States, she did exactly that, quickly making her intentions clear to special presidential adviser Harry Hopkins during their automobile ride from the airport. She indicated that a recent *Life* article that had attacked British policies in Asia accurately represented her views.[34]

After her medical treatment and a period of rest at Hyde Park, Madame Chiang headed for Washington in February 1943. Her arrival there immediately garnered favorable commentary from the press, an auspicious start to the way her entire visit would be received by journalists and the general public alike. The *Washington Post* called her the "world-famous wife" of the generalissimo and made specific references to her physical beauty and style: she "was as attractive as her photographs would indicate—and then some," the *Post* said.[35] The paper also ran an editorial praising the "Missimo"—as the Luce publications had nicknamed her—as "one of the most distinguished women of this generation." Her greatness, the editorial contended, had a twofold explanation. First was the function she performed as her husband's confidant and supporting partner: "No woman can be said to have dedicated herself to her man with the devotion of Mrs. Chiang Kai-shek," and her intelligence, abilities, and dedication— "her dowry"—had led to a definite rise in Chiang Kai-shek's "wisdom and influence." His outlook had broadened by her teaching him the ways and ideas of the West, so in "the best womanly as well as advisory sense she was his guide, counselor and friend in all affairs of state."[36] As for her own qualifications—separated into feminine and masculine categories—beauty was certainly considered very important: "Mrs. Chiang's beauty is as salient as her quick and alert mind." She combined "feminine charm and understanding with the vitality and directness which are supposed to be masculine traits," implying that women seldom achieved such stature as Madame Chiang on account of both her role as her husband's partner and her own abilities.[37] According to this perspective, she had successfully followed the recommendations of Orison S. Marden, who wrote in his book *Masterful Personality* (1921) that attractive women should develop "fascination."[38]

Madame Chiang's presence in the United States allowed the many members of Congress who were eager to express their excitement with America's allies the opportunity to extend to her the rare honor of addressing both Houses, albeit separately. She became the first private citizen and only the second woman to speak before Congress.[39] Her schedule in Washington called for a brief visit to the Senate on the afternoon of February 18, 1943. Thirty minutes later, before the House of Representatives, she was to give a longer address that was also broadcast over radio. In anticipation of her appearance, people crowded around the Capitol building during the morning in the hopes of getting a glimpse of "China's first lady." When she arrived, Vice President Henry Wallace escorted her to the Senate chamber and introduced her to its members. Then, as was reported in numerous periodicals and newspapers, the vice president asked her to make a few extemporaneous remarks. Supposedly caught off guard by his request, she nevertheless responded with a short but eloquent speech. *Time* magazine gushed, "After apologizing for not having a set speech, [Madame Chiang] knocked [the] silvery blocks off" the senators.[40] Her address would seem to be less spur-of-the-moment than was suggested, however, since the *Washington Post* reported that she was scheduled to deliver a few remarks before the Senate that very same morning. Nevertheless, the *Post*, the *New York Times*, and Henry

Luce's publications all emphasized the spontaneity of her remarks, which had the effect of making her eloquence seem all the more remarkable.

Madame Chiang's "impromptu" speech stressed the need for Sino-American unity. But she indicated that there already existed a great deal of mutual affection, admiration, and respect between the Chinese and American peoples. To illustrate her point, she related the experience of an American pilot who was forced to land in China after making a bombing run over Japan as part of the Doolittle raid. When villagers approached, the pilot waved his arms and shouted the only Chinese word he knew: Meiguo, meaning America (or literally, beautiful country), whereupon the peasants burst into laughter and hugged him "like a long lost brother." The pilot told Madame Chiang later that he had felt much at home because of the reception given him by the villagers.⁴¹

This perhaps apocryphal, perhaps true, story later reappeared in the 1944 MGM motion picture *Thirty Seconds Over Tokyo*, which starred Van Johnson, Robert Walker, Phyllis Thaxter, and Spencer Tracy. This film, with a script by Dalton Trumbo, and directed by Mervyn Le Roy, emphasized two themes relevant to wartime ideology and culture: the similarity between the American people and the Chinese, and the "home and hearth" ideology explored by Elaine Tyler May. *Thirty Seconds Over Tokyo* depicts the ordeal faced by the men who flew the first American bombing raid over Japan in April 1942. Logistics force the planes to land in China instead of returning to the American aircraft carrier from which they were launched. When the injured crew members of one plane are found and rescued by Chinese peasants, the pilot, Ted Lawson (Van Johnson), indicates that they are Americans and that they want to be taken to Chongqing, "Chiang Kai-shek, we're his friends, in Chongqing." Later, one American crew member says to another as they are recovering in a Chinese makeshift hospital, "I think the Chinese are a swell bunch of people." As Lawson is preparing to leave China to return to the United States, he says to a young Chinese who has helped them, "We'll be back. Maybe not us ourselves, but a lot of guys like us. And I'd like to be with them 'cause *you're our kind of people.*"⁴²

The domestic ideology of the war is brought out in several scenes. In one scene showing the training the men are receiving for their mission, the wives of three pilots sit near the airfield talking together, and one of the three women remarks that, however much her husband loves to fly, "he always comes back to me, especially when he's hungry." Later in the same conversation, another woman says: "I sometimes wonder how we'll feel when it's all over. Just think, being able to settle down in a little house somewhere and raise your children and never be in doubt about anything."[43]

Madame Chiang in her speech to the U.S. Senate in February 1943 used herself as a good example of the ties between the two nations. "I speak your language," she said, "not only the language of your hearts, but also your tongue. So coming here today I feel that I am also coming home." She then went on to underscore the common causes and aspirations that linked the people of China and the people of the United States. Most of the Chinese people could not speak in the same tongue as Americans, but if they could, "they would tell [Americans] . . . that we are fighting for the same cause, that we have identity of ideals." And she, like her friends in United China Relief, commented on the long Sino-American friendship, which she felt was based on the "great many similarities" between Americans and Chinese.[44]

Madame Chiang's speech in the House included many of the same themes as the Senate speech, but its chief purpose was to counter Roosevelt's Europe First strategy. She commended the Americans who were serving and fighting in China, and she paid a short tribute to the representatives and saluted the United States as "not only the cauldron of democracy, but the incubator of democratic principles."[45] Here, as in other instances, she alluded to the nation's frontier past, encouraging the members of Congress to seize the "glorious opportunity of carrying on the pioneer work of your ancestors, beyond the frontiers of physical and geographical limitations." The immediate problem that lay ahead was the growing strength of the Japanese empire. Many congressional members already felt the United States should direct more of its war resources at Japan because of Pearl Harbor; Madame Chiang's remarks played to that predisposition.[46]

The reactions to Madame Chiang's speech were overwhelmingly favorable. The *New York Times*, in one of several articles on the speech in its February 19 edition, reported that her comments had "made many converts to the cause of China" and had seemed to convince certain members of Congress that assistance to China was crucial to winning the war in the Pacific.[47] Another article proclaimed, "The First Lady of China smiled, spoke and conquered."[48] An editorial, "Lady from China," described how she had taken the "representatives by storm," and even went so far as to call her "one of the most influential women on earth," adding in similar fashion to an earlier *Time* magazine comment that she literally spoke for Asia. Indeed, the *Times* declared, she was "more than the beautiful Chinese girl educated in America": the nation could add a "certain paternal pride" to its "admiration" of her polish, poise, and grace. Madame Chiang's emphasis upon the common links between China and the United States "demonstrated not only how well she speaks our language but how much the thought and aspiration of China are like our own."[49] The overblown rhetoric of this editorial reflected both the paternalistic and the liberal-developmentalist assumptions that undergirded American national attitudes toward China.

The *Washington Post* on the same day called Madame Chiang "magnetic" and possessed of an "eloquence rarely heard" in Congress. According to the *Post*, spectators maneuvered for a better look, and senators and representatives had never seen anything quite like her performance. It had been spellbinding; the senators and representatives "sat as if enthralled" and then broke into thunderous applause "of the all out explosive kind"; at one point members of the House jumped to their feet "cheering and giving the rebel yell."[50] The *Post* editorial, which described Madame Chiang as charming and inspiring, predicted that her eloquence might spur Congress and the Roosevelt administration to increase American military assistance to China. It indicated that certain well-placed reports argued for 500 fully armed and equipped planes in order to defeat the Japanese air force and hamper Japan's industrial production.[51]

Life responded to Madame Chiang's appearance with customary admiration. Not to be outdone by the newspapers, *Life*'s coverage, with photos, said, "A gasp went around the galleries" when she entered the room. In an editorial, *Life* expressed its hope that America's founding fathers had been able to witness one of China's great leaders "in some ghostly fashion" because the "Missimo" "propounds the very principles that the Fathers had been at such pains to develop." The editorial recounted all the major points of her speech that *Life* felt coincided with the principles of America's first generation of political leaders and summed it up with the words, "Thomas Jefferson could hardly have excelled the clarity of [her] expression."[52]

In view of this enthusiastic reaction to Madame Chiang's appearance before Congress, the Combined Chiefs of Staff began to worry that her persuasive skills might actually bring about a reconsideration of the Europe First strategy. Roosevelt held his ground and the matter passed, but the president did order a greater air effort for China, which included rushing the newly developed C-46 into service before it had been adequately tested.[53]

By nearly unanimous consensus, then, Madame Chiang electrified the members of Congress and at least temporarily raised the issue of reconsidering overall war strategy. Journalists were obviously impressed, and even Franklin Roosevelt, an adept handler of the media himself, had trouble keeping up with Madame Chiang's adroitness. At a joint press conference held the day after her appearance before Congress, the two played out a curious spectacle before a packed room of over 170 reporters. The president talked of China's having become one of the "great democracies of the world" in the previous half-century, and he spoke of the closeness, "in thought and objective," between the Chinese and American peoples. Reinforcing what the president said, Madame Chiang echoed some of the ideas long promoted by American missionaries and other supporters in the United States. She noted that China throughout its history had "always had social democracy," and now the Nationalist government was moving toward bringing about political democracy as well. Then a reporter asked Madame Chiang exactly what her nation needed to help fight the Japanese. The president quickly interposed, saying that what China needed was "more munitions." Madame Chiang politely agreed, and she further supported that idea when she answered another question about the Chinese people's perseverance by observing that they could not fight the Japanese with their bare hands; they needed modern military weapons. But when queried as to how more equipment would reach China, Madame Chiang demurred: "The President has solved so many difficult questions, he has come through so many great crises with flying colors, that I feel that I can safely leave that answer to him."[54]

The reporters laughed at Madame Chiang's deft maneuvering. The president, not one to be easily outflanked, immediately embarked upon an answer long on rhetoric if not on substance. He outlined the existing logistical problems of supplying China, especially with the Japanese closing the Burma Road, and he continued with a discussion of the strategic realities of the Japanese position and how the Allied forces could best try to cut into that line and in the process provide more material for China's fighting forces. Toward the end of his lengthy response, Roosevelt noted that he understood why the Chinese would ask the simple but direct questions, when, how soon, and why not a little more? But he had an answer: "Just as fast as the Lord will let us." Madame Chiang's witty riposte was: the president had mentioned helping China as fast as the Lord would allow, but "The Lord helps those who help themselves."[55] The reporters exploded in a chorus of laughter and the incident of course was reported in most accounts of the press conference. The *Washington Post* related that after Madame Chiang's quip, the president "looked like the man who forgot to duck." The entire episode, the *Post* said, "establishes another precedent in her memorable visit to Washington."[56]

To a great many American women, Madame Chiang was now a symbol of women's ability to hold a position of power and authority. The *Washington Post*'s society columnist, Hope Ridings Miller, joined the chorus of admiration. Though she praised Madame Chiang in more traditional terms, for her stamina, her physical beauty, and her good taste in clothing, she made particular mention of her interest in women's rights as one of her most admirable qualities.[57]

A year earlier, a *New York Times* reporter, Harrison Forman, writing from Chongqing, had hailed Madame Chiang as representing "the awakening of Chinese womanhood."[58] Now, Anne O'Hare McCormick, a *Times* columnist, writing about China and the Lend-Lease debates, celebrated Madame Chiang for the prominent change she symbolized in the advancements women were making into positions of authority.[59] The *San Francisco Chronicle* called Madame Chiang "the symbol of women's power and achievement."[60] And Ruth Greene, in an article in a small woman's club magazine, praised her for drawing attention more generally to women's positions within society. Madame Chiang had made vividly clear to the entire world the role Chinese women were playing in the war effort, and this tribute to the women of China had served all women of the world by dramatizing their capabilities as they took "their place in every phase of [Chinese] national life." China was, in many respects, ahead of the United States in offering opportunities for women, Greene added. The People's Political Council, which Greene compared with the United States Congress, had twice as many women even though it had only about half as many members.[61] One woman, in a letter to the *San Francisco Chronicle*, expressed admiration for Madame Chiang this way: "To think she was commanding the attention of nations awed me, but how envious I felt, just being a wife and mother seemed relatively unimportant, yet still grand in the reflection of Madame's words." Madame Chiang's example and encouragement made her feel confident now in the role she was playing in the war effort, in spite of "the boundaries of my own home."[62]

In short, through the positions she held and through the words she wrote and spoke, Madame Chiang reinforced dual notions about Chinese women. Her work as leader of the New Life Movement during the 1930's, her activities on behalf of China's war orphans, her position as chairman of the Aeronautics Commission—all contributed to her image as a woman who had moved beyond the traditional confines placed upon women by both Chinese and American societies.[63]

As frequent translator for her husband, moreover, Madame Chiang clearly was involved in many facets of Guomindang rule, for access to Chiang often came through her. She did not cogovern with her husband—the situation in China was far too complicated for that—but the façade that Americans saw certainly suggested as much, and it was that larger perception that enchanted them to adopt China as a blossoming version of America.[64]

Despite her movement into traditionally male territory, certain commentators preferred to place Madame Chiang's actions in a feminine context. Carl Crow, for example, a prolific writer on China during the 1930's and 1940's, noted in one book that Madame Chiang's usual activities included preparing Chinese women for their duties as "mothers, wives, or sisters of men fighting to defend them." Her actions while temporarily head of the Chinese Air Force benefited from her "touch" as a woman, he said, and he commented on her skill at weeding out corrupt individuals: "Perhaps her feminine instinct helped her to detect the guilty ones." Her job completed, she returned to serving as "the spiritual mother of China. The work of the Bureau of Aviation had been principally a house-cleaning job and she had taken care of it like an efficient housewife."[65] It seems fair to say that in ascribing masculine attributes to Madame Chiang and at the same time diminishing the extent of her capabilities by placing them in a gendered framework, commentators like Crow and the editorial boards of various newspapers not only showed their provincialism but also were congratulating themselves as Americans, applauding their culture and nation for the splendid job it had done in shaping her character. It must be said, however, that Madame Chiang's own writings occasionally reflected a more traditional consideration of a woman's position within society. At one place in her book *China Shall Rise Again* (1940), she says that if a woman "is to make definite personal contributions to national advancement, [she] must be a good wife, a good mother, and a good citizen."[66] Being a good mother, she emphasized, was particularly important for raising the next generation of citizens.

Soong Meiling followed her successful address before Congress with an equally successful month-long tour across the United States, speaking to large and enthusiastic audiences in New York, Boston, Chicago, San Francisco, and Los Angeles. Wherever she went, she made a highly favorable impression. Her appearances were customarily accompanied by a considerable amount of fanfare organized ahead of time by her ardent supporters at United China Relief and Time Inc.[67] At her first stop, New York City, her arrival drew a crowd

of 50,000 at City Hall and another 50,000 when she toured Chinatown after the official reception.[68] "Probably never before has a mission from China been more effectively launched," the *New York
Times* observed, and the *New York Herald-Tribune* added in an editorial that China's struggle was America's and that Americans therefore must do everything within their power to help the Chinese.[69] In
a second editorial about aid to China in the same issue, the *Herald-
Tribune* commented that China's wants were rather modest, but the
airplanes, munitions, and gasoline that Madame Chiang had requested must be found, because rhetoric alone would not help China
fight Japan. America had to make a more concrete demonstration of
its resolve to assist China in the immediate future.[70]

Madame Chiang's main appearance in New York was at Madison
Square Garden, on March 2. Before the Garden speech, she was asked
to be the guest of honor at a dinner, largely arranged by Henry Luce.
The distinguished guests, some of them faithful United China Relief
supporters, included John D. Rockefeller III, chairman of the New
York committee to welcome Madame Chiang; Wendell Willkie; Lieu-
tenant General Henry H. Arnold, chief of the Army Air Forces; Paul
G. Hoffman, who was now head of UCR; T. V. Soong; New York State
Governor Thomas E. Dewey; and the governors of eight states in the
region, including Charles Edison of New Jersey (later, chairman of
UCR).[71] Madame Chiang, pleading delicate health, did not attend, but
she did agree to see a select group before her Garden appearance.[72]

The rally at Madison Square Garden was attended by an enthusiastic crowd estimated at between 17,000 and 20,000.[73] After prelim-
inary speeches by the governors, each of whom paid a handsome tribute to Madame Chiang and the people of China, and some brief remarks from General Arnold and Dr. Henry Sloane Coffin, president
of the Union Theological Seminary, Madame Chiang finally arrived,
looking exotic but sounding American. The *Times* declared that although she was obviously Asian, with "her shiny black hair brushed
back to a knot . . . green jade earrings, a velvet gown high on the neck,
golden embroidery gleaming in the front," her language "sounded so
completely Western that she seemed to be understanding China
rather than explaining it."[74] In an editorial, the *Times* expounded
upon its coverage, reiterating the point that Madame Chiang's "perfect command of our language" and her "perfect command of ideas
which are received with equal sympathy here and in China" brought
the two countries closer together, and that these two shared cultural
notions—language and ideas—had created a mutual understanding
and strengthened the bond between the two nations. China was no

longer a strange, mysterious land to America: "The very laughter of democracy that is trying to be born in China had a familiar note to us." In a rhetorical flourish seldom permitted in the normally reserved *New York Times*, the editorial concluded: China has "risen to a new and splendid destiny. Freedom is being born beside her great rivers and in her mountains. In freedom and the hope of freedom she is not divided from us by the widest of seas."[75]

Of the press reactions to her speech, *Time* magazine, not surprisingly, managed to surpass all the others with its excessive adulation. *Time*'s account said that Madame Chiang, in her "long black dress, gold-trimmed, wearing earrings, [and] black gloves . . . looked more like next month's *Vogue* cover than the avenging angel of 422,000,000 people."[76] *Vogue* had already published a number of articles on Chinese women, and it is worth noting that its piece on Madame Chiang's American tour, in the April 15, 1943, issue, made a rather greater point of her intellectual qualities than *Time* did.[77]

The *New York Herald-Tribune* ran three editorials on China and Madame Chiang in three days. The newspaper declared in one that there was "nothing exclusively or esoterically Oriental" in the ideas she espoused. Her words expressed ideas that Americans had long considered "their particular, if not exclusive, property." Indeed, Madame Chiang's Christian conviction and her emphasis upon social and political democracy were both familiar to Americans. "Perhaps," the *Herald-Tribune* ventured a guess, "this supplies a clew to the spiritual kinship which so many Americans have discovered, on closer acquaintanceship, with the Chinese."[78]

With her arrival in Chicago later in March, Madame Chiang appeared to take another city by storm with her charm and dignified presence, speaking at a daytime rally in Chicago's Chinatown section, where an estimated 15,000 to 20,000 gathered to hear her, and before an audience in Chicago stadium of 20,000.[79] As with her other appearances and speeches, this one attracted its share of favorable commentary. One Chinese woman who had heard the speech on the radio wrote to Madame Chiang, "I have to confess that neither have I ever enjoyed a speech so much, nor have I before realized the magic worth of radio. Please accept my personal thanks for the half hour of your broadcast which passed as if it were half a second."[80]

From Chicago, Madame Chiang traveled to San Francisco, and then on to her final stop, Los Angeles, where the *Los Angeles Times* immediately set a Hollywood tone to the entire affair: Madame Chiang, it said, is "the international Cinderella for whom midnight will never come."[81] Henry Luce, with specific help from UCR's area director,

David O. Selznick, pulled out all the stops to give the "Missimo" a Hollywood-style welcome. In addition to a parade through the city and a reception upon her arrival on March 31, Madame Chiang attended a "special tea" with 200 Hollywood stars. At a banquet held for 1,500 celebrities at the Ambassador Hotel on April 2, she was joined by Selznick and a cast of admirers that included Bob Hope, Samuel Goldwyn, Loretta Young, Barbara Stanwyck, Gary Cooper, Rita Hayworth, Edward G. Robinson, James Cagney, and Frank Capra.[82]

Madame Chiang's final public address, at the Hollywood Bowl, drew her largest audience, estimated at 30,000, and probably her most sympathetic, or at least the most receptive to her speaking style. *Life* reported that her description of the destruction her homeland had suffered brought tears to the eyes of many spectators.[83] One newspaper columnist, Kimmis Hendrick, called the whole Selznick production "thrilling" and "magnificent." With consummate skill, Selznick had managed to bring together a large group to honor one of the leaders of America's fighting ally in the Pacific. "Only Hollywood," Hendrick wrote, "could have provided a setting of this kind." The impression of the Hollywood Bowl appearance had been so powerful that Hendrick still found himself humming parts of the Chinese national anthem days afterward.[84]

Madame Chiang's impact upon Americans did not fade with the conclusion of her tour and her return to China that summer. Frank W. Price, the Presbyterian missionary who was also Chiang Kaishek's personal adviser and friend, wrote to her offering his congratulations on accomplishing so much: "You won a unique place in the hearts of the American people, and you succeeded, to a far greater degree than we had even expected, in your presentation of China's struggle and hopes and in preparing the way for China's larger place in the total war strategy and plans for post-war reconstruction."[85] An article in the *South Atlantic Quarterly* the following October seemed to summarize the favorable sentiment that continued to permeate American perceptions of China. This article asserted that Madame Chiang spoke on behalf of a China that possessed "an identical belief in democracy, [and] an identical mainspring of thought and action": "Missimo," as China's "*envoy extraordinaire,*" spoke "for a people who are of essentially the same democratic stuff we are—appreciative of the same ideals of human rectitude, wanting the same simple fundamentals of free action and unfettered opportunity." The authors concluded: "Anyone who has known Chinese people well knows them as one of the most naturally democratic peoples in the world, much more nearly kin to ourselves in this respect than many a European nation of 'our own race.'"[86]

Madame Chiang's public appearances in the winter and spring of 1943 were the high point of her public influence in the United States, but they did not mark the end of her involvement in Sino-American relations. Privately, she continued her political activities in the late fall of 1943 in an effort to keep Lt. General Joseph W. Stilwell in his post as commander of the China-Burma-India theater. Moreover, her subsequent appearance at the Cairo Conference in November was further proof of one of the unique aspects of the public impression she had created for herself as the cogovernor of China. The period from February 1943 until the end of the year, then, represented the zenith of her personal impact upon Sino-American relations, publicly as well as privately.

As the military situation in China deteriorated during the course of 1943, Stilwell and Chiang, who had never got along well, grew increasingly at odds over the question of the proper course of military action for China. The situation finally came to a head when Chiang became determined to request Stilwell's recall.[87] Stilwell's superior, General George C. Marshall, even went so far as to draft a message informing Stilwell of his termination, citing "the attitude of the Generalissimo" as the reason.[88] Stilwell blamed two people for this development: Chinese Minister of War He Yingqin and Madame Chiang's brother, T. V. Soong, who at the time was serving as foreign minister.[89]

Countering these forces were Madame Chiang Kai-shek and her sister Ailing, wife of H. H. Kong, a wealthy Chinese financier and prominent member of the government. The stage was set for behind-the-scenes maneuvering in a battle of family in-fighting for the control of China. Stilwell's aggressive plans for the training and equipping of a mixed British-Chinese-American land force capable of attacking the Japanese found favor with Madame Chiang, who, Stilwell noted on two separate occasions, was keen on beginning military action.[90] But the generalissimo was reluctant to commit his troops to battle for fear they might suffer casualties that would diminish their later effectiveness in prosecuting the civil war against the Chinese Communists, whom Chiang thought the greater threat. He wanted to attack Japan from the air, with the ample help of the American air power embodied in Major General Claire L. Chennault's command.

For the sake of Allied harmony, Stilwell's time in China appeared limited. In fact, when Vice-Admiral Lord Louis Mountbatten arrived to take over as Supreme Allied Commander of Southeast Asian Command (SEAC), he informed Stilwell that the generalissimo had requested his removal; Stilwell wrote in his diary, "I guess that's that."[91] Having earlier informed Stilwell that convincing her husband to change his mind was a complicated and delicate task, Madame Chiang and her sister requested that he see them at eight o'clock on the evening of October 17. Stilwell was told that "there was still a chance to pull the fat out of the fire." After talking with him at length and getting him to agree to admit to some past mistakes, the three went immediately to see Chiang. The matter was ultimately resolved, and Stilwell retained his position—if only for one more year—in large part because of Madame Chiang's efforts.[92]

Another meaningful event for Madame Chiang—this one public—that bolstered her reputation occurred when she and her husband met with President Roosevelt and Prime Minister Winston Churchill at Cairo in late November 1943, before Roosevelt and Churchill went on to meet with Joseph Stalin in Tehran. The Cairo Conference represented one of the most significant boosts for the Nationalist government during the war. Roosevelt's invitation to Chiang (accompanied by Stilwell, who was now back in favor) to join himself and Churchill at Cairo for discussions on finishing the war and the direction the postwar peace would take symbolically raised Chiang's status to one of the major wartime leaders. Roosevelt's reasons for inviting him were twofold: first, he hoped to quell Chiang's ceaseless clamoring for more military and financial assistance. He felt he could use the famous Roosevelt charm on the Nationalist leader to get him to understand the priorities of the Allies as well as sympathize with the difficulties they were facing in attempting to resupply China. Second, by raising Chiang to a position of equality, Roosevelt could presumably count on his vote against Churchill and Stalin if such a need arose in future negotiations. That way Roosevelt could guarantee he would never be vulnerable to a Russo-British collaborative effort to outmaneuver the United States. Thus, despite Churchill's contentions that the Americans paid too much attention to a minor actor in the prosecution of the war, Roosevelt invited Chiang to Cairo, and he readily accepted.

Upon arriving in Egypt, however, Chiang was immediately disappointed that neither Churchill nor Roosevelt greeted him at the airport. From the Nationalist government's standpoint, the conference went downhill from there. Army Chief of Staff Marshall informed Chiang that the United States could not afford to increase the number of supply planes flying into China in the foreseeable future. American forces in the region would need assistance from his armies in forc-

ing the Japanese from Burma. Although Roosevelt publicly assured
Chiang that the United States was still committed to an amphibious
operation in Southeast Asia, privately the president sided with the
British, who wanted to postpone the plan indefinitely.

Roosevelt's confidential dealings were not reported in the American press, but pictures of the big three—FDR, Churchill, and
Chiang—and Madame Chiang, sitting together apparently engaged
in friendly conversation, appeared in all the newspapers and periodicals, and were later placed into history textbooks. One widely repro-
duced official photograph shows the generalissimo at camera left.
Next to him is the president, leaning toward Chiang in an apparent
attempt to share some wry observation or witticism, Chiang smiling
as if to acknowledge the president's remark, which, of course, he
could not since he did not speak English. Prime Minister Churchill,
in a full white suit with black socks, is seated on the president's left,
and to his left is Madame Chiang. While the president acted for the
cameras with Chiang, Churchill and Madame Chiang, who were not
on the most cordial of terms, appeared to enjoy the proceedings in an
amicable fashion. The picture gave the impression that the leaders of
China had joined the ranks of the first circle. Along with that admission came the conclusion that China was an equal partner in the prosecution of the Pacific war and would be instrumental in carrying out
the postwar peace settlement for Asia. Madame Chiang appeared at
the conference not only as the wife of the generalissimo but as his
partner. The picture of her sitting with the three leaders seemed to
confirm her station as a woman who virtually cogoverned China with
her husband. That, in turn, reinforced her status as a woman who exercised a great deal of authority.[93]

Privately, Madame Chiang attended at least five meetings during
the Cairo Conference where she served as translator for her husband.[94] Moreover, she persisted in her efforts to bring about a change
in her husband's reluctance to commit China to military operations.
After one particularly exasperating episode, Stilwell noted that Madame Chiang had done her best to convince her husband of the need
to reconsider his stance. "She realizes the implications and it drives
her nuts." The next day Stilwell added, "[Meiling] said she *prayed*
with him last night. Told me she'd done 'everything except murder
him.'"[95]

The Cairo Conference produced the usual pronouncements about
the unity of the Allies in purpose, strategy, and policies. More importantly, it provided evidence that the heavy propaganda of the previous
eleven months had been well justified. Madame Chiang had spoken

eloquently during her visit to the United States. Now, the Roosevelt administration supported her rhetoric with the symbolic, but meaningful, gesture of elevating Chiang's government to a position of equality.

The president backed up the public move toward greater cooperation with China by pressing Congress to repeal the Chinese exclusion laws that had been in effect for half a century. Pressure, in fact, had begun earlier in the year when Madame Chiang made her triumphant tour. In speaking to T. V. Soong in June, Secretary of State Cordell Hull indicated that he and other members of his department had been drawing the attention of members of Congress to China's desire for truly equal treatment.[96] Congress had originally passed the exclusionary measure in response to the intense pressure from the Western states and territories that feared an influx of Chinese laborers. The act continued to bar Chinese immigration during the twentieth century despite China's new position as America's exalted ally in the Pacific. The Roosevelt administration correctly saw this as a national insult. A month before leaving for Cairo, the president made a request to rescind the law, and upon his return, FDR was pleased to announce that he had signed a measure repealing the law. Although only a little over 100 Chinese were admitted under the new provisions, the change, as Roosevelt said in announcing the policy, was symbolic of the general good feelings and American affection for China.

To emphasize these notions of Allied unity, especially with China, President Roosevelt broadcast a Christmas Eve fireside chat from Hyde Park in which he told the American people of the accomplishments made at the Cairo and Tehran conferences. In discussing the growing Sino-American harmony, he said, "Today we and the Republic of China are closer together than ever before in deep friendship and in unity of purpose."[97]

During World War II Soong Meiling literally captivated the United States with her public appearances. From her speech before Congress on February 18, 1943, to her final performance at the Hollywood Bowl six weeks later, over a quarter of a million Americans saw her, and countless thousands more heard her over the radio.[98] Along with the positive image she etched for all things Chinese, Madame Chiang symbolized the message American missionaries had propagated for decades: a democratic, Christian China appeared on the verge of realization. The enthusiasm and optimism generated by that thought infected numerous commentators on Sino-American relations. Madame Chiang succeeded in personalizing China. However much she may have been set apart from the political and social changes that were taking place in China, she worked to make herself a central issue in American considerations of future relations with China. She did so by dramatizing in a very compelling way the similarity between the United States and China: she was indeed the tangible proof that Americans wanted to see in their earnest efforts to transform the rest of the world in their own image.

For the larger war effort, Madame Chiang conveniently reinforced existing notions about gender. "Even during the war," Elaine Tyler May has noted, "Americans were heading homeward toward gender-specific domestic roles."[99] The fighting men abroad fought for "home and hearth"—an attitude that itself reinforced traditional ideas about gender constructs. The preservation of this "culture of domesticity" combined with an American "cultural offensive" abroad resulted in an application of domestic standards about proper relations between men and women to other nations, in this case China.[100] The belief that the China of Generalissimo and Madame Chiang Kai-shek was fighting to attain a similar standard of gender relations in turn further solidified the belief that China was becoming increasingly like the United States. American commentators placed Madame Chiang within their own nation's social parameters as well as within distinctly American "cultural constructions" of gender.

Ironically, however, as a figure who transcended traditional notions about women and their abilities, Madame Chiang attracted the attention of many women who saw in her an important model for change. Like a good politician, Madame Chiang simultaneously played to these two contradictory expectations—of maintaining the status quo and of bringing about change—when she wrote and spoke to Americans.

The impressions she made during the war continued to have an effect long after the Japanese were defeated. Despite critical reports, unflattering articles, and other publications that focused on Guomindang deficiencies and corruption (most of which appeared after the war), Madame Chiang retained her highly favorable image in the United States while her husband's reputation declined along with his government.[101] Even three years after the war was over, in December 1948, she ranked second, after Eleanor Roosevelt, as the woman Americans (of both sexes) admired most.[102] A year later, even after the Nationalist government had collapsed on the mainland and fled to the island of Formosa, she still managed to place in the top five.[103]

There can be no doubt that her husband was also vital in fostering certain illusions about China and the future of Sino-American relations, but he could not match his wife in many fundamentally important ways. Because she managed to appear both Chinese and American at the same time, Americans long interested in China could not have asked for a better symbol to express their hopes than Madame Chiang Kai-shek.

At a time when the United States was engaged in a bitter war with one Asian nation, Madame Chiang offered the prospect of an Asian people remarkably like Americans in their political aspirations, their social organization, and even in their sense of humor. If the war between the United States and Japan was a "war without mercy," then Madame Chiang presented a diametrically opposed picture, one of cooperation between Americans and Asians. With her commanding public presence, her physical attractiveness, her wit, charm, grace, and fluency in English, she captured the emotions of Americans because she coincided with the nation's search for cultural as well as military allies.

CHAPTER SIX

The Underside of Sino-American Relations During World War II

The idea of China being called a World Power to me is a big joke and I am afraid someday in the not too distant future we are going to pay dearly for this propaganda.
—Gus Paton to John R. Hutchinson, 1944

Underneath the façade of Sino-American cooperation and harmony lay a complicated alliance full of disappointments and antipathies. Madame Chiang Kai-shek may have captured the emotions and sentiments of much of the American public with her well-coordinated appearances, but she could not ameliorate the general discord created by differences of opinion over wartime strategy. Many American military and diplomatic personnel stationed in China viewed Chiang's entire effort as one predicated upon accumulating all the war matériel possible while largely allowing the United States to assume the burden of defeating Japan. Such a strategy clashed with the American hope that China would actively engage the Japanese and tie down a large number of units from the Kwantung army.

Chiang's initial elation over the news of Pearl Harbor meant that he immediately grasped the long-term ramifications. With the United States in the war, not only would China no longer have to fight alone, but it would also mean a significant boost in the amount of American military and economic aid China received. Because that aid would help solidify his political standing, he hoped at the end of the war to be in a strong position from which to launch an attack on the Communists, eliminating them once and for all.[1]

The Sino-American partnership, then, worked on two levels. On the one, the partnership seemed to embody mutual hopes and aspirations for the future. But there was another, more immediately serious level, concerning the two quite opposite strategies; at this level, the problem was the friction that developed when the American attempt to secure a more concerted military effort from Chiang met with his equally determined resistance to pursue a different strategy.

Because Madame Chiang had traveled around the United States to such universal acclaim, inspiring fabulous impressions in the process, certain commentators began to worry that Americans were gaining inflated ideas about Chinese abilities and endowing the Chinese with selfless motives beyond anything that was reasonably accurate. Some American supporters of the Nationalist government even began to fear that a backlash would result when it was discovered, as it certainly would be, that the Chinese people were not as ingenious, hard working, and steadfastly committed to the achievement of a democratic political system as some people had insisted. One of the first and most influential persons to forward a cautionary note publicly was Pearl Buck. As a principal contributor to the development of romantic notions during the 1930's with her novels and articles, she appeared to back away from her earlier position with a warning about the damage that might result from the perpetuation of these ideas. Her decision to speak out illustrated the heights that the celebration of China had reached in wartime America. Somewhat surprisingly, *Life* magazine published her concerns in May 1943—an editorial decision that Luce supporters have since cited as evidence of his balance in describing conditions in China. But a close reading of the article reveals that instead of discussing China's real problems, Buck echoed the line of ardent romantics by blaming the United States. In submitting her piece to *Life*, Buck purportedly sought to counter the highly emotional temperament that had inflated American expectations, and Luce supposedly agonized over whether to publish the article.[2] It would appear, however, that his hesitancy had less to do with her criticisms, such as they were, than with the tone, which was a good deal less sentimental than most recent American commentary on China. Buck asserted that caution was required in viewing China, but not because of endemic corruption or because of any failings on the part of Chiang Kai-shek or the Nationalist government; rather, the worsening political and economic conditions had developed from the failure of the Roosevelt administration to secure the delivery of vital war matériel to Chiang's government. Specifically, she argued that because of America's "policy which has relegated Japan to the place of a secondary enemy," "undemocratic forces" had recently gained momentum. Their rise was especially tragic because the Chinese were "historically a democratic people." Moreover,

Chiang had valiantly led his people through many years of hardship and determined resistance, prompting her to characterize his actions as typical of "the leadership and genius of Generalissimo Chiang Kai-shek."[3]

Later, in repeating her assertion that America had served as an accomplice in strengthening Chiang's undemocratic competition, Buck charged that the Roosevelt administration's policy of financial assistance instead of concrete military aid was responsible for the problems. The United States had "stopped sending . . . trucks and parts and gasoline" to the Chinese with the closing of the Burma Road, she wrote, implying that the United States had taken this as a voluntary and unilateral action, when in fact it had been brought about by the Japanese military. Throughout the article, she echoed the widely held belief that America alone determined the course of action wherever it touched, quite unencumbered by regional and local conditions. Roosevelt, not the Japanese, was to blame for Chiang's predicament. Toward the end of the article, she underscored this point by observing gratuitously that America's present policy of denying military equipment to the Nationalist government certainly had to be meeting with approval in Tokyo.[4]

In explaining to *Time*'s correspondent in China, Theodore H. White, why he had decided to publish the article, Luce acknowledged that there were often considerable differences between expectations and reality, but he assured White that an overall optimism about the future of China was justified and he wanted White to continue to convey to *Time*'s readers an overt faith in Chiang: "It is still the faith— and not the defects of faith—which it is most of all important to communicate."[5]

A few months after Buck's article in *Life*, the *Reader's Digest* published an article by Hanson W. Baldwin, the military correspondent for the *New York Times*, that delved into some of the existing problems created by the sentimental and overly optimistic thinking about China. Like the Buck article, this one has subsequently stood as further testimony to the changing nature of Sino-American relations in 1943.[6] Baldwin was hardly an apologist for the generalissimo, to be sure, but instead of discussing the deteriorating military and political conditions in China and the mistakes of the Nationalist government, he warned Americans against the notion that air power alone could defeat the Japanese. Chiang Kai-shek had, of course, long sought American air support as a way of fighting the Japanese without committing his troops to battle. Specifically, he backed General Chennault, who, as head of the 14th Air Force in China, believed in the ability of air power to cripple Japan militarily. Baldwin sought to address this confusing tangle of issues by praising the Chinese people for their courage and stamina. "The Chinese spirit has not been broken," he declared; although "missionaries, war relief drives . . . and the movies" may have oversold China, it was only in how China would be "the royal road to victory in the Pacific." The Japanese were going to present tough problems for American military planners, but just as plainly, the Chinese would play their part. "China's great and continuing contribution to the victory" came through its ability to tie down substantial numbers of Japanese troops. With their courage and their "patient fortitude and philosophic resignation," the Chinese people were without peers, and the conclusion was certain: "China will play its noble part in this strategy of encirclement."[7]

A minor example of the caution with which certain American periodicals began to treat China in general, and in this instance Madame Chiang in particular, came with the publication of an article by Ernest O. Hauser in the *Saturday Evening Post*. Even more so than the Buck article in *Life*, Hauser's article was extremely mild in its content and was in no way intended to undermine Madame Chiang's tremendous public reputation in the United States. But whereas Hauser had nothing but praise for the generalissimo, who had "captured the imagination of the world's least romantic race," he seemed to be emphasizing the strengths of Chiang and lessening the importance of his wife, placing her significance in a more restricted context. "The influence of Madame Chiang has been overrated abroad," he said, and her primary importance came through her activities on behalf of China's war orphans and through her role as an intermediary between her husband and those seeking his attention. He also pointed out that she did not have the political power in China that certain American commentators had attributed to her.[8]

These tentative reappraisals in the public press were as nothing compared with private expressions of increasing doubt about the unmitigated American celebration of the Chiangs and everything Chinese. Some who began to ask questions were military men, others were in the administration. Whiting Willauer, assistant to General Chennault during the war and an important member of the China Air Transport afterward, noted in a diary entry in May 1943 that the American attitude was getting out of hand. He mentioned the problems created by the missionaries' predilection for viewing everything in a good-versus-evil framework. As examples, he listed a few ideas he said had gained widespread acceptance without having much, if any, basis in fact. First, the suggestion that China was democratic either in fact or in inclination was patently untrue. Second, Americans had been fooled into believing that every Chinese was fighting selflessly and that the only obstacle that prevented more Chinese from engaging the Japanese was a lack of military equipment. Third, China was simply not a country united behind the leadership of Chiang Kai-shek. He blamed the creation of these myths upon American sentimentalists, official Chinese propaganda, and Madame Chiang. "Selling these things," he noted, had "been Madame's major activity."[9] There was much that was good about China, but he feared that as long as these exaggerated claims continued to gain widespread acceptance, more damage would be done in the end than anything else. His observations are especially interesting given his dedication to General Chennault, a prominent and ardent supporter of the Chiangs throughout his life.

Presidential adviser Lauchlin Currie also had misgivings, which he expressed mainly in comments he traded with Foreign Service officers stationed in China. In 1943, when Madame Chiang was on her travels across the United States, Currie wrote John Carter Vincent at the American embassy in Chongqing, indicating that many members of the administration were "peeved about her speaking tour." Not only had her public comments inspired criticisms of the administration's war strategy, but she had lobbied certain senators and representatives just a little too vigorously, he thought, trying to force an Asia-first turnabout. He noted that some of her recent public statements were "increasingly erudite," and cited a speech in San Francisco in which she used the words "mendacity," "disjunctive," and "postulates" in one lengthy and convoluted sentence.[10]

In fact, Currie had expressed some misgivings as early as 1942. In a memorandum to the president on the state of Sino-American relations in June of that year, Currie remarked that China's cooperation was "helpful" but not essential in defeating Japan, whereas that same cooperation was "indispensable" to Chiang. He made a number of other observations, including one involving a recent *Time* article that was critical of the administration. Evidently, it had been "inspired" by the Chinese.[11] At about the same time, Currie's sarcasm got the better of him in a letter to John Carter Vincent. Admitting that he was "feeling rather low about the Far East . . . both from the military and political side," he asked Vincent about recent official Guomindang statements concerning China: "One is that it is a classless society, another that it is a true democracy, and a third that there is full freedom of thought and speech." Having run through the standard litany, he then asked, "Why haven't you told me this before?"[12]

These thin strands of discontent grew ever thicker as other problems developed over the course of the next year. Currie began keeping track of certain financial matters relating to Madame Chiang and her entourage during her tour of the United States. Large cashier's checks of $100,000, $61,000, and $59,000 were issued in May, and by mid-June of 1943, Currie recorded that the total amount transferred to her stood at $800,000.[13] President Roosevelt, obviously irked, referred to her as China's "prima donna" in a conversation with Walter Judd and further suggested that "it might be well if Madame Chiang were to plan her return to China soon in order that these irritations might subside." Judd tried to defend her actions as a physician. After all, he responded, the strain caused by her long journey, demanding schedule, not to mention "the greatest acclaim ever accorded to a woman in this generation," had undoubtedly left her a little overwrought at times. The president understood, naturally, but in the best Roosevelt fashion, he expressed his worry that her admirable successes not be undermined by petty sniping. It was not that he personally had anything against her, of course.[14]

Further questions about Madame Chiang, these raised publicly, came up in the summer of 1944 when syndicated columnist Drew Pearson wrote on a recent trip to China by Vice President Henry Wallace.[15] Pearson's sources indicated that China was the number one problem facing the Allies, "much tougher than the American public realizes." Moreover, reports that Chiang had taken up with another woman meant that Madame Chiang's influence was clearly waning. He noted that Chinese popular sentiment would support the generalissimo as long as Madame Chiang bore him no children. He also served warning on the fractured state of relations between Stilwell and Chiang by mentioning *New York Times* correspondent Brooks Atkinson, whose diary would "blow the lid off" the appearance of Sino-American harmony and unity if the *Times* published its contents.[16]

Indeed, if anything had a negative impact upon American conceptions of China during World War II, it was President Roosevelt's decision to remove General Stilwell as commander of the China-Burma-India theater in the fall of 1944, and the subsequent articles about the tumultuous situation there written by Atkinson for the *New York Times* and the equally critical ones put together by Harold Isaacs for *Newsweek*. Stilwell's recall unleashed a storm of anti-Chiang criticism in the United States, but the tempest was quickly over. In fact, the overall media response was ambiguous, in part because of the Roosevelt administration's determination to downplay the episode, coming so close to the election as it did, by preventing Stilwell from talking publicly. It subsided quickly on account of other considerations as well.

The fundamental difference between "Vinegar Joe," as he was known for his caustic remarks about every subject without fail, and the generalissimo came down to how Chinese troops could best be employed in fighting the Japanese. Chiang wanted to preserve his units for the civil war he anticipated with the Communists after the defeat of Japan. Rather than sacrifice the very soldiers that made his rule possible, he favored a two-pronged approach. First, he saw the progress American forces were making in the Pacific. As long as Japanese troops were tied down on the mainland, the Central government served an important military purpose in not allowing those units to be relocated. Second, he endorsed the overall strategy pushed by General Chennault, who insisted that with enough bombers and fighter planes he could effectively cripple Japanese shipping in the area and seriously weaken the nation's industrial capacity to wage war. For Chiang, this plan offered the value of not forcing him to commit large numbers of troops to battle.

On the other side of the strategic debate sat General Stilwell, who believed that an aggressive air war would have to be backed up with sufficient troops to protect the bases from which the planes flew. The only real way to dislodge the Japanese from their positions was to engage them in ground combat; that required well-equipped, properly trained, and capably led troops. Stilwell's first priority lay in reopening the Burma Road, the important supply line running from Allied-controlled areas in Burma through parts of the Himalaya and into southwest China. It had been cut by Japanese troops in the spring of 1942, and since then supplies had been flown by cargo carriers of the Air Transport Command over the Hump into China, a risky mission for the pilots and necessarily inadequate in terms of matériel that could be transported.

The rancorous debate between Stilwell and Chennault extended all the way back to Washington, where journalist Joseph Alsop worked on Chennault's behalf, aggressively advocating an increased commitment to air power. Before the American entrance into the war, Alsop had been employed by T. V. Soong's China Defense Supplies. As a distant cousin of Franklin Roosevelt, moreover, he was able to use his various personal connections to gain access to presidential adviser Harry Hopkins. Later, he traveled to China where he hooked up with Chennault and in the process received a military commission at the rank of captain.[17]

In keeping a regular correspondence with Hopkins, Alsop insisted on numerous occasions that the China war theater was "preeminently an air theater." He stated the case vigorously in a letter he wrote in March 1943: "*China, from the global standpoint, is preeminently an air theater[;] we should make mounting a China air offensive our first concern.*"[18] Given Chennault's successes so far, which Alsop characterized as stunning and complete in view of the limited resources at his disposal, the general had managed to place the Japanese "over a barrel in the air in China." In short, with Chennault requesting a greater share of the Hump supplies, "There couldn't be a better preparation, at smaller cost, for the ultimate major effort in the Far East."[19]

Even more than military reasons alone, Stilwell's deficiencies, somewhat substantial ones according to Alsop, also warranted a redirection of the limited American resources. A major ground offensive in China required a great deal of its commander: "Gifts of imagination, open-minded, patience and cautious diplomacy which Stilwell, alas, is almost wholly without." Further contributing to Stilwell's liability was his low opinion of the efficacy of air power; in fact, Alsop suggested, the Chinese had yet to request his removal only because they feared something worse. General Chennault, on the other hand, if given a proper chance, could seriously weaken the Japanese war-making capability: "He has never lost a fight, nor launched a plan that miscarried."[20] Two months later, Alsop wrote again to inform Hopkins that the situation in China was now so serious that he feared an internal collapse. The Japanese had established a position that made it possible to launch an attack upon the Nationalist wartime capital of Chongqing. Unless Chennault had more in the way of supplies and planes, Chiang doubted he would be able to prevent the Japanese from taking the city.[21]

Complicating matters even further, while Alsop and Chennault lobbied for greater support for their aerial campaign, other summaries of deteriorating conditions in China were reaching the White House through Lauchlin Currie, by way of Harry Hopkins. One report put together by two foreign doctors on the situation along the Ichang front—the one from where Chennault, Alsop, and Chiang feared the Japanese would strike at Chongqing—detailed the shocking physical deterioration of many soldiers. Their diet now consisted mostly of years' old rice and some pickled vegetables, salt, and red pepper—equally old and nutritionally valueless—and regular epidemics of typhus, dysentery, and smallpox were decimating numerous army units.[22]

Another report, which came while Madame Chiang was attracting the tremendous adoration of Americans with her well-organized appearances, was sent by Theodore White, who was in North China. This dispatch described the terrible famine in Henan province in the winter of 1943. In touring the area, White noted that all the while he and members of his party were treated to official banquets consisting of "spiced lotus, peppered chicken, beef, water chestnuts . . . spring rolls, hot wheat buns, beancurd, chicken and fish . . . two soups and three cakes with sugar frosting," peasants tried to subsist on "elm bark, peanut shells, [and] pondweed." The extraordinarily bleak conditions had been caused by two years of poor crops, 1940 and 1941, followed by a spring wheat failure in 1942. Throughout this period, the Central government continued to collect taxes in grain. Peasants whose taxes exceeded their supply were forced to sell their livestock and belongings, and in many cases their land, to come up with the required amount. Failure to pay often led to beatings. The results were staggering: dead and dying men, women, and children, including infants, littered the roads. Some people had resorted to cannibalism, while others killed their families and themselves rather than continue to suffer. In a province of 20 million people, White estimated 5 million had died from malnutrition and starvation; another 3 million were refugees. Neighboring provinces refused to send their surplus grain for fear that the prices of their existing stocks would rise. The Central government responded slowly and ineffectively, earmarking $100 million (Chinese) to the region. Two problems with the money, however, were immediately evident: paper currency had already lost so much value that the government chose to collect taxes in grain rather than money, and the region needed food most of all. Allocating financial assistance only further delayed the arrival of the desperately needed grain.[23]

White's account of the tragedy in Henan was not seen only by the president; part of it made it into print, in *Time* magazine, of all places, which published a heavily edited version in March 1943. Madame Chiang, on her way from New York to Chicago amid all the fanfare, reacted angrily and insisted that Luce fire his reporter. Luce refused, and White remained in the employment of Time Inc. for another three years.[24] Luce's reasons for publishing the news of the famine may well have had more to do with his missionary instinct than with any desire to criticize the generalissimo and his government; he could not deny that the tragedy had occurred, but what he could do was stimulate the Chinese government to action without assigning blame. White in his article clearly laid out the faults of the provincial and national governments for failing to prevent the onset of massive starvation, but *Time*, in a fatuous prefatory note, absolved the responsible parties: "How ageless are China's problems and how bitterly Chinese history repeats itself in cycles of wars, floods and famines, TIME Correspondent Teddy White could tell last week from firsthand knowledge."[25] White's report to the president had warned that peasant support for Nationalist armies could not be guaranteed in areas like Henan because the government's response to the desperate conditions faced by the local population had been so paltry. No such warning appeared in the *Time* report.

The consequences of the famine, combined with the persistent corruption inside the Nationalist government, became clear in the spring of 1944 when the Japanese launched a major offensive called Operation Ichigo. Defeats in the Pacific at the hands of American naval and air forces led the Japanese Imperial Headquarters to conclude that a secure position in China and Southeast Asia could ensure Japan's continued resistance almost indefinitely. Beginning in April 1944, Japanese troops advanced south of the Huang river into Henan province.[26] Chinese troops in the area were quickly routed, in part because peasants rose up against their own countrymen and disarmed some 50,000 soldiers according to one estimate.[27] In this way, the famine had tremendous military ramifications, for the Japanese swiftly moved farther south, inflicting casualties and jeopardizing the entire military situation.

The Japanese success, including the overrunning of many of Chennault's forward airbases, led Roosevelt to conclude that Stilwell had been right.[28] When Army Chief of Staff Marshall concurred and then asked Roosevelt to request Chiang to place his forces directly under Stilwell's command, the president signed on in July. Chiang was now faced with the unattractive, and ultimately unacceptable, prospect of losing control of his forces to someone whom he had come to loathe. But instead of rejecting Roosevelt's firm suggestion outright, he stalled, asking for an American intermediary to facilitate the change in the command structure. Roosevelt acquiesced and decided to send the former secretary of war under Herbert Hoover, General Patrick J. Hurley. Hurley's somewhat naïve view of the world, based mainly on Republican-Democratic political differences in his home state of Oklahoma, hardly prepared him for the complicated world of Chinese politics, and he was quickly ensnared as the military situation worsened. In September, Roosevelt sent a strongly worded message, but Stilwell's elation turned out to be premature. Hurley sided with Chiang, who now requested Stilwell's recall, citing personality conflicts; he indicated that somebody else would be satisfactory, however.[29]

Additional contributions to the White House picture of the situation came in the form of reports from John Paton Davies, a junior Foreign Service officer attached to Stilwell's command. In the fall of 1944, he noted that widespread dissatisfaction with the leadership of the Guomindang could easily precipitate sectional breaks from the Chongqing government. Therefore, he concluded, the United States should not continue to make the mistake of "personalizing [its] support of China." The whole concept of the Big Four was "dangerous and misleading in the case of China."[30] Having written earlier that Chiang was "probably the only Chinese who shares the popular American misconception that Chiang Kai-shek is China," Davies noted that his unwillingness to change stemmed from a firmly held belief that eventually the Americans would come to his rescue.[31]

Roosevelt was faced with two unattractive alternatives: he could back Stilwell and try to pressure Chiang into making specific reforms, or he could extemporize by agreeing to Chiang's demand for a new commander. The first carried with it the possible loss of China, as Hurley was quick to point out in one message to the president; the second essentially wrote off the Chinese theater for any serious operations in the future. After some delay, on October 18, Roosevelt opted to bring Stilwell back to the United States. He chose as his replacement General Albert C. Wedemeyer.

Stilwell's dismissal was made easier, at least in part, by the recent successes in the island-hopping strategy in the Pacific. With the securing of the Mariana Islands by September, American B-29's could strike directly at the Japanese home islands from airbases on Saipan and Guam, making China less important strategically. Thus, by the end of 1944, changes in the military situation in the Pacific impinged upon the sentimental emotionalism that had infected early Sino-American relations.

The incident certainly generated a considerable amount of reporting, despite the best efforts of the administration to keep it quiet. Front-page stories across the United States signified the importance the event held not only for Sino-American relations but also for American military policies in the Pacific. Brooks Atkinson broke the story in the *New York Times* on October 31, and the newspaper quickly ran three editorials in the next four days. Each was more notable for its conciliatory tone, however, than for any strong argument in favor of fundamentally reconsidering the status of Sino-American relations. The *Times* immediately cautioned its readers to acknowledge certain "facts" before jumping to conclusions about the Stilwell affair. Chiang had been diligently fighting the Japanese since 1937 and had refused Japanese offers for peace despite their undoubted appeal at various times. Chinese resistance, it added, although declining in effectiveness, nevertheless continued to detain a large number of Japanese troops: "We thus owe a debt to the soldiers and people of China which nothing we can do will repay." Moreover, it was still possible for Chiang to improve overall conditions in China. Should he make those necessary changes, his prestige would "be enhanced, not diminished." Regardless of his ultimate actions and reforms, the *Times* declared, "we cannot fail in our friendship for the Chinese people. We cannot fail in gratitude to Generalissimo Chiang Kai-shek, who has met the supreme test and refused to surrender. Peace in the Orient without a stable and prosperous China is unthinkable."[32]

A follow-up editorial the next day continued the effort to cast a positive light on the new information coming out of China. Though recent events indicated a certain amount of disorganization there, they nevertheless demonstrated that "Chiang Kai-shek, in spite of his errors and *much more the errors of those surrounding him*, can still command the allegiance of the Chinese people."[33] In other words, as many of his American supporters were wont to claim, Chiang was not responsible for the corruption and mismanagement of the Nationalist government. The *Times* later wrote (November 4) that perhaps he was not to blame for the manner in which the Nationalist government failed to prosecute the war either. Instead, the newspaper hypothesized, "It may be that to some extent the fault rests with us here in the United States, and especially among the best friends of the Chinese people." The logic behind such a conclusion ran as follows: earlier in the war, Americans had been quick to point out that time was on the side of the Chinese, because of their nation's vast size and enormous population. Sooner or later the Japanese would become exhausted. The problem came when the same Americans who had pushed this suggestion not too long ago forgot their earlier comments. As the *Times* noted, "Having sold to the Chinese people this idea that they have all the time in the world, we here at home proceeded to forget our own argument, and we have lost patience with Chiang for practicing what we preached."[34]

A third, longer, *Times* editorial took a rather different tack. Despite the present crisis, Roosevelt's China policy was not a failure: "Every American who has died in the Pacific war has died for the freedom of China as well as for the principle of freedom everywhere." And de-

spite the obvious internal problems that had to be solved by the
Chinese themselves, it once again lauded Chiang Kai-shek as the one
man who could continue to unify China and bring about needed reforms. China was a nation that Americans admired and respected,
and the *Times* offered the hope that an American military landing on
the Chinese coast would allow the "'trickle' of aid . . . [to] become a
mighty torrent."³⁵

In only a slightly less conciliatory vein, the *Washington Post* on
November 2 printed an editorial acknowledging that perhaps the recent disillusionment was the natural reaction to the overly sentimental and optimistic attitude that had previously clouded American perceptions. Chiang was apparently ready to bring about essential reforms, and his continued rule remained an important part of the
American strategy for the Pacific.³⁶ In the same issue, columnist Barnet Nover remarked that although recent information from China
had thrown a "valuable light" on conditions there, there was a danger
that too much unnecessary heat would seriously damage Sino-
American relations. Conceding that Chiang certainly appeared to be
a dictator on paper, Nover went on to explain how the intricate nature
of his position required a deft political hand to maintain the various
coalitions with regional warlords all in an effort to keep China in the
war.³⁷

Even as the editorial pages of some of the most respected newspapers across the nation sought to salvage something from Stilwell's
dismissal, a less flattering portrait of the war in China emerged principally from the reports filed by Brooks Atkinson and Harold Isaacs.
Atkinson, whose story had to wait for his exit from China in order to
avoid the censors, described the long-standing feud between Chiang
and Stilwell from a perspective clearly more sympathetic to the latter. He characterized Chiang as possessing the mind of a warlord,
which meant that he saw military forces for their political value. The
Guomindang government had become "bureaucratic, inefficient and
corrupt," and Stilwell's recall denoted a victory for the "moribund,
anti-democratic regime that is more concerned with maintaining its
political supremacy than in driving the Japanese out of China." The
United States, he said, was now committed "at least passively to supporting a regime that has become increasingly unpopular and dis-
trusted in China, that maintains three secret police services and concentration camps for political prisoners, that stifles free speech and
resists democratic forces." Atkinson tried to end on a small note of
optimism by arguing that even though its recent actions indicated
that the United States was "acquiescing in a system that is undemo-

cratic in spirit as well as fact," the Chinese people themselves remained "good allies."[38]

Harold Isaacs's two articles for *Newsweek* corroborated Atkinson's
views: Stilwell had lost his battle "against inertia, corruption, inefficiency, and questionable motives," Isaacs said, and the success of
these very forces meant clearly, "China has been written out of the
plans for defeating Japan."[39] Isaacs's second article detailed the conditions faced by the Chinese soldier. In this story, hardly the usual
line about the jolly conscript dedicated to fighting the Japanese,
Isaacs asserted that the deaths of Chinese officers, which made up
fully one-half of all Chinese casualties, could have been avoided
through the use of proper military techniques.[40]

Another very outspoken critical appraisal was that of Thoburn
Wiant, writing out of London for the Associated Press. Wiant did not
equivocate: "Democracy does not exist in China. There probably is
no more effective dictatorship than that of the Kuomintang Party.
There is no freedom of speech; or of press; or of much of anything
else." Addressing the issue of Stilwell and his recall, he praised the
general and added that he deserved "unique recognition for his long-
suffering, conscientious, loyal, skillful service."[41]

Atkinson, Isaacs, and Wiant were the only three journalists who
consistently forwarded negative portrayals of conditions in China.
Other periodicals, some wholly committed to China, continued their
vested support for Chiang and the Guomindang and flung wild
charges. The *Christian Century* even accused the United States,
Great Britain, and the Soviet Union of joining Japan in attacking
China. Roosevelt's demand that Stilwell be placed in charge of
Chinese forces was simply unacceptable; it was no wonder the generalissimo insisted upon his recall.[42] Other media assessed the entire
affair from a politically partisan viewpoint and in so doing laid much
of the blame at Roosevelt's feet. The *Wall Street Journal* accused FDR
of bungling America's relations with China. The recent picture of
Chiang was that of a man who had "some virtues and a great many
defects," not unlike "a good many men in other parts of the world."[43]
The *Chicago Daily Tribune* added its strongly anti-Roosevelt voice
to the controversy: Chiang's request was not "altogether unreason-
able" given the situation, and the crisis in Sino-American relations
was proof not only of how "Mr. Roosevelt can't handle Chiang" but
also of the fallaciousness of Roosevelt's claims to foreign policy ex-
pertise.[44] The same argument also appeared in the *Wall Street Journal*
in an article by Raymond Moley, a former brain-truster and assistant
secretary of state under Cordell Hull, who had left the administration

after becoming disillusioned with the New Deal's turn to the left in 1935. As a Columbia University professor in 1944, he wondered what mistakes Republican presidential nominee Thomas Dewey could make "in dealing with Chiang, that Mr. Roosevelt has not already made."[45]

Overall, the media reaction to the Stilwell firing was mixed. But the effort to shine the best possible light on China continued, despite the harsh criticisms offered by some commentators. Once again, Pearl Buck came to the rescue. Writing in the *New York Times Magazine* in December, she insisted that if China had been given its proper place in the war, Chiang's position would have been strengthened to the point where he could have exercised the necessary authority to broker a genuine coalition with the Chinese Communists. That he remained too weak to bring about such unity was on account of the policies pursued by the Roosevelt administration. The Chinese welcomed the recent reconsideration of Chiang because it meant that Americans had discarded their too sentimental and romantic notions about China, which, Buck said, the Chinese had been uncomfortable with from the very beginning. The Chinese continued to hold their leader with the same affection as "the Russians do Stalin and the English do Churchill, and even as [Americans] do . . . Roosevelt." She then, by way of illustration and to underline her criticism of Stilwell, drew a preposterous analogy: "In spite of the likeness between Churchill and Chiang Kai-shek, the American people have not been encouraged to criticize our ally England as they have been encouraged [to criticize] our ally China—this, although China has fought far longer on our side than anyone else."[46] She finished on an optimistic note, not surprisingly, as she attempted to blunt some of the recent stories. Out of the present darkness, she saw China as already beginning to forge a dedication to creating national unity and political democracy.

Chiang was apprised of the American public's reaction. Frank Price, the Presbyterian missionary who was Chiang's close friend, noted in a letter to him: "Recent opinion in America has not been very favorable to China and that public opinion greatly influences government policy." Price offered a number of suggestions about how Chiang could turn American public opinion around, starting with a "radical reorganization of the gov[ernment] and army under [the] Gen[eralissimo]'s leadership, and [the] bringing of new and able men into service of the central gov[ernment]." Despite the recent spate of unfavorable publicity, Price took heart in a recent *New York Times* editorial, and he ended his letter by quoting Jesus, suggesting that through supreme sacrifice for China, Chiang and the Guomindang would "gain greater life and glory."[47]

Several months later, in February 1945, Price made additional suggestions about how Chiang should play to American public opinion. He warned that a further weakening of American confidence in the Nationalist government would have a detrimental effect on military decisions: "We must do everything possible to hold American confidence in the Nationalist government and to give evidence that its policies are liberal, reasonable and democratic." In order to demonstrate such sensible and moderate intentions, Price advocated making Guomindang offers to the Chinese Communists public so that if they were refused, the public onus would be placed on them.[48]

Still, changes were not forthcoming, at least not according to the various reports arriving at the White House. Instead, they indicated that conditions in China were continuing to deteriorate. Lauchlin Currie passed along to the president a copy of Harold Isaacs's uncensored background assessment, which was much more detailed than his *Newsweek* articles.[49] Evaluating the impact Stilwell's departure had had in the United States, Isaacs despaired of an American press that after having "flared in a pyrotechnic display on the Chinese question," had managed to publish only "a few hard truths," which were in turn "promptly buried in recriminations, smothered in half-truths, and editorial pap. The fireworks gave out and the show ended in a smoky fog of confusion." Both Chiang and Roosevelt had their reasons for trying to patch over the unseemly matter, he noted, and now because of the superficial changes that had been instituted "the public prints oozed with mutual goodwill." Replacing Stilwell with Wedemeyer and allowing Hurley to continue his mission had not produced any tangible results. In fact, Isaacs observed, the burly Oklahoman with the white, handle-bar mustache had got in over his head: "Hurley has fallen among men whose brand of politics is a little too finely spun to compare with the Oklahoma frontier push-and-pull." His dramatic attempts to reach an agreement between the Nationalists and Chinese Communists had gone nowhere. Militarily, Chiang's forces continued to wait until the United States finished defeating Japan.

With General Wedemeyer's replacement of Stilwell, the China-Burma-India theater was split into two commands: the first, China, came under Wedemeyer's jurisdiction; the second, Burma and India, fell under the direction of General Dan Sultan. In reporting to Marshall in February 1945, Sultan remarked about how well Stilwell had trained the Chinese divisions he had managed to work with. Some of the units were now as good "as any commander could wish." Of even greater interest was the fact that Wedemeyer also defended Stilwell's strategy for handling military matters in his area. Disagreeing with both Chiang and Chennault, he argued that "a disproportionate amount of tonnage" had been allocated to Chennault's forces if effective offensive operations against the Japanese were planned; Stilwell's prediction that air power alone could not stop the Japanese had been correct. In short, he called for a greater percentage of the Hump tonnage to be allocated to ground units over the next few months. Only then could a coordinated, ground-air effort be made against the Japanese.[50]

America's military and diplomatic relations with China during World War II differed sharply from the rosy portrait painted by United China Relief and Time Inc. But the true picture lay largely hidden from the American public's view. Some critical reports did make it into print, to be sure, but on balance, members of the media, like the Roosevelt administration itself, were chiefly interested in promoting the image of Sino-American cooperation and harmony for the overall war effort.

As for Franklin Roosevelt, one historian has characterized his handling of foreign policy during the war as that of a skilled—and self-professed—juggler, a public performer who tossed the balls of Europe, Africa, South America, and so forth, into the air with the understanding that he would deal with each one when required.[51] China was certainly one of the largest balls he attempted to handle. His intentions were based on future prospects, on the enticing opportunities offered by China. As Roosevelt wrote to Louis Mountbatten about getting China included as one of the four great powers in 1943, "I really feel that it is a triumph to have got the four hundred and twenty-five million Chinese on the Allied side." But in expressing no illusions about their present military capabilities, he added, "This will be very useful twenty-five or fifty years hence, even though China cannot contribute much military or naval support for the moment."[52]

The problem with Roosevelt's plan was that as skilled as he may have been in his juggling act, he did not live long enough to finish his performance. His sudden death in April 1945 left Harry Truman to try and catch the balls before they hit the ground. Truman had shown little interest in China prior to Roosevelt's death, and he more or less subscribed to the established view begun by American missionaries and perpetuated by Henry Luce and company. Upon assuming the presidency, however, Truman came to realize that China was not a nation in the Western sense of the word; instead, he later wrote, it was "only a geographical expression."[53] But his discovery would not become widespread knowledge for a few years.

The more ambiguous impressions made by the Stilwell affair notwithstanding, his recall did signal an end to the uncontested hyperbole surrounding certain expectations and aspirations for China. Yet the subsequent change in American thinking did not come about any faster, simply because too many people had worked for too long to give up so easily. Besides, the United States stood victorious at the end of the war in such a way as to make the future appear not only bright but perhaps limitless. And that was what China was all about.

CHAPTER SEVEN

The Dawning of the American Century

We offer China a way of life beaten out on an anvil of actual experience. From Plymouth Rock to our present position as the richest country in the world, ours has become knowledge anyone can check.
—*News of China* editorial, April 1949

There's a China in your future.
—Proposed United China Relief slogan

China, in effect, is to the West what the vast American continent was to Europe after its discovery—a land for pioneers on an ever expanding frontier. But the new frontier that is China is a vast frontier, far exceeding in complexity that which confronted the Pilgrims.
—Leon Loeb, *China Clipper*, 1946

At the end of World War II, the United States stood militarily triumphant, economically prosperous, and politically confident. American armed forces had participated in the destruction of fascist aggression in Europe and Asia, but unlike the other nations involved in the fighting, the United States had suffered virtually no damage itself. Instead, the nation's Gross National Product soared from just under $100 billion in 1940 to over twice that by the war's end.[1] American liberal principles, as expressed in such pronouncements as Roosevelt's "Four Freedoms" speech and the Atlantic Charter, offered a beacon of hope to oppressed peoples around the world. This historic combination of military and economic power intersected with a seemingly altruistic political ideology, all of which gave the appearance of bringing about the realization of Luce's "American Century."

Like the nation itself, Time Inc. prospered during the war. It grew so substantially, in fact, that by 1945, there were 5.4 million American subscribers to *Time, Life,* and *Fortune.* Added to that were 95,000 overseas editions of *Time* printed every week, and "The March of Time" newsreel, which attracted millions of domestic and international viewers. By the end of the war, Luce's three periodicals so surpassed their competition that they exceeded the combined number of readers for the *New Republic*, the *Nation*, the *Saturday Evening Post*, and the Sunday edition of the *New York Times*. Over 1.1 million Americans read *Time* magazine every week compared with less than 600,000 for its nearest competitor, *Newsweek*. And Luce's empire sustained its growth after the war. By 1947, it reached nearly 6.5 million American readers, more than the combined figures for *Newsweek*, the *Saturday Evening Post*, and the Sunday editions of the *New York Times* and the *Los Angeles Times*.[2]

In addition to propelling Luce's corporate-journalistic juggernaut, World War II served to validate much of his political ideology in tangible ways. The war largely discredited the isolationist bloc of the Republican Party. Such stalwarts as North Dakota Senator Gerald Nye and New York Representative Hamilton Fish were voted out of office. Others, like Senator Arthur Vandenberg of Michigan, converted to the internationalist cause with some assistance from the Roosevelt administration. The lessons of the 1930's generally, and Munich in particular, indicated that appeasement and isolation, rather than preventing American involvement in European conflicts, contributed to its probability. The world had simply become too small to retreat behind the vastness of the Atlantic and Pacific oceans. During the course of the war, the president and members of his administration worked carefully, and resolutely, to prepare the American people for their postwar obligations. As a reference to the nation's failure of just a generation before, Roosevelt kept a portrait of Woodrow Wilson on a wall in the War Cabinet room to remind everyone of that mistake, one he wished to ensure would not be made again.[3]

Despite his past criticisms of Roosevelt's policies, Henry Luce could not find fault with the idea of the United States accepting a greater share of responsibility in world affairs. On the contrary, he, too, worked during the war to prepare Americans for their new role in international relations. As he said in "The American Century," the United States was ultimately responsible for the world in which it lived. Already, he argued, American culture had spread around the globe as part of a new and dynamic internationalism. The country needed to follow this up with a firm commitment to share the best of its political legacy with other nations. Included in his list of standard American writings were the Declaration of Independence, the Constitution, and the Bill of Rights. He wanted political thinkers from Thomas Jefferson to Abraham Lincoln to receive the wider recognition they richly deserved.

Not everyone agreed that the United States should involve itself in events thousands of miles away. The Truman administration's decision to station Marines in North China in the fall of 1945, for example, was especially unpopular with certain citizens who felt that the United States was unnecessarily meddling in the internal affairs of another country. In an extraordinary example of this sentiment, one private citizen expressed his feelings vehemently in a letter to the Secretary of the Navy, James V. Forrestal.[4] The letter contained a tirade of invectives, calling the secretary a "sneaking, low life, murdering cur . . . drug store cowboy . . . arm chair soldier . . . Hitler in knee britches . . . filthy scum." In the same harsh language, the writer insisted that Forrestal immediately remove all American soldiers from China.[5] The administrative aide who brought the letter to Forrestal's attention made a note that although the language used was more "vigorous" than in most cases, it nevertheless expressed the prevailing opinion of those who had written in about the decision to station the Marines in North China.

Shortly thereafter, in November 1945, Forrestal forwarded a copy of the letter to Luce as an example of the intense public sentiment against leaving American soldiers abroad to assist in the postwar reconstruction of other nations. Women were even sending baby booties to senators and representatives along with notes about wanting daddy home. But despite the concern of military planners like Army Chief of Staff General George C. Marshall, who feared that the drastic, unilateral, and rapid demobilization of American forces would jeopardize the nation's strategic positions in Europe and Asia, the politicians quickly folded in the face of the popular drive to "bring the boys home." In short order, they effectively dismantled the bulk of the country's armed forces.[6]

Luce responded by thanking Forrestal for the "obscene blatherskite" and for the reminder of the public pressure faced by government officials. In his cheerful response, he passed along a short letter he had received from the president of Standard Brands, who, after having spoken with him, indicated that if only Americans understood the issues at stake in China, they would impel the administration into "carrying out what amounts to our very real obligations" there, instead of criticizing this effort to fulfill the nation's new international assignments.[7]

Luce was certainly not one to be intimidated by the emotion to remain uninvolved in other countries' affairs, and he did his best to influence public opinion into supporting an American presence in China. In a *Life* editorial on the domestic cry to bring the soldiers home, he chided Americans for their selfishness, which he attributed partly to ignorance and also to a certain amount of Communist propaganda. Americans should realize that it was their duty to continue to assist Chiang Kai-shek and the Nationalist government. "In the confusing aftermath of the war," the editorial concluded, "the safest thing for us to do is to rededicate our wartime alliance with China and its government."[8]

In a larger sense, Luce's efforts tried to bridge the gap from the long-standing emphasis upon an Open Door internationalism to the Truman administration's conception of a world divided into two blocs, one Soviet, one American, where the bulwark became the new operating metaphor. Luce's paternalism, with its focus upon converting China, had easily fitted into Roosevelt's idea of "four policemen," which implied lifting China up to the level of the United States. Now it coincided, at least for a time, with the switch to containing the Soviet threat, because Luce envisioned this danger as it specifically related to China. Part of saving China for the United States meant protecting China from other, presumably evil, forces. Forrestal, like many of Truman's other advisers, and along with Stilwell's replacement, Lieutenant General Albert C. Wedemeyer, also insisted that Soviet designs for world domination included China as well as Europe. Thus, these two viewed developing events from the same ideological and strategic perspective as Luce. Many other members of the administration, however, including Dean Acheson and George Marshall, focused primarily on Europe. The problem ultimately developed into one where Luce saw China as the bulwark against further Communist expansion in Asia, whereas members of the Truman administration, particularly George F. Kennan, saw Japan as playing that role. The importance this had for the intracultural dynamics of American attitudes toward China became clear when Luce's paternalism, ever expansive and benevolent, collided with the cold realities of America's limited resources. The Truman administration found itself facing choices about where to apply containment and in what fashion. China was simply too large for the kind of commitment envisioned by people like Luce. Still, and in spite of discovering that China was "only a geographical expression," Truman relegated over $2 billion in military and economic assistance to Chiang Kai-shek's government after the war. But even that could not save the Nationalists from collapse. Although the American Century in China was apparently within sight, reaching that illusive dream required spanning a chasm of unfathomable proportions.

*

Though the swiftness of Japan's capitulation caught many people off guard, Henry Luce was not one of them. He had already prepared Time Inc. to run cover stories on the two great heroes who, he believed, had contributed much to the Allied victory.[9] The first was General Douglas MacArthur, the second, Chiang Kai-shek. Luce cabled *Time*'s correspondent in China, Theodore White, assigning him the Chiang Kai-shek story. But White's experiences in China had given him a completely different conception of the situation. He did not share Luce's views on the prospects of democracy ever coming to China under Guomindang auspices, and he no longer looked upon Chiang as the savior of China. In the late 1930's, when Nationalist forces stubbornly resisted Japanese aggression in their retreat to Chongqing, he had viewed Chiang as something of a hero, but the failure of the Nationalist government to respond to the basic needs of the Chinese people, along with Chiang's persistence in fighting a civil war against the Communists while the Japanese ravaged China, had given him a markedly different opinion. He cabled Luce his refusal. There was another exchange, in which White made it clear that their perspectives on China had diverged. Luce ordered him back to New York, and when White returned, he immediately took advantage of a six-month leave of absence coming to him. With Analee Jacoby, he wrote a book on the historical forces unfolding in China. A confrontation with his boss finally came about in the summer of 1946 when White showed him a copy of the manuscript. The two met to discuss their differences, but nothing was resolved. Luce wanted him to accept any assignment given to him in principle; White decided that he could not accede to such an ultimatum. Not knowing whether he had quit or been fired, White prepared to leave his office when he received word that the book he and Jacoby had recently completed had been chosen as a Book-of-the-Month Club selection. *Thunder Out of China* thus enjoyed widespread circulation, with total sales exceeding 450,000 copies.[10]

The book's importance arose as much from its iconoclastic approach to Chiang Kai-shek and the Nationalist government as from its surprisingly brisk sales. It vividly described conditions in China and discussed why the Chinese Communists had been so successful in gaining support from the population. The Communists were sharply contrasted with the Nationalists, whose inefficiency, corruption, and basic disregard for the peasants alienated them from the largest segment of the population. Guomindang sympathizers in America encountered another problem with the book: its authors' eloquence. "It is just too bad that 'Thunder out of China' was written so well," wrote John H. Baker, the chairman of United China Relief (now known as United Service to China): "Its effect has been to practically kill United Service to China's campaign out here."[11] Missionary Frank Price concurred. In a letter to Madame Chiang, he explained that because the book was "brilliantly written and a best seller," it had "done a great deal of damage to China's cause" despite being marred by factual errors.[12] Luce's opinion was blunt and unfair. Years after its publication, even after Chiang's government had fled to Formosa, he mistakenly commented that when George Marshall arrived in China in December 1945 to mediate between the Nationalists and Communists, he was carrying "that book by that ugly little Jewish son of a bitch."[13]

Theodore White observed that best-seller success can provide an illusory sense of influence and importance. *Thunder Out of China* sold well, and although White continued to enjoy public attention for the first half of 1947, the postwar mood of the country was concerned with the fundamentals of domestic, peacetime life. The revolutionary developments in China seemed too far away and too intricate, and in the end too distracting, for most Americans. By early 1948, White found himself in a predicament. In the increasingly conservative political climate, his liberalism was viewed askance by many employers. Subsequently, he had some difficulties in finding a job. His book with Jacoby had sold very well, and in the process, it had focused some attention, however briefly, on conditions in China, but its importance within the larger scope of events was ephemeral at best.[14]

Time Inc., on the other hand, continued as before. After all, Luce was not about to let go without a fight, and he had far greater resources at his disposal. In one week in 1946, for example, *Time* reached over three times the number of people who bought copies of *Thunder Out of China; Life* had a subscription rate of nearly 4.7 million in 1947, over nine times the number of books sold.[15] In addition to his flourishing media empire, Luce possessed an inner determination—a missionary's righteousness—that precluded any reconsideration of his convictions. Eric Hodgins, former managing editor of *Fortune* and someone who held his boss in high esteem, remarked that Luce "stuck utterly and completely to Chiang Kai-shek until the day of his death."[16] He clung to this vision without qualification and promulgated it vigorously. The result was reporting by his three major magazines that highlighted Chiang's strengths, excused or rationalized his faults and weaknesses, and focused on how much the United States should be doing to help him survive.

Time began the postwar onslaught with another cover appearance for Chiang, an unprecedented sixth, in its issue of September 3, 1945. The story, in typical *Time* style, applauded Chiang's tenacity in resisting the Japanese. It insisted to his American critics that his strength did not depend on corrupt or authoritarian practices but on his huge popularity among his people. His conduct during the war and his leadership qualities had finally "justified those who had long held that his Government was firmly embedded in popular support."[17]

Coupled with this notion was its ubiquitous counterpart: namely, that China's fate lay in the hands of Americans, especially those of the nation's foreign policy makers. Fortunately, assistance was forthcoming, and it included ferrying Chiang's armies from their positions in the south and west to the cities along the eastern seaboard. In one instance, C-54 transport planes flew the 35,000 men of the 94th Army to Shanghai. All in all, American military forces facilitated the movement of between four and five hundred thousand of Chiang's best-trained and -equipped troops to places like Shanghai and Nanjing.[18] This action, coupled with the occupation by U.S. Marines of key cities until the Nationalists arrived, helped deny nearly all the urban centers to the Communists. *Time*'s September 3 cover story noted that American actions coincided with a Soviet "back of [the] hand to Manchurian Communists" to create a highly favorable situation for Chiang's government in its efforts to regain control over most of China, especially Manchuria. Time Inc.'s interpretation of events was that Mao, despite his initial reluctance, was being forced into accepting an invitation to negotiate the integration of the Communists' army into the Central government.[19]

In celebrating this apparent triumph, the corporation's public posturing reflected its internal discussions. A lengthy unpublished special report on Chinese-American relations prepared by Alfred Jones (a Time Inc. employee) commented favorably on the immediate prospects for Chiang's government and, in the process, summed up Luce's prevailing sentiment with the statement, "In short, Chiang has promised to make China the model democratic country of Asia."[20] It seems "probable," Jones said, "that Chinese-American relations are about to enter their era of greatest intensity, in which the dreams will be fulfilled and the good American policy of the past justified."[21] He defended this conclusion by noting that observers of Chinese history would do themselves a favor to look at the situation with "the eye of an ethnologist." Such a perspective offered the view that "the Chinese appear to have a tremendous democratic potential and a minimum of receptivity to the appeals of totalitarianism."[22]

Jones's analysis relied in great part on the old historical analogies, and the supposed lack of any tradition of social hierarchy in China. He commented at one point, "In China there is hardly a trace of caste, or of aristocracy, or any of the social leftovers of feudalism that characterize almost every other civilized people." This bland assertion ignored the foundation for Chinese society and glossed over centuries of Confucian influence upon every aspect of Chinese life, from the structure of the government to proper familial relations, and indeed the Confucian emphasis upon hierarchy, but it was exactly suited to Time Inc.'s grand postwar conception of harmonious Sino-American relations. Jones's comprehension of Chinese character and life verged on the absurd when he argued that an analysis of daily events provided evidence of a society keenly democratic at its core: "This free-market environment of haggling and voluntary decision is what has made the Chinese individualistic, argumentative, and stubbornly, if passively, attached to the basic values of democracy—freedom and equality."[23] He might as well have claimed that the air they breathed was suffused with the fragrance of liberty. But the point was obvious: with a passive, yet innate, attachment to the fundamental tenets of democracy instilled through centuries of daily food purchasing, the Chinese people simply needed an enlightened leader to direct them along the proper course toward creating a truly democratic nation. Who else but Chiang Kai-shek? With the generalissimo's lucid sense of a political mission clearly defined for all to see through Time Inc., with the Chinese Communists apparently fading into relative unimportance, and with the military and economic might of the United States so definitively established, the future of Sino-American relations overflowed with unrestrained optimism. Luce's desire for Sino-American harmony, predicated upon the natural disposition toward democracy underpinning both societies, appeared closer to realization than ever before.

The prospect for the American Century was clearly there, beckoning, entreating, and luring those capable of recognizing it. And it was obviously part of the larger idea espoused by Luce that the war had provided the United States with another unprecedented chance to remake the world, something he first publicly advocated in his senior address at Yale University in 1920. Even twenty-five years earlier, his driving intellectual and ideological thinking had revolved around a powerful America wisely and judiciously exercising its political, economic, and, if called upon, military power in an effort to create a global community compatible with the nation's interests. Through the tremendous destruction it had wrought, the war just finished had effectively crippled any competitors for years to come. Luce believed that this unique moment in history had been granted to the United States, of all the world's countries, as part of its providentially ordained mission. Decidedly internationalist, yet at the same time staunchly Republican, he worked assiduously to promote a new and more involved program for his party toward directing the nation's course in the postwar world.

In that vein, Luce immediately went after the State Department. A September 1945 *Life* editorial assessed its readiness, comparing it to an old lady "set in [her] ways" many of which were "not of this generation." *Life* went for the obvious conclusion that the nation needed a coherent foreign policy, especially in light of the current gravity of the world situation. "In the next few months Europe and Asia will be reformed," and as it stood, the State Department was unprepared to deal with the task at hand. "Our decisions," *Life* intoned, "will not only affect American lives but help determine the future of half the human race. It is an immense responsibility."[24]

In China, the prospects for a political settlement boded well. Recent Sino-Soviet negotiations had apparently isolated the Chinese Communists, stripping them of their only real leverage, and the Nationalist government was preparing to re-form as a constitutional, multiparty government. This political evolution afforded the United States a unique opportunity to assist in the transformation of Asia through a concentrated program of military, economic, and financial assistance.

But if everything looked bright immediately after the Japanese surrender, the situation changed during the fall of 1945. Evidently, the Chinese Communists were not as weak and isolated as Time Inc. wanted to believe. Mao's forces, as some journalists and observers had reported, did have considerable support from the peasants, and it appeared that, with or without Soviet assistance, the CCP was continuing to spread its influence through programs of land reform and tax relief. The Communists even demonstrated an ability to manage the city of Harbin.[25] This success gave them the confidence to continue to resist any agreement with Chiang. Chiang had turned on them violently in 1927, and the Nationalist army had attacked them during most of the 1930's and had continued its attacks throughout World War II while the Japanese destroyed much of China. The Communists were not ready to dismantle their military forces unilaterally or place them completely under Chiang's authority without some concessions on his part.

During the subsequent negotiations, battles for North China broke out as each side vied to control more territory. The primary difference in strategy between the two lay in Chiang's concentration on regaining his urban bases of support. Although the Communists also tried to occupy key industrial centers whenever possible, the Nationalists' overwhelming military strength gave them the edge. Mao and his commanders Zhu De and Lin Biao satisfied themselves with retreating into the countryside in the best guerrilla warfare fashion in order to preserve their strength to fight another day.[26]

As the undeclared civil war escalated in the fall, Time Inc.'s rhetoric became more strident in saddling the United States with ultimate responsibility for events. A *Time* "Report on China" in November stated that the realization of genuine peace depended upon how much America helped. "We have put Chiang's key armies in the ring with U.S. ammunition," *Time* misleadingly reported. The United States, as *Time* undoubtedly knew, had supplied and trained some of Chiang's troops to increase their fighting effectiveness against the Japanese during the war. Chiang's decision to move against the Communists was his own, and he undertook it against the advice of key American military advisers.[27] Nevertheless, *Time*'s message to its readers was that stockpiles of ammunition would run down at some point: "To make their handsome weapons work," *Time* concluded, "we must continue to supply the U.S. ammunition." *Time* further said that the United States had predicated its foreign policy on the assumption that a Sino-Soviet agreement signed in August would preclude civil war by isolating the Chinese Communists. With rather suspect logic, it argued that the failure of this treaty to make good on that promise placed a burden upon the Truman administration to enforce the implied provision. The consequences of not doing so would be tremendous, of course. A refusal to keep open the supply lanes would constitute "a great failure" for the United States, because a cutoff of aid would force the nation to "take responsibility for stranding [Nationalist forces] without ammunition and letting the Communists mow them down, with weapons taken from the Japanese."[28] Such a policy of betrayal would undoubtedly come back to haunt America.

On the same day, *Life*, in a double-barreled barrage from Time Inc., appeared with a two-page editorial (something of an event in itself) that predictably argued for a sustained campaign of American support for the Guomindang. It took a somewhat different tack, admitting that Chiang's government had "often been justly criticized as a dictatorship," but that was only a journalistic flourish, for the editorial went on to explain that up till then, conditions in China had not been completely under the Nationalist government's control, and therefore it could not be held accountable for all that had happened—inflation, corruption, and other unfortunate circumstances. These problems notwithstanding, *Life* proclaimed, the Chinese people took great pride in their government, faults and all; indeed, Chiang's group of assistants was "man for man . . . probably as able and as 'liberal' as Truman's cabinet."[29]

As if this were not enough to strain any intelligent reader's credulity, *Life* then proceeded to make the old exaggerated comparisons between China and the United States. Under Chiang's direction, China had recently found new unity, culturally as well as theologically, the editorial said. Its 400,000,000 people were "much more homogenous than, for example, the people of the U.S." Americans had been deceived about the differences in dialects between the various regions. In a statement so blatantly false as to be embarrassing, the magazine reassured its readers that at "least 300,000,000 Chinese speak a language which varies no more than the dialects of Vermont and Alabama."[30] Once again, aspects of Chinese history, society, and culture were placed within the context of how they pertained to the United States. If Chiang's cabinet could be compared with Truman's and if Chinese language dialects could be understood by their relationship to those of American Yankees and Southerners, then the Chinese themselves could not be all that much different from Americans.

Almost as if in response to its onslaught, Time Inc. very quickly had new ammunition when Major General Patrick Hurley resigned his post as U.S. ambassador to China, charging the State Department, particularly its China staff of Foreign Service officers, with having interfered in his efforts to bolster the Nationalist government. These officers had, he said, undermined his authority by purposely circumventing him in reporting back to Washington. His accusations subsequently led to the assertion that China had been lost by American subterfuge and betrayal; but for the more immediate concerns of late 1945, they instigated an enormous amount of commotion as events in China began to slip slowly from the confines of the nation's paternalistic aspirations.

Time, applauding Hurley's attack, hoped that his charges would force the Truman administration to develop a specific policy of supporting Chiang, rather than staying with the vague policy that had languished for too long. This "handsome, irascible Major General Patrick Hurley," *Time* said, had once killed a "fractious mule by bashing its head with a two-by-four"; now he had "killed an official attitude" by bashing an "indecisive State Department" with his resignation and follow-up statement before Congress. His actions received such favorable commentary because they "turned the beam of public interest on the State Department" and its more dubious assumptions about China. In his salvos against State, Hurley had not shied away from naming the people he thought were responsible for sabotaging his mission—among them George Atcheson, Jr., John S. Service, and John Carter Vincent, Lauchlin Currie's correspondent, who later served as the State Department's head of the Office of Far Eastern Affairs. Even Secretary of State James V. Byrnes could not escape blame, *Time* added, if Hurley's charges proved to be accurate.[31]

State Department officials and China correspondents like White and Jacoby were well acquainted with Hurley's often bizarre behavior and realized how totally unfit he was for the job of ambassador.[32] The Truman administration had seriously considered replacing him earlier in the fall of 1945 and had only reluctantly asked him to stay on in order to maintain continuity in the discussions with the Nationalists and the Communists. But Hurley, after reassuring Secretary of State Byrnes on the morning of November 27 that he would indeed remain, that afternoon in a speech before the National Press Club announced his resignation, with the string of fantastic charges already mentioned. The public nature of his allegations drew Congress into an investigation; hearings were held in December, and Hurley once again made himself a public spectacle, but a very useful one as far as Luce was concerned. Meanwhile, Albert Wedemeyer in China made some suggestions to Chiang on how his government could best promote its designs for the postwar era. At the generalissimo's request, moreover, Wedemeyer looked into a number of personnel who might be able to serve as a propaganda and publicity director. Specifically, Wedemeyer wanted someone "of fine character, scrupulously honest and unselfish in his desire to serve China" so that he could counter "the distortions and untruths being promulgated by certain opposing forces." After making a few recommendations, Wedemeyer indicated that, whoever was selected, the most important thing was to spread the word about Chiang's plans for the "democratization" of China. He closed his memo on the subject by adding that he expected to hear from his "old personal friend" George Creel, the former director of the Committee on Public Information during World War I, who had some experience in the matter of selling governmental programs.[33]

Hurley's actions and public statements had brought out the usual commentators on the subject of Sino-American relations. A month after Hurley's resignation, the radio show "America's Town Meeting" devoted another one of its programs to China under the question, "What Should Be Our Policy in China?" This time Walter Judd and

Donald M. Nelson squared off against journalists Vincent Sheean and Theodore White. Nelson introduced a new wrinkle into the fabric for understanding Chinese society. When asked about the difference between the Soviet and Chinese forms of communism, he replied: "The Chinese people are individualistic people. [Their] nation has been built around the family, whereas in Russia, Communism is collective Communism."[34] Judd, as usual, brought in historical analogies, this time comparing Chiang with Abraham Lincoln not once but several times during the broadcast. In reply to comments about the number of people killed in the Chinese civil war, he said, "Abraham Lincoln killed even more in his desperate attempt to save this Nation from being split." And later, he added, "Just as Abraham Lincoln succeeded, after a long struggle, in putting down a rebellion in this country," Chiang was working to put down his own rebellion. Finally, he observed, "Chiang has always said, as Abraham Lincoln said, 'If you're willing to come along, we'll work together.'" Theodore White's retort was: "Abraham Lincoln never set up concentration camps throughout the northern United States. He never executed students for the possession of Southern literature. Abraham Lincoln never had a gestapo that went into every home, and that seized professors from their universities for what they said in class."[35]

Hurley's resignation and the furor it caused forced the Truman administration to react quickly. Secretary of Agriculture Clinton Anderson proposed General Marshall for the job of ambassador, in part, according to Forrestal, to "take headlines away from Hurley's resignation the following day."[36] Because Hurley had apparently spurred the government into action, Time Inc. found his actions laudable, especially when the president picked Marshall to succeed him in trying to mediate the Chinese conflict, and Luce's periodicals expressed their admiration for Marshall as a man exceptionally well suited for the task ahead. Late in December, for example, *Time* covered Marshall's arrival in Chongqing by noting that this "rugged, aging General of the Army on whose shoulders the hopes of East Asia rested, bore the burden confidently."[37] His appointment seemed to signal that the Truman administration was prepared to give China a higher priority on its foreign policy agenda. The problem with the Communists would undoubtedly be brought under control by the Nationalist government now that there was a clearer definition of American policy.

The future appeared to herald such bright prospects for Sino-American relations that *Life* published a major, surprisingly candid, article just before Christmas on the subject of conditions in China and the prospects for peace. Editor Charles J. V. Murphy wrote the story after spending three months surveying the situation, and although his conclusions remained consistent with the corporation's well-established attitude, he did make some unusual admissions and acknowledgments. In Time Inc. fashion, he argued generally that the Guomindang represented the only legitimate government of China. Chiang, the Nationalist government, and the Guomindang party all wanted a democratic China and a reformed government, and the cabinet was "the most liberal and honest in recent Chinese history." All the evidence pointed to Chiang's intention to fulfill his promises of bringing democracy to China, a fact that only the Communists refused to believe.[38] His confidence that China would soon realize peace stemmed not only from the generalissimo's ability to make good on his political promises but also from the improving military situation. Nationalist military movements into the north were "the teeth of a comb," and these forces would no doubt subdue the Communists in short order; the exact amount of time required depended upon a number of factors, but a surprisingly woeful performance by the CCP greatly abetted Chiang's enterprise.[39]

But after these standard Time Inc. preliminaries and the usual predictions of amicable Sino-American relations, Murphy, in a seeming awareness of the real situation, said that China throbbed with "a pent-up reform," which would soon become a torrent that would have to be appeased. The problem, he said, was that neither party could do the job alone, and he mentioned positive contributions made by the Communists toward China's political development. Regardless of their ultimate fate, which he indicated would include some form of political assimilation, either peaceful or violent, they were responsible for introducing "a genuine democracy into the bottom of Chinese life." He credited the CCP with "crushing the grip of the rapacious landlord and tax collector" in certain places and, more generally, with awakening "the political consciousness of the Chinese peasant." Having thus allowed the Communists a pat on the shoulder, Murphy wound up, inevitably on the old side of Time Inc.: Luce and company assumed that the Nationalists had the situation solidly under control, so there was no harm in acknowledging a few of the Communists' better points.[40] After all, events in China were progressing along the track laid out by Luce in his postwar proposal for the world. Hurley's resignation had forced the Truman administration to reconsider its China policy; Chiang Kai-shek gave all the assurances of making the political reforms he had long been touted as favoring; the military situation favored the Central government; and finally, the

Communists had not received the kind of assistance from the Soviet Union that they had expected and Luce had feared. The situation, on balance, appeared to favor the Nationalist government decisively. An American Century of China moved apace.

At the same time that Time Inc. set about to convince Americans of the need to help ensure a peaceful and prosperous postwar world, United China Relief was faced with a different set of problems. Even before the Japanese surrender, the organization had begun to debate the question of whether or not to continue its work after the war. In assessing matters and, in turn, arguing for a continuation of the agency's efforts, B. A. Garside estimated in a letter to Luce that UCR had been responsible for a five- to tenfold increase in the number of Americans "actively interested in China."[41] Dissolving UCR into its former agencies would cause most of these new people to be lost, and furthermore UCR provided a valuable service because it offered Americans a comprehensive picture of China, something the eight agencies could not do as separate entities. Garside's arguments apparently won the day. In December 1945, the board of directors decided unanimously that the agency should continue for at least two more years.

The money-raising efforts of UCR gave a certain confidence. Garside calculated that, all told, including estimated receipts for 1945 of over $11 million, UCR had raised slightly over $40 million in the years 1941–45. Barring incompetence, bad luck, or a series of unfortunate events either in China or the United States, he thought UCR should be able to raise another $13.8 million for the years 1946 and 1947. But this figure was predicated upon a highly problematical second general assumption: "That China will during the next few months find some means of avoiding serious and wide-spread civil war, and during the next few years will not have more than a reasonable amount of factional strife and bad press in America."[42] As he and the others were soon to discover, that was not to be the case.

Just the same, United China Relief carried on its public support of Chiang Kai-shek and the Nationalist government. The agency's latest president, Dr. James L. McConaughy, stated in November 1945 that Chiang was the only one who could "lead a United China toward democracy."[43] Luce continued his work for United China Relief, and on behalf of Chairman Charles Edison, he wrote to the board of directors that the work that had been so "uniquely effective in demonstrating American good will toward the Chinese people" during the war had to be continued despite the onset of peace. The display of resolve and goodwill, he added, "is the firm foundation for the friendship which we seek in a progressive and democratic China."[44] A list of UCR's board of directors contained the usual names, and a few new ones: Justice William O. Douglas, Henry J. Kaiser, Eleanor Roosevelt, Walter Judd, John D. Rockefeller III, David O. Selznick, and Henry P. Van Dusen, president of the Union Theological Seminary.

In their postwar efforts to continue aiding the Chinese, UCR's officers debated whether to keep the old name or change it to something that was less closely associated with the war; members discussed how the American public now reacted unfavorably to the word "relief" because of the number of organizations that had sprouted up with it in their name. In the summer of 1946, after much deliberation, the board of directors voted to change United China Relief to United Service to China.[45] In considering various alternatives, President McConaughy noted at one point that the phrase "United China" was no longer used so as to avoid any implication that the organization concerned itself with the civil war.[46]

Talk about the name change also included serious discussion of postwar policy. At one meeting in June 1946, the acting field director in China, Lennig Sweet, said, "China has a more moral, Christian civilization than any of the other nations." Not only had China never attacked another nation, but also the nation "allowed freedom of religion." Both statements were unmistakable distortions. China did indeed have a long history of trying to dominate Southeast Asia, the most recent incident having occurred when roughly 150,000 Chinese Nationalist troops entered the northern half of Vietnam at the end of 1945 ostensibly to accept the surrender of Japanese units. Chiang used the opportunity to install Vietnamese favorably inclined toward him wherever possible, and, in an ironic repetition of Soviet actions in Manchuria, his troops looted much of the area north of the sixteenth parallel.[47] It was the fear of another Chinese invasion, in fact, that led Ho Chi Minh to reach an accord with the French that allowed them back into their former colony. Ho's frequently cited line to his colleagues underscored the reverberations past Chinese interventions had upon Vietnamese thinking immediately after World War II: "Don't you remember your history! The last time the Chinese came they stayed a thousand years. . . . If the Chinese stay now, they will never go. As for me, I prefer to sniff French shit for five years than eat Chinese shit for the rest of my life."[48] Sweet also seemed to forget Chinese hostility toward foreign missionaries in the nineteenth century—hardly a painstaking observation of freedom of religion. The animosity increased over time and included the beheading of one of Henry W. Luce's contemporaries during the Boxer Uprising.[49]

President McConaughy's prediction for the future was equally blind. He saw "no indication that China wants to adopt Communism as it exists in Russia." And if he was more accurate in predicting that Asia would be the next economic boom area, his thinking conformed to UCR-USC logic: "It is to America's advantage," he noted, "for the sake of peace to see China rise to her own feet."[50] A moral nation with freedom of religion and the next boom area—what more could Americans want?

Part of United Service to China's new program looked very similar to its former one. The renamed agency created a speaker's kit containing statistical information on China, anecdotes, tips on how to present a concise and informative speech, and ways to answer questions from the audience; it explained that USC had been reorganized "under a mandate from the American people" to continue the work it had started. One section quoted former Secretary of State Edward R. Stettinius, Jr., to the effect that the Chinese were very much like Americans: "Their desires for education for their children, peace, health and freedom from want are as deep rooted as our own." A statement by former president McConaughy—now governor of Connecticut—sustained the paternalistic attitude that pervaded much of the American thinking: Americans "must help China to grow strong and healthy," and they must "nurture [China's] democratic growth."[51]

As it turned out, Garside's worries about the political conditions in China proved to be warranted. The civil war seriously eroded popular support in America for philanthropic efforts designated for China, and though USC tried to portray its activities in a favorable light and pushed ahead with various educational and fund-raising programs, it continued to stretch the point that the two nations were essentially alike. Part of the postwar effort included the production of new films. The film created for the 1946–47 campaign depicted two typical towns, one American and one Chinese. According to a UCR memorandum, *Bridge to Yinhsi*, as it was titled, needed to "have a good sales arguement [sic]. We must sell China first, then UCR. The movie should be lengthened so that it will bring across the salesmanship."[52] After some changes, the final version, some twenty to twenty-five minutes long, compared living conditions in Junction City, Kansas, with those in the Chinese village of Yinhsi, the point being to show how much the two places had in common in spite of their obvious differences. The directors chose Junction City because, as a set of pre-showing remarks observed, it was "located close to the geographical center of the United States," and it was "as representative of the U.S. as a 'home run.'"[53] The postshowing remarks repeated the central theme of the film: as a "strong, productive, friendly" nation, China was prepared to "stand beside the United States . . . joining . . . in one world of peace and friendship."[54]

United Service to China also launched an educational and publicity campaign designed to demonstrate how the organization could affect public thinking about China. This campaign, called the Pottstown Project, revolved around a sample publicity operation conducted in Pottstown, Pennsylvania. The idea was that by showing how effective it was in educating the citizens in one "representative American town," changing attitudes about aiding China in a microcosm as it were, the success could spur larger successes in a national campaign: "Pottstown, Pennsylvania was selected . . . because it is a representative American community whose citizens' views could be deemed typical of those of their fellow Americans throughout the country."[55] The people of Pottstown belonged to organizations like Kiwanis, Rotary, and Elks, thus solidifying their status as solidly middle American.

The plan was that USC would first poll a representative sample of Pottstown's 20,000 residents (with another 25,000 in surrounding communities) in order to gauge the general public's attitude toward China. That was set up for November 1946. Then USC would carry on a month-long educational saturation, including the new film and other publicity and promotional programs. A second poll would test the results, and would also compare them with polls taken simultaneously nationwide.

The program continued through November 1946. The results were not as dramatic as some had hoped, but they were encouraging. United Service to China found that while the percentage of Americans nationwide who thought contributions to China were very important dropped 3 percent from the time of the first poll in early November to the second poll at the beginning of December, the percentage of Pottstonians who felt contributions were very important actually rose nearly 3.5 percent. Moreover, the response to the film was overwhelmingly positive: 91.2 percent at one location expressed favorable sentiments, rating *A Bridge to Yinhsi* good, very good, or excellent.[56] The agency concluded: "It proves that the American people are deeply interested in helping China and that, regardless of the kind of news coming out of China, that interest can be increased by an effective campaign of education and publicity."[57]

The organization also discovered that of all the countries of the world, Americans were most interested in aiding China. Initial surveys ranked China first, ahead of Great Britain, Germany, the Soviet Union, and France in this category.[58] A USC summary noted afterward, "China is at the top of the list of countries in which [Americans] believe we should be interested."[59] After studying the results of the experiment, USC concluded that Americans were indeed interested in China, and educational programs such as the Pottstown Project had made a difference: "That both the movie 'The Bridge to Yinhsi' and newspaper publicity [were] *necessary to sell the people*"; and the work just completed could serve as a starting point for any future campaign.[60] The success of the film in Pottstown was judged to be so persuasive that during the week of February 21–27, 1947, it was run over and over again in a show window at R. H. Macy's in New York City, where it was seen in whole or in part by an estimated 150,000 people.[61]

Finally, and perhaps most importantly, USC ascertained that the majority of the people who expressed opinions about China received their information and impressions primarily "from pictures in [the] media" and not as much from "news or educational articles."[62] Such a finding tended to sustain the importance of *Life* magazine in influencing attitudes; in fact, when different media were mentioned by name, more people listed *Life* as their source than any other periodical or newspaper.[63] The results of the Pottstown Project suggested that USC could have a limited impact. Ultimately, of course, that impact depended upon the outcome of events in China, so even if United Service to China and Time Inc. worked together to sustain the wartime popular interest in China, their vigorous efforts faced the mounting difficulties created by China's civil war.

On the surface at least, the Guomindang had come through the year 1946 as victorious over their rivals for power. Although George Marshall could not in the end bring about a permanent peace settlement for China, he did manage to construct a temporary cease-fire between Nationalist and Chinese Communist forces, announced on January 10, 1946. Both sides continued to struggle for position, despite the cessation of hostilities, and Nationalist forces made gains in North China and Manchuria over the course of the year. On account of his efforts, Marshall outshone even the Chiangs in the Luce press for much of the year. In a March 1946 cover story, for example, *Time* described him as tall and having a face "in which there was the visible touch of greatness." He had accomplished "the most significant mission undertaken by a U.S. citizen since the end of WWII." *Time*'s hagiography went to great lengths: Marshall walked alone around the streets and hills of Chongqing in rapt contemplation, or he would drive out to the surrounding countryside, where, "far from his own acres [he] could sample another good earth." And in the evenings,

Marshall, "over a cup of jasmine tea or a Bourbon old-fashioned, would mull over the day's progress." Marshall was thus shown to transcend cultural differences, which in some kind of bizarre cosmological sense seemed to *Time* to suggest that he could bring about a permanent settlement between the Communists and Nationalists. The homey portrait, after the manner of Norman Rockwell, also took note of the two pictures of his wife on his desk that "looked at him reassuringly."[64]

With Marshall's celebrated efforts, the Truman administration had apparently embarked upon one of the primary recommendations set forth by Luce in his "American Century" essay. But the tenuous cease-fire that was managed in early January had not really solved the problem: the situation was still so complex, so fraught with friction, mutual distrust, and animosity, that neither the Nationalists nor the Communists accepted these efforts in good faith. Both sides continued their aggressive actions especially when Soviet forces withdrew from Manchuria in April. They had planned to leave the previous December, and then again in February, but both times the Nationalist government requested that they stay. Chiang's forces were not yet prepared to move into the area, and a Soviet withdrawal would have left it open to occupation by the Chinese Communists. When Stalin's army finally began its pullout, Nationalist and Communist forces rushed to fill the void. Chiang's army secured most of the major cities, except Changchun, where, in violation of the cease-fire, the Communists established control. Incensed over this, Chiang ordered his troops to continue their movement north in spite of the military inadvisability of such action. Nationalist troops captured Changchun on May 23, but in so doing Chiang seriously overextended his forces, leaving Nationalist supply lines vulnerable to harassment and interdiction.[65]

Marshall had returned to the United States in March to discuss the situation with President Truman; by April, when he arrived back in China, the situation had deteriorated dramatically. He negotiated another cease-fire, this one signed in June, but like the earlier truce, it did not last. Maneuvering from an apparent position of military strength, Nationalist forces extended their tenuous control over Manchuria and North China during the remainder of the year. Upset at what he saw as the deliberate scuttling of peace, Marshall responded by prohibiting further military shipments from the United States in an attempt to use the only leverage he had. It produced little change, since the United States had already supplied Chiang's forces with enough arms and ammunition to render the cutoff ineffectual.

146   *The Dawning of the American Century*

During the period of the embargo (August 1946–May 1947), the
Chinese Ministry of Defense continued its rearming of second-line
troops, something that it presumably could not have done had it not
had adequate equipment for its front-line troops.[66] Chiang was so confident of final victory that he later insisted that the Nationalist government would not need any foreign assistance for at least two years.[67]

Although Marshall was disgusted with the refusal of both sides to
negotiate in good faith, especially the Nationalists after June, he persisted throughout the remainder of the year in an attempt to reach
some kind of accord. He believed, correctly as it turned out, that a
military solution favored the Communists, and he expressed as much
to the generalissimo in July.[68] Nevertheless, Chiang pushed his military plans forward, assuring himself all the while that his forces could
achieve that which they had been striving for since 1927: the elimi-
nation of the Communists.

Luce's empire echoed this optimistic perspective: Chiang's "big-
ger, better-equipped armies might score quick victories if they were
unleashed," *Time* commented in July 1946. Its assessment also included boasts by conservative members of the Guomindang that Nationalist forces would soon eliminate the Communists.[69] *Time* noted
that American observers thought this judgment overoptimistic, but
by early fall the Nationalists did seem to be sealing the victory:
"Everywhere the Nationalist armies smashed ahead," *Time* reported
in September.[70] The victories continued to mount with deceptive ease
as Nationalist armies rushed to occupy the large cities of North
China and Manchuria. Although the movement lengthened Guomindang lines of supply and communication beyond what was considered prudent, Chiang pressed forward with greater zeal in a grand
dash to try and quash the Communists once and for all. "Chiang Kai-
shek won his greatest victories in years over the Communists last
week," *Time* proclaimed in its issue of October 21.[71] The military success convinced many Chinese that Chiang could now achieve a settlement with the Communists through force if necessary, and in its
next issue *Time* elaborated upon this thesis, comparing the generalissimo's recent offensive with a boxer's punching combination and
arguing that his proposals for negotiations were genuine offers made
from a position of strength.[72]

There seemed no stopping Chiang now. "With surprising but by
now familiar ease," *Time* confidently declared, Nationalist forces in
"well coordinated offensive[s]" captured more cities. Each new conquest represented a greater victory than the last. Flushed with the gid-
diness of victory after victory, Chiang confidently declared that he

could "defeat the Communists in the field."[73] The generalissimo seemed to hold a decisive military advantage, which would, given time, make it possible for him to unite the country despite the best efforts of the Communists to the contrary. To have peace, *Time* concluded, the civil war needed to be "fought to some kind of a decision."[74]

The piling up of these victories seemed to indicate that the Chinese Communists were no longer a real threat. Yet Time Inc. remained unconvinced that it should alter its recommendations for American policy toward the Guomindang. Several articles acknowledged the lack of direct Soviet support for the Chinese Communists, but there was a strong note of skepticism. For example, Henry P. Van Dusen, president of the Union Theological Seminary and speaker at various UCR-USC functions, argued in a *Life* editorial that despite this lack of present support, the Soviets had already strengthened the Communists tremendously by handing over captured Japanese equipment.[75] Moreover, the potential for Soviet assistance remained a distinct possibility, and any determined Soviet entry into the situation would have global ramifications. Soviet intervention remained such a distinct possibility because the United States had been stingy in assisting the Nationalist government. *Time* added to the alarm, warning of a Soviet-controlled China that would result in "a U.S. strategic retreat to the Mariana Islands."[76] In Van Dusen's view, the American public's ignorance of the connection between the Soviet Union's global expansion and events in China had to be brought up short: "China in Communist hands would be the most probable, one may say certain, prelude to World War III."[77] Coupled with that idea was, as *Time* pointed out, the crucial question about the future of American security and stability in connection with China: "Should the U.S. throw its full support behind Generalissimo Chiang Kai-shek's Government or permit China (with its nearly 500 million people and vast resources) to become directly or indirectly a Soviet satellite?"[78]

But these were cries of alarm. The fact remained that the Soviets were not giving significant help to the Chinese Communists, and the situation appeared to favor the Nationalist government. Their defeats had evidently made the Communists far more "willing to submit to Chiang Kai-shek on considerably less than the blackmailing terms by which they had hamstrung" Marshall's earlier attempts at peace.[79] Thus as 1946 ended, *Time* continued to report confidently on China's rapid progress toward democracy. Marshall returned to the United States in January 1947 to become secretary of state. His mission had turned out to be an exercise in futility. As he left, he blamed intransigent elements in both camps for spoiling the chances for peace, but *Time* reported only on Chiang's urgent pledge as to his government's "democratic intentions."[80]

Marshall's mission may have failed, but his reputation had soared to such heights during the year that even the dissolution of the truce could not lower his stature. Time Inc. had anticipated that a political agreement at one level did not necessarily translate into peace, and Luce's publications did not exhibit any surprise over the breakdown of the settlement. Chiang's victories on the battlefield obviated the need for a negotiated agreement. The generalissimo's "brilliant military victories" received full coverage, and the Communists' rapid and unexpected demise was blamed partly on the failure of their revolution to live up to its claims. The Chinese Communists had, so it seemed, undermined their own position among the peasants by pursuing a guerrilla strategy that alienated the population. In late 1946, Time Inc. could even indulge in the luxury of letting Marshall off the hook. "No blame could be cast on George Marshall" for the failure to secure peace, *Time* insisted. Although dissatisfied with the Truman administration's tepid show of support for the Nationalist government, Time Inc. did not assign specific blame because Chiang appeared to be on the verge of consolidating his hold over all of China. As long as he kept the strategic advantage, Luce's publications continued their praise of Marshall and his efforts.

The immediate postwar period saw an attempt by Time Inc. and UCR-USC to extend the wartime façade of Sino-American harmony to suit postwar circumstances. Much of that effort, of course, focused on Chiang Kai-shek: as a military genius, he smartly outmaneuvered the Communists and appeared on the brink of uniting China; as consummate political operator, he guided his nation carefully down the path toward constitutional democracy; and as an enlightened religious leader, he laid the foundation for the continued spread of Christianity. The picture could hardly have been more auspicious, except perhaps for a more coherent foreign policy for the region on the part of the Truman administration.

Despite a new name, United Service to China followed established policies. It kept its overall focus on providing humanitarian relief by selling China to the American people. Unfortunately, it found itself competing against the very force that it sought to distance its efforts from: the Chinese civil war. Unlike World War II, which had benefited UCR's money-raising endeavors, this conflict had the opposite effect.

George Marshall had failed to secure a lasting peace for China; nevertheless, the situation appeared to bode well for the realization of Luce's dream. Chiang's military gains gave all appearances of signaling the collapse of the Communists' resistance. The sudden reversal of fortune was still around the corner, and along with it, the highly emotional repercussions. At least for a short time, an American Century for China appeared within reach.

CHAPTER EIGHT

The Collapse of the American Century

Whether we like it or not—and I like it—[Americans] are
predominately a moral people, who believe that our nation
has a great spiritual heritage to be preserved.
—John Foster Dulles, September 1952

Our moral obligation to China is clear.
—Charles Edison (late 1947?)

I think it not at all unlikely that historians a hundred years hence
will agree that the death knell of Western democratic civilization
was sounded in China in the autumn of 1948.
—Henry P. Van Dusen, December 1948

In 1947 the two forces grappling for control of China collided
in a way that served as a prelude to the final outcome of the conflict.
Chiang's earlier victories were quickly proved to be the serious strategic mistakes certain American advisers had predicted. In his rush
to reoccupy North China and Manchuria, Chiang had placed his
forces in highly exposed positions. Supplies had to come over miles
of rail lines or else be flown in by plane. The first was vulnerable to
guerrilla attacks, and the second was not only expensive but logisti-
cally defeating in that it taxed the Nationalist air force beyond its capabilities.

By the summer of 1947, Chinese Communist forces, under the
leadership of Zhu De and Lin Biao, switched from the guerrilla tactics
they had employed for so long to conventional warfare. Despite stiff
resistance from some Guomindang divisions, Communist victories
began to mount as Chiang's troops were isolated and cut off from
further supply. With the Communists in command of the countryside, many Nationalist units, including the American-trained and
-equipped ones, became demoralized by the pillbox strategy and were
defeated, or surrendered. Either way, the Communists began to amass
a substantial amount of American military equipment. By the end of

the year, the military and political situations in China had a completely different look.[1]

The Central government's rapid deterioration continued in 1948. Incompetent military and political leadership at almost every level, including the very top, worsened an already bad situation. Then, in the fall, two important battles took place. The first engagement resulted in the Communists' capturing the cities of Changchun and Mukden, thus securing their control over Manchuria. The second, an even greater disaster for the Nationalists than the first, took place in the waning months of the year. Having been relieved of the "formidable burden," as he put it, of maintaining troops in Manchuria, Chiang decided to make his stand at Huai-hai, the barren plain outside the city of Xuzhou, about a hundred miles northwest of Nanjing.[2] There, from November 1948 until January 1949, Communist and Guomindang troops engaged in an enormous battle. Chiang personally overruled his officers in selecting what one historian has called the site of his very own Waterloo.[3] Further complicating the tactical situation were the contradictory orders given by the generalissimo.[4] The final ignominy came when a relief column of Nationalist troops became surrounded by Communist forces. The Central government decided to bomb part of its own army rather than allow the troops and their equipment to fall into enemy hands. Upon learning of this decision, the commander of the column surrendered, thus ending the battle for North China on January 10, 1949. It was a black defeat: during the last four months of 1948, the Nationalist government lost nearly one million men through death, desertion, or capture, along with a huge quantity of military equipment.[5]

By 1949 the promise of Luce's postwar world showed ominous signs of collapse. In his beloved China, Chiang Kai-shek's triumphant position as one of the victorious allies no longer seemed relevant to the nation's rapidly changing circumstances. Although his wartime reputation as one of the Big Four—and the accompanying illusions about his political abilities—continued to influence some Americans, the situation in China unfolded in a manner markedly different from the earlier predictions offered in the pages of *Time*, *Life*, and *Fortune*.

Chiang had avoided implementing any social, political, or economic changes to alleviate the deplorable conditions facing the peasants. Instead, he contented himself with continuing the same unresponsive policies that had characterized his government since its beginning, all the while paying only lip service to democratic reforms. He had confused his early military victories in the immediate postwar period with popular success and was disinclined to make revi-

sions in the party's rule. In the end, poor military leadership combined with unenlightened political and economic policies, and it all
manifested itself in the low morale within Nationalist army units and
the general population alike.

Further undermining the Central government's position was the
devastating inflation that the Guomindang proved unable and unwilling to check. Although the government made a much-heralded
attempt to combat rising prices in the fall of 1948, its refusal to bring
expenditures in line with revenues made the effort futile. The mostly
middle-class Chinese who obeyed the provisions of the new program
by turning in their hard currency and precious metals suddenly found
themselves bankrupt. Entire savings were wiped out in a matter of a
few months.[6] Overall, the unpopularity of the Nationalist government contrasted sharply with the growing acceptance of the Chinese
Communist Party. Apparently, Chiang's mandate had been revoked.
The speed with which the Guomindang collapsed during 1948 and
1949 reflected its tenuous relationship with the people. Unresponsive, corrupt, and inefficient, Chiang's party had based its support for
too long in the landlords, the bankers, and the industrialists. With no
real vision other than self-preservation and no adequate program to
extend its influence to the overwhelmingly peasant sector of the population, the National government collapsed as a result of its own de-
crepitude.

The Chinese Communist Party, meanwhile, spread its influence
throughout the countryside. From its virtual extinction at the beginning of the Long March in late 1934 to its phoenix-like rejuvenation
during the war against Japan, the CCP showed a remarkable ability to
regroup and continue its organizational activities. By the end of 1948,
the contrast between the two forces contending for control of China
could hardly have been more pronounced.

Despite this dramatic change in the relative strengths of the two
sides, Luce refused to give in to critics of the Guomindang and Chiang
Kai-shek. The situation in China may have been dire, but he argued
that a collapse was not inevitable. A quick, bold stroke of economic
and military assistance to the Central government would shore up its
deficiencies and demonstrate a much-needed resolve to thwart the
spread of communism in Asia. America had an obligation, Luce
maintained, to assist a longtime ally in its desperate fight against
communism. He tried to modify his paternalistic thinking to fit
within the new circumstances of the Cold War. To accomplish that,
he immediately set about excoriating the Truman administration for

its failure to do more in assisting Chiang's government; at the same time, he implored his readers to keep up the fight.

United Service to China faced a much more serious problem than did Time Inc. Unlike Luce's media corporation, which went about its business in a highly partisan manner, USC simply wanted to carry on with its philanthropic activities and provide humanitarian assistance to China's destitute, keeping in mind, of course, its efforts to portray a China thoroughly American in its aspirations. Yet however much it tried to distance itself and its activities from developments in China, USC could not escape the truth of the civil war.

At the end of World War II, B. A. Garside had estimated USC's fund-raising potential for 1946–47 at nearly $14 million.[7] Initially, his projection appeared to be on target with $7 million raised in 1946.[8] Another comparable year and the goal would have been reached, but events in China undermined his projections, and USC suddenly found its ability to raise money severely circumscribed. It managed only $1.5 million in receipts for 1947. The next year saw a further decline, so that for the first time since its creation in 1941, United China Relief–United Service to China raised less than one million dollars. In 1949, USC raised less than $600,000, and the next year saw income drop again by more than half. In the three years from 1946 to 1949, USC's ability to raise funds deteriorated exactly on account of the forces Garside had hoped could be kept at bay.[9]

Fund-raising weaknesses became evident in the specific reports coming in to the national headquarters as early as 1947. For example, William P. Spear, the state director for Connecticut, ran into a wall of reluctance on the part of individuals and corporations to give money. In his final report for the year, he assessed the state on a town-by-town basis. Typical of his remarks was the conclusion he reached for the towns of Waterbury and Watertown: "Another glaring example of the utter apathy shown everywhere toward China this year." For Hartford, a city where he assumed that the local organization was solid enough to surpass its quota, he found instead that nothing got off the ground on account of a general indifference among the population. Despite extensive efforts by USC people there, they encountered "the same feeling against China" that prevailed throughout the state. To underscore the travails endured by all, he recounted the experience of one fund-raiser, Judge Leo Hamlin, from Berlin, Connecticut, a respected member of the community and a successful campaigner for other causes in the past. Judge Hamlin finally gave up on trying to raise money for USC, because in his words, " 'Why should I get myself

disliked by my friends and the rest of the folks in town just because
I can't make them see the light on China?'"[10]

It was clear that the changed situation in China had everything to
do with USC's fund-raising problems. In March 1947, the same
month that President Truman went before Congress and asked for
$400 million in aid for Greece and Turkey to protect those nations
from communist aggression, a USC internal evaluation listed six factors as impeding any new agency efforts to raise money. The two most
important were a general feeling of apathy about foreign relief and the
confusion generated by the civil war in China. The memorandum
listed the proliferation of campaigns, causes, and other types of public
requests for money as an additional complication and suggested that
USC's recent campaigns had lacked proper focus, having been targeted too broadly. The organization needed to concentrate on those
people already known to be interested in China. A new emphasis on
previous contributors might allow it to salvage something, however
small, from present circumstances. Along with other special measures, like reindoctrinating the top personnel at USC, such a reori-
entation might preserve something for later. But the situation did not
seem promising. Regardless of the changes instituted, the future appeared so dismal that the memo ended with the dreary admonition,
"Prepare your friends in China . . . that all is not well."[11]

The gloomy forecast did not stop USC from trying to put the best
possible light on the situation, though it no longer displayed the same
vigor. One appeal letter argued that the world balance of power rested
in China. Resolving the situation there to America's benefit would
be determined, in part, by how much humanitarian assistance Americans provided. To simplify matters, the letter explained that Americans were fortunate because the Chinese people liked them and even
preferred their way of life.[12] Another solicitation discussed the long-
term financial investment the United States had made over the years.
Was this simply going to be forsaken, it asked, or were Americans
going to help the "450,000,000 Chinese—⅕ of the world . . . live in
fruitful democracy?"[13]

Walter Judd, ever loyal to the cause, equated the defense of China
to the defense of the United States, and with his customary skill
turned the criticisms of inefficiency and corruption in the Nationalist government into a positive argument: "Yes, there *is* waste, inefficiency, corruption," but such conditions only made financial assistance that much more imperative, or as he phrased it, "All the more
reason to help." The problems of Chiang's government were more the
"results than causes of the chaos in China," he added.[14]

Other supporters of the Chinese Nationalists made much the same argument. Former ambassador to the Soviet Union William C. Bullitt told a hearing of the House Committee on Foreign Affairs that the corruption in China was the result, not the cause, of the fantastic inflation, and there was still hope: "The remarkable thing is that there are so many honest people, under the circumstances."[15] General Claire Chennault, too, excused the conditions; in his testimony before a congressional committee he invoked the obvious truism that corruption was a worldwide phenomenon, and not one exclusive to China.[16]

Throughout 1948 and 1949, USC continued its effort to solicit money for a rapidly deteriorating cause. Judd urged Americans to concentrate on what could be done now, not on what should have been done earlier. To say that it was too late to help China was to whisper the sweetest words the Kremlin could hear. He insisted that, despite the difficulties facing organizations like USC, Americans should continue "to help those who are trying to preserve in China the things we believe in."[17] But these persistent efforts to maintain some semblance of hope were losing propositions. The declining financial returns after 1946 bore that out. A USC survey of mail appeals for the period May 1948–April 1949 showed that in spite of sending more than 145,000 letters to former contributors, USC managed to raise only a little over $150,000.[18]

Its efforts having clearly been undermined by Chiang's crumbling government, USC was faced with the disintegration of its conception of a Christian, democratic, and friendly China. In a letter to Luce early in the summer of 1948, Garside evaluated the immediate future for the organization, for China, and for the dreams of people like himself who had sought to raise a malleable, almost childlike, nation from its subordinate status up to the level of the mature and successful parent. He lamented that the unity of World War II had been only a temporary phenomenon. The recent setbacks in fund-raising indicated a lack of interest in the conditions in Asia, and there seemed little justification in expending the money, labor, and time to mount another campaign when the outcome was certain to be a disappointment. "There is no longer any hope of getting the general American public to support a general philanthropic program in China," Garside concluded.[19] The time when private organizations could lead the task of helping China was gone; the responsibility now lay with the American government.

Toward that end, people long involved in UCR-USC lobbied for greater assistance to Chiang. Former chairman Charles Edison telegraphed Senator H. Alexander Smith (Rep., N.J.), who was a member of the Senate Committee on Foreign Relations, urging him to push for economic assistance to the Nationalists because a massive Communist conspiracy was at work. He implored Smith to recognize that "a smart and subtle game is being played by the communists with the objective of diverting American attention to Europe while 450 million Chinese are being brought under communist domination."[20] The monolith of international communism was spreading in Asia while the United States blindly focused its energies exclusively on Europe. If China fell, it would threaten to destroy the American way of life. With that in mind, USC found itself struck between two equally unattractive positions. On the one hand, the agency faced the inexorable advance of the Chinese revolution and the resulting reluctance of Americans to contribute money toward China's social and spiritual salvation. On the other hand, the organization wanted to maintain its distance from the increasingly acrimonious and politically partisan debate over what to do about the situation.

Luce faced no such quandary. His magazines had never hesitated from politicizing events, and he firmly believed that as a journalist and publisher, he should educate Americans as to their domestic and international responsibilities. With the realization of the American Century in doubt, there was no reason to think *Time, Life,* and *Fortune* would change their approach now.

Luce's publications immediately set about to convince their readers that the situation in China was of enormous importance to the United States. The seriousness of Chiang's military reversals could not be exaggerated. In a January 1949 issue, *Time* dragged out William C. Bullitt's remarks of eight years earlier on the magnitude of the stakes in China. The former ambassador's interest in bolstering the reputation of the Nationalist government had been established years ago when he had recorded a message for one of UCR's participating agencies. In it he spoke of how China and the United States coexisted as sister republics and mentioned that their two peoples believed in "the same moral code" and spoke "the same moral language." At the head of the Chinese people, most notable for their remarkable similarity to Americans, was none other than Chiang Kai-shek: "A great leader of a great people." His role in forging a new patriotism along with a new national fighting spirit made him a great man. Playing upon a favorite theme of Time Inc. and UCR, Bullitt compared Chiang's military plight with the one faced by George Washington in the winter of 1777–78: from the Chinese wartime capital of Chongqing, "he stands at China's Valley Forge."[21] That was the same year

UCR was created—1941. *Time*'s point was that, eight years later, Chiang faced a situation even more serious than Washington's. Bullitt, said *Time*, argued that the world was at "one of the turning points in human history" and that America could "not afford to be wrong in [its] decisions, since the stake may be not only the independence of China but also the independence of the United States."[22]

Communism's march toward global conquest, especially as its elaborate scheme unfolded in China, appeared as the larger menace threatening the national security of the United States. That external dynamic, moreover, had its domestic counterpart: subversion or infiltration. Truman instituted a loyalty program well before Senator Joseph McCarthy began his search for Communist intruders. This fear of being undermined from within played itself out in politics and popular culture in a curious manner for women, especially in terms of how it reinforced traditional ideas about gender roles. Madame Chiang had been celebrated during the war in part because of the socially constructed function she had displayed as wife to her husband and symbolic mother to China's war orphans. She had fitted into Americans' preconceptions about appropriate obligations for women, notions that coincided with the "home and hearth" ideology of the war. A new set of exigencies was operating now, however. The onset of the Cold War and the American response in the form of the Truman Doctrine stipulated that the containment of the Soviet Union abroad was necessary for the nation's safety. To some, such an approach seemed to reinforce traditionally rigid assumptions about gender. Promiscuous, or sexually independent, women imperiled the very social fabric of the nation. Popular fiction and movies reflected and fortified this supposed danger. Mickey Spillane's detective hero, Mike Hammer, ably resisted the temptations offered by Communist vixens in order to protect the nation's secrets from espionage attempts. As the historian Elaine Tyler May suggested of him, Hammer "had to save the nation from its own moral failings because other men were unable to contain their sexual passions. If they had been able to resist temptation and if the women had behaved themselves, there would have been no need for the hero's bloody deeds."[23]

To explore this evidently very real, and perverse, threat offered by Communist seduction, Time Inc. in 1946 had recruited Arthur Schlesinger, Jr., to write an article on the American Communist Party. The Harvard historian got to the point immediately: communism promoted sexually abnormal behavior, though he did not mention specifically what these aberrations were. Just the same, he delved into how the party furnished its members with an outlet for their unusual physical and psychological needs. It filled "the lives of lonely and frustrated people, providing them with social, intellectual, even sexual fulfillment they [could] not obtain in existing society."[24] He compared the American Communist Party and the dedication of its members to certain religious groups, including the "Jesuits, the Mormons [and] Jehovah's Witnesses."[25] Although not as fantastic and melodramatic as later Time Inc. articles on communism, his account nevertheless distinctly averred that communism posed a moral threat to American society; as such, it could not be viewed as simply another political organization like the Republicans or Democrats.

Schlesinger's approach in 1946 had been relatively mild. Two years later, the situation was far more threatening. Picking up on these earlier threads, John McPartland wove together an exposé for *Life* titled, "Portrait of an American Communist," in which he delved into communism's socially aberrant nature and the racy, lusty, associations with free love. Beginning with the innocuous manner in which the party enlisted new members, McPartland told the story of one impressionable youngster, later given the name "Kelly." "Kelly" attended a few simple high school social gatherings that led to additional picnics and beach suppers at which the older boys engaged in political discussions while the girls admired them for their "intentness and their verbal brilliancies." Insidious developments were at work, however: "A magic seemed to be operating. Each time ['Kelly'] was welcomed as a fine fellow by these suave intellectuals, pretty girls appeared and responded generously to his clumsy lovemaking. What more could a boy want than this?" Intrigued by the intellectual challenge and then literally seduced by "pretty party girls," "Kelly" found himself unable to resist the temptations placed before him. In emphasizing the moral depravity of this scenario, McPartland stressed a peculiar collection of talents and interests these girls evidently possessed. Though they were intellectually sharp and politically active, more importantly, "they danced and went to bed." Unfortunately for "Kelly" and somewhat naïvely on his part, he did not take notice during his seduction that these girls "went to bed in much the same way they carried placards—as a service to the party."[26]

In focusing upon communism's alleged inculcation of sexual promiscuity, *Life* reflected the thinking expounded by certain members of organized religion. In 1938, the Christian author Earl Cressy had discussed Communist attitudes about love, sex, and familial relations in a pamphlet titled, "China Marches Toward the Cross." In directing his comments toward whether or not communism was suitable for China, he concluded that in order to gain greater acceptance, it would have to move in the direction of the Central government. He supported his speculation with the statement, "Communist theories as to free love have made on the whole little inroad on the traditional family morality of China."[27] The alien nature of communism hindered its acceptance by the Chinese people, and to gain wider appeal it must therefore adopt a more acceptable moral code of conduct. A decade later, *Life* reported little change since the time of Cressy's assessment. Communism continued to expand its appeal, not by conforming to Western standards of decency, but through a whole set of deviant sexual practices. Confirming this was an article written for the official publication of Catholic University of Peking in 1948 by Father Raymond de Jaegher. He delved into communism's success by examining its techniques of seduction. In a section devoted to perversion, he described events in North China, where in the past the people had achieved a "moral elevation" matched by few other civilizations. Aggressive "Red" tactics had brought about a rapid decline in the region's morality, leading him to quote one Chinese man as crying, "There's no more virtue! Where is China going?"[28] The real question was where communism might be headed after it completed its moral destruction there. The answer, of course, was right for America. This social threat combined with other dangers—economic, political, and strategic—to create a desperate need for coherent foreign and domestic policies to thwart its spread. The United States had to take note of its allies around the world and coordinate their efforts to create an effective bulwark against the advance of communism.

In Asia, America's ally clearly had to be Chiang Kai-shek. In selecting a person to honor for the year 1947, *Time* chose Secretary of State George C. Marshall for his recent stand against the spread of communism in Europe as evidenced in the Truman Doctrine and the European Recovery Program (Marshall Plan). *Time* argued that Marshall had finally come to fathom the dimensions of the Communist threat. This acknowledgment came none too soon, for the secretary of state had been blind to the impending danger during his involvement in mediating between the Chinese Nationalists and Communists.[29]

The Truman administration also finally received some credit for proposing and then constructing a bulwark against the spread of communism in Europe. Senator H. Alexander Smith joined in, praising the Truman Doctrine for its stance against communism in Europe, but indicating that the barrier needed to be extended to Asia. He suggested that because "history may one day record that . . . Mr. Tru-

man's first Administration saved Europe under Marshall," he hoped
that the president's second administration would "save Asia under
Acheson."[30] He later compared Truman's containment of world communist aggression with the accomplishments of Washington, Lincoln, Wilson, and Roosevelt. The president could complete this picture and secure his place in history by expanding his doctrine to include Asia.[31]

Truman's refusal to underwrite Chiang's government ended all the
praise from Chiang's American supporters, and Truman was soon
caught in the cross-fire of attacks from certain members of Congress
on the one side and those in the press and the business community
on the other. In particular, he and his advisers became the targets of
the informal China lobby—Judd, Smith, Luce, and so on—who complained that the United States must develop a policy for China like
the European Recovery Program. Chiang deserved the assistance because he had long been aware of the danger posed by communism. In
fact, *Time* pointed out, he had known the enemy the United States
now faced for decades. His experience in fighting communism made
him an invaluable ally in Asia.

In a more general critique of American postwar policy toward the
Nationalist government, a *Life* editorial commented that Chiang had
been the victim of a propaganda campaign, in part stimulated by the
Truman administration. The State Department and much of the
American press were responsible for the tide of anti-Chiang propaganda that had permeated the discussion of America's China policy.
The latter, *Fortune* reported, "talked about . . . the venal Chiang government" while the former had refused to address the problems inherent in bringing the American soldiers home so quickly after the
end of World War II.[32] The Chinese Nationalists faced a wall of prej-
udice against them in the United States, but *Fortune* explained that
the Central government's weakness "in public relations" and its
overly polite manner in responding to outside criticism compounded
the problem.[33] The same article, however, acknowledged that during
the war the Guomindang had hired the influential Washington lob-
byist Thomas G. Corcoran, and that Tommy the Cork, as FDR had
nicknamed him, acting as legal counsel for T. V. Soong's company,
China Defense Supplies, had lobbied aggressively for military and
economic aid to the Nationalist government.[34]

It was, of course, apparent that Chiang clearly recognized his American allies and treated them appropriately. Luce was the most important of all. Commenting on how Chiang's government handled Luce,
Theodore White wrote that his boss was a natural resource almost as

valuable to the Chinese Nationalists as "the Yangtze gorges from which the government hoped to draw hydropower once they were dammed after the war." When Luce visited China in 1941, Chiang's government treated him more graciously and granted him more extensive privileges than any other visitor: "No visitor I had seen previously in China," White wrote, "no eminent journalist, no diplomat, no Asian eminence, not even Jawaharlal Nehru, was received with the deference given to Luce and his wife Clare Boothe Luce."[35] Stanley Karnow, another one-time Luce employee, remarked that when he and Luce visited Taiwan years after the Nationalists had fled the mainland, Chiang Kai-shek and Madame Chiang treated his boss as a supremely honored guest: "They flattered him ceaselessly, they told him how important he was to them, how dependent they were on him, how great a man he was."[36] Wesley Bailey quipped about Luce's visit to China in October 1945 that no foreign visitor had been so welcome since Marco Polo.[37] The extraordinary treatment, the compliments, the banquets, the unique privileges, and special transportation arrangements with access anywhere in China—all were at Luce's disposal. If, as *Fortune* declared, Chiang was naïve in the field of propaganda and public relations, he certainly knew which one, of all Americans, he could count on to lobby on his behalf.

Throughout 1948 and 1949, Time Inc. routinely attributed the deteriorating conditions in China, in what became standard company practice, to President Truman and his "half-a-loaf" policy. *Life* made the case more stridently when it characterized American policy as one of "disastrous neglect half-ridden by irrelevant sermonizing."[38] Because of its refusal to give Chiang even more economic and military assistance than it had already done, the United States government supposedly restricted the generalissimo to halfway measures and partial successes. In the pages of *Time*, Judd found a sympathetic venue to blame the United States for developments in Asia, not that the former medical missionary lacked outlets through which to express his opinions. He seemed to seize any opportunity to make his case. As part of a Town Meeting in early 1948, he again compared Chiang with Lincoln in what was becoming a predictable reply to criticisms of the generalissimo's actions. One listener, quite convinced, wrote to congratulate Judd on his "quick-witted responses, the Blue Ribbon going to the allusion to Abraham Lincoln."[39] Later in the year, Judd was at it again, debating Harvard historian John Fairbank on the dilemma China presented to the United States.[40]

Life tried to suggest that a rethinking of the nation's foreign policy toward China was imminent on account of the public's dissatisfaction over the continuing spread of communism in Asia. One particularly scathing editorial, in March 1948, castigated the administration for its refusal to support an important ally in a time of desperate need.[41] Chiang and his government had been "doing more active fighting against Communism than any other government in the world—and with guns." A select group of stalwart Americans had finally begun to break down the wall of anti-Chiang propaganda, but until recently, this distortion, along with the Truman administration's vacillation, had only amounted to "a lesson in blunder and failure." By turning its back on Chiang Kai-shek, a "pro-American statesman who has been fighting Communism for 20 years," the government continued to lead the United States toward its biggest foreign policy disaster ever.

That catastrophe now appeared inevitable. In its issue of March 29, 1948, *Time* published an ominous warning about the international conditions closing in on the United States in an article titled "Struggle for Survival," in which it insisted that the nation faced a graver challenge than at any other period in its history. Recalling Dean Acheson's example of how "apples in a barrel [are] infected by one rotten one," *Time* illustrated the danger communism posed to strategically vital locations by two maps, in color, showing how countries could be affected. One map, of Europe and parts of Africa and the Middle East, dramatized what might happen if the Communists won in the upcoming elections in Italy. The map showed the handle of a Soviet sickle superimposed over Italy with its long curving blade stretching down through the Mediterranean, across parts of eastern Africa, and up into a Saudi Arabia dotted with oil wells. As the map and the accompanying text insisted, a Communist Italy would threaten the entire area south and east of it including the critical region of the Middle East. This dire prediction was hardly more than the one that Undersecretary of State Dean Acheson had made only a year before, when he told congressional leaders that the Communist "corruption of Greece would infect Iran and . . . would also carry [the] infection to Africa through Asia Minor and Egypt." That imagery had been utilized to sell the Truman Doctrine in 1947, effectively so. *Time*'s tone was rather more alarming, however, in that it compared the present situation to the darkest days of World War II: "If the Communists win Italy in a free election, that will have an effect equal to the fall of Singapore and Manila in World War II."[42]

Time's second map showed Asia. Here, the handle of the sickle was superimposed over China with the blade curving down around Southeast Asia through Singapore and northwest over to India. Similar disasters could be expected to befall the region should communism engulf China. But here, the situation held even greater potential for danger: "A Communist China would hold the Indian subcontinent's 385,000,000 in a pincers, overhang the South China Sea, from whose opposite shores come 80% of the U.S. natural rubber."[43] Furthermore, with Japan cut off from its Asian areas of trade, the United States would have to foot the expensive bill of maintaining the island nation.

"Struggle for Survival" also mentioned a possible Soviet airborne occupation of Alaska if China fell to communism. Such an operation, "not regarded as impossible by U.S. military men," would give the Soviets bases from which they could launch an airstrike on Detroit.[44] In fact, *Time* suggested several times in the article that American vulnerability appeared to be growing in the face of communism's global onslaught. Luce's potential nightmare included an anti-American, Communist-dominated world stretching from Italy all the way across to China. The Truman administration had used similar tactics when it "scared the hell" out of the Congress in presenting the need for the aid to Greece and Turkey the year before, but Luce was now making the same argument with regard to China.

The text accompanying the maps did more than analyze the immediate peril. The article went on to speculate on the situation the United States might find itself in ten years later, using the traditional Goldilocks options to suggest the proper response. Option one was too cold: "a divided, stunned and defeated U.S. . . . trying to adjust itself to a Communist-ruled world." The second was obviously too hot: "a weary, mangled and victorious U.S. . . . trying to salvage what it can from the radioactive wreckage of the world." The third, and the one that would follow Time Inc.'s recommendations, was just right: "a busy, peaceful U.S. . . . helping to push forward the frontiers of freedom everywhere in the world."[45]

In a sense, Luce was using his magazines like a theater to direct the public's attention toward communism's purported encroachment: the audience could watch the unfolding drama much the same way as the Truman administration had informed a reluctant Congress of the enormous Soviet threat facing Europe in 1947. In describing his meeting with congressional leaders to convince them of the seriousness of the situation in Greece and Turkey, Acheson later wrote, "I knew we were at Armageddon. . . . The Soviet Union was playing one of the greatest gambles in history at minimal cost."[46] Luce switched the focus to China, and after setting the stage, he introduced the central characters, Chiang Kai-shek and Mao Zedong. In reporting on these two, however, Time Inc. created caricatures, symbols representing the forces of good and evil in the titanic battle for global supremacy.

Time's cover story on Chiang Kai-shek, the savior, the messiah of China, in the issue of December 6, 1948, was its eighth cover story on Chiang in the eighteen-year period 1931–49.[47] Like many of the previous ones, the cover portrait showed a handsome and thoughtful Chiang, gazing off into the distance to his right with the Chinese Nationalist flag in the background. The legend under his picture read, "The howitzers could now be heard in Kansas City." The text underlined the approaching doom: "Asia's howitzers could now be heard in Kansas City, although the U.S. still had only a partial notion of how big its stake was in the China war."[48] The American heartland, as symbolized in Kansas City, was an important theme in *Time, Life,* and even *Fortune* because Luce wanted it that way. Although many of his writers and staff members came from Eastern, especially Ivy League, schools, he insisted on keeping his magazines aimed toward middle America. One employee wrote that Luce did not want *Life* to become "a sophisticated, big-city magazine." To protect against this, it consistently ran stories on items of interest to farmers, including a grasshopper plague and "an Iowa corn-and-pig farm."[49] Directing himself to this point, Luce once said to his staff, "I want more corn in the magazine. Yes, I know you don't like it, you're too Ivy League and sophisticated, but we need more corn in it."[50]

Time placed Kansas City within the context of the Chinese civil war and at the same time underlined Luce's concern with "corn" by making a number of assumptions about the United States, China, and the readership of *Time*. In writing about how the howitzers could be heard in Kansas City, *Time* alluded to the remark made by Nebraska Senator Kenneth Wherry in 1940, when he had said of Americans, "With God's help, we will lift Shanghai up and up, ever up, until it is just like Kansas City."[51] *Time* referred to the worsening military situation by equating the Central government's southward retreat and the Communist advances toward Shanghai with the global movement to envelop the United States, or Kansas City as it were. The spread of communism in Asia, *Time* suggested, if not checked, would pose a serious threat to the United States by striking at the geographical and metaphorical heartland of the nation.

Time's cover story on Mao Zedong two months later, appropriately timed to coincide with the Chinese New Year celebrations, was another example of *Time*'s mixture of exaggeration and innuendo, blending presumed fact with trivial detail to present an unflattering portrait. The previous Chinese year, *Time* noted, had been "the Year of the Rat—and the year of the Communists." Obviously, it implied, Mao was not a fit leader: whereas Chiang always made a neat and crisp impression, Mao "frequently sat with his feet propped on the table and in warm weather he unceremoniously stripped to the waist." He smoked, chewed seeds, and until recent advice from doctors against such consumption, "used to wash down his heavy meals with ka-oliang (grain liquor)." The recent absence of alcohol had apparently turned him into "something of a hypochondriac."[52] Furthermore, he often attended Saturday-night dances, where he could be found danc-ing with his wife, the wives of other Communist leaders, or "pretty Communist office girls." (Undoubtedly, these were the same type of "party girls" who were seducing the likes of "Kelly" in the United States.)

Perceptive readers may have realized that by the end of 1948, the struggle to preserve the American Century in China had degenerated into a feeble and unbelievable last attempt to invoke an emotional and alarmed reaction from Americans. By depicting the success of the Chinese Communists as a gain for Soviet designs on the rest of the world and emphasizing how the outcome in China would affect life in the United States, *Time, Life,* and *Fortune* revived claims to Chiang's leadership as a positive moral figure for the Christian way of life. *Time* mentioned his moral crusade, the New Life Movement, which "symbolized the new China" with its "strictures against every-thing from bribery to wiping the nose on the sleeve."[53] Aside from cleaner shirts, Chiang evidently brought Christianity to the highest level of government. His morning ritual included a cold splash of water on his face, twenty minutes of exercises, followed by morning prayers and reading from the Bible.[54] But he did more than wake up with God every morning; he lived his life in a thoroughly Christian manner. The continual and repeated emphasis upon his Christian faith, despite the rapid deterioration of the Central government's po-sition, began to fall upon the sympathetic ears of some influential people, who in turn took up the case for Chiang Kai-shek and the Chinese Nationalists.

One such person, H. Alexander Smith, who had been the Republi-can senator from New Jersey since 1944, used his position as a mem-ber of the Senate Foreign Relations Committee to bolster the Nation-alist cause. The persistent emphasis upon the strength of Chiang's Christian convictions and his role as the Christian leader of a non-Christian country struck a responsive chord in the senator because of his own deeply held religious beliefs. Smith's pivotal position, and his later proposals to deny Formosa to the Chinese Communists and to provide economic assistance to stop the spread of communism in Asia, placed him in the good graces of Time Inc. but at the same time positioned him squarely in the path of the Chinese civil war.

Like Luce, Smith viewed the situation in China from the perspective that Christianity could play a decisive role in determining the outcome of events there. His perspective was shared by many of his friends and relatives, including John Roots. Roots, born in China, the son of an Episcopalian bishop, kept in close touch with Smith from Europe and frequently passed along his thoughts about Chiang, China, and the need for Christian guidance in trying to devise a positive program to combat the gains made by the Communists. "God knows Chiang and his crowd have been difficult in many ways," he wrote Smith in the summer of 1949, but added, "Chiang is still a Christian—very much so."[55] In a draft of an article for *Reader's Digest*, he explained: "At the head of the most populous nation in the world stands a man of lion-hearted courage—physical and moral— and of serene and unconquerable faith. It means that in Chiang Kai-shek the Far East has a leader who, whatever his faults . . . will in the final count stand like a rock for the traditional values of Christendom and for those moral concepts which are at the heart of Christian democracy."[56]

Another person who shared Smith's belief in the strength and quality of Chiang's Christian commitment was the senator's son-in-law, H. Kenaston Twitchell. Twitchell corresponded regularly with his father-in-law about the situation in China, and his ideas apparently reinforced Smith's thinking. Twitchell worried that faith, and not sight alone, was necessary to see a clear solution to the problem. As late as June 1949, while the Nationalists were in the process of transferring their government to Formosa and the Communists were extending their control over much of the area south of the Chang river, he maintained that there was still a chance to reverse the Communist tide. He proposed a program of "ideological indoctrination."[57] The plan called for "injecting a new spirit into the remainder of the Nationalist group" in the hopes that with its new-found training this group could arrest Guomindang decay, halt the Communist military advances, and completely reverse the situation in China.[58]

The emphasis upon an ideological approach to solving America's dilemma in Asia became Senator Smith's trademark in speaking on the situation. Although generally vague as to what exactly comprised his ideological approach, Smith's son-in-law provided some clues. In one letter, for example, he wrote of it as a "beachhead for democracy in China."[59] Roots described the strategy as encouraging the creation of Christian commandoes, as it were. He thought that by maintaining the Christian institutions in China—the thirteen Christian colleges for example—even after the imminent Communist takeover, the Christians could make it possible for the United States "to infiltrate communist China, provided that teachers, technicians, missionaries, and traders were themselves ideologically equipped."[60] Smith himself wrote that with Shintoism and Buddhism failing to fill the spiritual needs of Asians, a vacuum had developed, which could be filled by an "aggressive, practical and inspiring Christianity."[61] A morally sound, Christian program based on stealth and infiltration would allow the West to regain the initiative. Roots suggested that Dean Acheson should be sympathetic to such a program, for, as he noted, the secretary of state was a Christian and his father had been a bishop just like Roots's father.[62]

The ideological strategy was meant to counter what Smith argued had been Moscow's sustained twenty-five-year effort in China. The Soviets were reaping the rewards of their planting because they had infiltrated China with a solid and consistent program of education and ideological indoctrination. To counter that, he thought the United States should use religious and educational institutions, as well as the Boxer indemnity money, in a similar fashion.[63]

Although Smith did not define his program beyond what he called an ideological approach, he did make it clear that, with respect to mainland China, he was not proposing any more military assistance to the Nationalists. The Guomindang had failed, he said in a statement broadcast over NBC radio, in part because its leaders had not fully understood the precepts of Western democracy; that is, they had not started with the proper Christian framework necessary to make democracy work.[64] Chiang's government deserved American Christian attention, but not its military assistance. In commenting on the inadvisability of sending military supplies, he acknowledged that such assistance would have to be accompanied by a substantial number of troops and officers. And that, in turn, might very well lead the nation down the path toward a third World War.[65]

For those reasons, Smith stayed away from the more extreme calls for an American bailout of Chiang Kai-shek, but he frequently brought out his respect for Chiang's religiosity. In a draft of a memorandum on how to reverse the setbacks in China, he managed to mix in some ideas made popular by Luce's magazines. He noted of the generalissimo, "He is a Christian, whose conversion in 1927 has been compared to the conversion of Constantine." In another section on Chiang, he added: "The Bible is his daily companion. He rises at five in the morning for meditation and prayer. His address on the Person and Sacrifice of Christ are unique in the annals of statecraft since the days of Oliver Cromwell."[66]

Given his more general interest in the Christian leadership of all nations, and not just China, the fact that Smith would take up Chiang's cause reflects the broader attraction the China situation had for other American political leaders as well. John Foster Dulles, for instance, maintained a substantial interest in the success of Christian governments around the world. In commenting on the situation in China, he once remarked: "Sentiment, rather than materialism, is, indeed, the essence of the relationship of the American people with the Chinese people. . . . Always the contacts have been primarily cultural and spiritual, notably through missionaries."[67]

As far as the challenge communism posed to the Christian nations went, even George Kennan provided another example—a somewhat surprising one given his commonly assumed emphasis upon pragmatic political concerns. At the end of a *Foreign Affairs* article describing the motivations behind the Soviet challenge, he wrote that God had presented the United States with a tremendous test in the form of the Soviet Union. This had been done so that Americans would fulfill "the responsibilities of moral and political leadership that history plainly intended them to bear.[68] Kennan thus expressed ideas very similar to the ones that Henry Luce had long since decided should be the foundation for American expansion.

Senator Smith was not the enthusiast that Walter Judd and some other members of Congress were, and though his position on the Senate Foreign Relations Committee placed him in the center of the debate, he did not use it as a propaganda base for Chiang.[69] At the same time, however, his strong convictions about the need for Christian morality made him genuinely concerned about the effect of communism in China and elsewhere. As he noted on one occasion in his diary, the real issue facing the world around 1950 was "God vs. atheism."[70]

The Protestant missionaries had traveled to China in the nineteenth century because of their desire to convert its people to Christianity. That same feeling motivated Smith a half-century later. For him, as for Luce and the members of United China Relief, Chiang was a leader in trouble, and regardless of his faults, he was a Christian. That fact alone drew Americans to his side. In the worldwide struggle between godless communism and the Christian, democratic nations of the West, support could not be apportioned only to those who were absolutely pure and without sin. Chiang had erred, it was true, but in the end, only he could help bring about the realization of an Americanized version of China.

The collapse of the concept of a Christian, democratic China portended a search for culprits. Chiang and the other Guomindang leaders could not be held accountable because, whatever their faults, they were Christians. Misunderstanding and naïveté at best, incompetence and ignorance more likely, and Communist infiltration and betrayal at worst—those were the reasons for the collapse of an American Century for China.

Coming at the time that it did, the Chinese Communist revolution upset the plans laid out by Henry Luce in his vision for the United States and China. Mao's declaration of the creation of the People's Republic of China in October 1949 put an end to the days of celebrating a Chinese people remarkably like Americans and a Chinese nation determined to become more like the United States. The Communists' success, moreover, raised disturbing questions: if China had its George Washington, if Chiang had been through his own Valley Forge, if the Chinese people laughed at Charlie Chaplin and Laurel and Hardy, then what did their inability to resist the global onslaught of Communist aggression mean for the United States? If China, a nation supposedly so much like America, could fall to communism, what were the chances of the United States succumbing to this same evil?

Some commentators, like Henry P. Van Dusen, saw in the Guomindang collapse one consequence of the American refusal to accept the global responsibilities clearly intended for the nation, a failure that had begun with Munich in 1938 and continued down to the Chinese revolution in 1949.[71] What, in turn, did that mean? He answered the question by insisting that this refusal to acknowledge the natural course of history for the United States would eventually lead to the nation's ultimate and premature demise. For Luce, the prospects were equally dispiriting. His grand conception of America included China playing a central role in fulfilling the country's evangelical mission. After all, China provided an unmatched opportunity. In a speech for United China Relief, he had once contended, "You know the remarkable thing about China is that everyone who comes here becomes enchanted with the tremendous possibilities for achieving whatever it is they want to achieve."[72]

Of God and Mammon, J. A. Hobson wrote, "We find from the earliest times in various countries of the ancient world a reciprocity of services between God and Mammon—religion and industry."[73] In its potential for religious conversion or as a market for trade, China symbolized the perfect combination of these forces. Regarding exactly this sentiment, the historian Jonathan Spence has written about certain foreigners, from Jesuit missionaries in the seventeenth century to Soviet advisers in the 1950's, who tried to transform China into what they wanted it to be: "Implicit in most of their actions was a more complex motive, a desire not so much to help China as to help themselves."[74] Although Spence did not include Luce in his survey of Westerners who had traveled to China seeking to change it, his words apply to him with equal validity.

When Chiang proved himself unable to hold China against communism, in the eyes of many Americans he failed as the Christian leader of a nation. John Foster Dulles saw it that way. He possessed a deeply personal conviction about Christianity and its importance in guiding American foreign policy. Van Dusen, summarizing Dulles's feelings on Chiang's collapse, could just as easily have been speaking of Luce.[75] According to Van Dusen, Dulles "could never reconcile himself to the Communist takeover. He said, 'What about the Christian leadership? What's become of this Christian cause that's supposed to be at the heart of the government of China?'" Dulles expressed "bitter disillusionment" when the Nationalist government was justly charged with corruption. A Christian government had failed in the face of a communist, atheistic movement. In Van Dusen's words, it had failed to hold China "within the community of democratic nations." In the same way, the loss of China struck Luce on a personal level. When former Secretary of War Henry L. Stimson made critical remarks about Chiang in an excerpt from his memoirs published in *Ladies' Home Journal*, Luce quickly wrote him, "I cannot think of any utterance which ever hurt me so much as your recent statement about Chiang Kai-shek and China."[76]

In the end, Luce could not separate his personal feelings on China from his views about what the United States ought to do there. He was devastated by the Chinese Communist takeover. It seemed almost a personal betrayal. One longtime editor at Time Inc. commented that Luce "thought there was something dreadfully wrong about China turning on America when he knew he loved China and he thought China ought to love him and America too."[77] The pain he felt over the loss of his China—"the misery of China" as he himself once wrote—led him to react emotionally, and his reaction, reflected in his publishing empire, did a great deal to poison the domestic political climate.[78] The ultimate effect, one commentator has noted, contributed "squarely to the excesses of the McCarthy period."[79] Undoubtedly so, but of equal importance was Luce's insistence on retrieving his lost vision of China, a search many other Americans embarked upon in their desperate attempt to save the American Century for China.

CHAPTER NINE

Coming to Terms with the Emotional Attachment to China

It is a pity that the Chinese crisis has weakened the American sense of invincibility. As a people we are at our best—if not our most ingratiating—when we believe that nothing is impossible for us.
—Anne O'Hare McCormick, January 1950

In a democracy, foreign policy is based on the decisions of the people.
—Harry S. Truman, April 1950

Americans should abandon ill-founded assumptions that they can transform China internally.
—Nancy Tucker, *Foreign Affairs*

The success of the Communist revolution in 1949 disabused most Americans of the notion that China was fast on its way toward becoming an equivalent of their country. The dragon had awakened, and, rather than turning out to be a friendly one predisposed toward the United States, it instead seemed to confirm the anxieties of those who had looked across the Pacific in fear of a hostile entity. The Yellow Peril was now a part of the Red menace.

In discussing the "loss of China," however, the question still remains: what, if anything, was lost? Nothing, according to one knowledgeable academic, since Asia was not America's to have or to lose in the first place. At a round table discussion of the nation's China policy in October 1949, Owen Lattimore asked the question that paternalists took for granted: "Since when and by whom was Asia given to America to solve all its problems?"[1] Perhaps, then, the better question is, what did people like Luce and Judd think was lost? A partial answer can be found in a comment made by Edward Said, who, in his exploration of the relationship between Europe and the Middle East, noted that the latter helped to define the former in important ways. "*Orientalism*," he wrote, was "a way of coming to terms with the Orient that is based on the Orient's special place in European Western experience."[2] If China is substituted for Orient and the United States for

Europe, certainly much the same can be said for the relationship envisioned by an American Century of China.

China helped to define the United States through its opportunity—
a seemingly boundless opportunity given China's huge population
and its purported cultural malleability. Initially attractive to missionaries and business leaders, it later became a potentially important ally and market for American foreign policy makers as they
sought to maintain a regional and global balance of power that suited
their interests. "By denigrating other cultures as . . . malleable," one
historian has observed, Americans acquired "false expectations that
it is an easy enterprise to induce and direct political change and economic development" in order to serve their larger concerns.[3]

Connected with this idea was the notion that China allowed the
United States to act out its pretensions to exceptionalism. By becoming such a powerful magnet for missionary efforts, China appeared
ready to demonstrate the applicability of Christianity as spread by
Americans, many of whom came to assume that in addition to religion, the nation's culture and political ideology were equally trans-
ferrable. Success in transmitting these ideas abroad directly reflected
the country's relative international position vis-à-vis competing
states in the constant struggle for wealth and power. The concepts of
white man's burden, *mission civilisatrice*, and Manifest Destiny all
played important roles in confirming pretensions to international
preeminence for Great Britain, France, and the United States, respectively. Part of rising to and maintaining a global position of power and
prestige meant bringing the nation's ways of doing things to other
peoples.

In this case, culture and diplomatic influences worked together to
foster a sense of control—one of the keys to Sino-American relations.
Luce's prescription for postwar China was easily compatible with
Roosevelt's designs for Asia. The two complemented each other
rather nicely, in fact, since both were clearly paternalistic propositions at heart. The ambition to determine the focus and pace of the
bilateral relations took form in the apparently more benevolent
strands of racial paternalism as cultural, political, and economic aspirations for China were defined and interpreted according to an
American scale. Thus, the American Century rested upon an ability
to control the relationship in an effort to secure a China capable of
serving the interests of the nation's larger dreams and aspirations.

When the last possibility for achieving those expectations vanished
at the end of 1949, one of the principal tenets that had defined America's position in Asia for the previous half-century vanished. The

original site of the Open Door was gone. Diplomatic contingencies
were already in place because Japan had moved to the central position for American plans for Asia by 1947; that was part of a containment framework, however, certainly a more conservative approach to foreign affairs, especially when compared with the liberal-
developmentalism of the Open Door.[4] The ideological and practical
realignment evidenced in this focus upon Japan caused considerable
dislocation and disaffection for people who had developed highly
emotional attachments to China.

The broader domestic ramifications were contradictory, and public
opinion polls—not a precise means of measurement in the first
place—reflected the ambivalence. An April 1948 Gallup poll indicated that 55 percent of those responding favored increased military
assistance to Chiang, but by the end of the year only 32 percent approved of sending him $5 billion in aid, with 34 percent opposed. The
significant drop can be linked, at least in part, to the different wording
used in each question. The first had to do with aid in general, whereas
the second mentioned a specific figure. The polls also indicated that
a growing number of Americans had come to view Chiang unfavorably, even though the plurality of respondents expressed no opinion
on him at all.[5] The public's ambivalent, and highly pliable, feelings
about Chiang immediately raise the question of how efficacious
Luce's propaganda campaign for the preceding two decades had been.
How could Americans so quickly and willingly have abandoned their
symbolic counterpart in Asia without more of a protest, especially if
Luce and company had reflected what the general population wanted
to believe? The answer to this question is complex, but a good start
begins with an examination of the simplistic way Americans have
frequently come to understand other countries and their political
leaders, and also the consistently inferior status they have accorded
Asian nations and their peoples.

The apparent ease with which Americans abandoned long-standing
sentimental notions about the Chinese did not really constitute
much of a change at all, since most of those ideas were quickly transferred to the Japanese. China and Japan simply switched sides on the
paradigmatic coin of Asia. As the journalist Harold Isaacs observed,
"The Chinese heroes of the 1940s became the Chinese monsters of
the 1950s without having to move very far from the one compartment
to the other in anyone's mind."[6] Meanwhile, the Japanese found themselves falling under the paternalistic rubric that remade them into aspiring Americans. According to the historian John Dower, General

Douglas MacArthur's "guiding philosophy" toward the Japanese during the occupation meant treating them like twelve-year-old children. Furthermore, in discussing what he termed "the true resilience
of code words concerning the Other," Dower has traced this pattern
in how it pertained to images of the Japanese both during and after the
war: "Not only are such concepts capable of evoking constructive as
well as destructive responses; they are also free-floating and easily
transferred from one target to another, depending on the exigencies
and apprehensions of the moment."[7] The forces of racism and ethnocentric paternalism directed at the Japanese and Chinese during
World War II suddenly became policy instruments in a Cold War context, as one wartime plasticity was replaced by another.

Luce, whose internationalist, open-door, and paternalistic outlook for China had been appropriate earlier, as part of a liberal-
developmentalist framework, found himself fighting on the wrong
side. Containment was applied to Japan, not to mainland China,
though the Chinese people could, and were, subdivided into Communists and Nationalists. In the end, the United States did not abandon Chiang once he brutally reconstituted his government on Formosa. The Cold War paradigm for Asia necessitated as much, especially after the outbreak of the Korean War.[8] But Luce's ambitions
were more grandiose, and he never could reconcile himself to the fact
of a mainland Communist China.

Another trend became apparent as the Nationalist government's
position deteriorated. When asked in late 1948 whether they believed
that the Chinese Communists took their orders from Moscow, 51
percent of the Americans who had heard of the Chinese civil war responded yes. Two years later, after the Chinese had intervened in Korea, over 80 percent of the population believed that China had done
so under orders from the Soviet Union.[9] This expanding belief in the
monolithic nature of communism, especially as it spread in Asia, coincided with the idea that the primary responsibility for the collapse
of the Nationalist government lay with the Truman administration,
despite its best effort to convince the American people otherwise.
Over half of those who had heard of *The White Paper* put together by
the State Department indicated that the United States had blundered
in its relations with China and should have given more assistance to
Chiang. That opinion was held twice as often as the notion that the
United States had done the best that it could have done under the circumstances. Thus, a reluctance to send material help to China—in
effect to refuse to back Chiang in his attempt to retain his position

on the mainland—did not necessarily translate into an exoneration
of the Truman administration for the demise of the Nationalist government.[10]

The decision to compile and publish *The White Paper* revealed the
administration's desire to counter the powerful image of China that
had been created by Luce and others. As the date of its distribution
neared, Chiang became sufficiently worried to suggest lobbying
the State Department to withhold publication. Walter Judd advised
against making such a request, cabling the generalissimo that such a
petition would have an "unfavorable effect on American public opinion for [the] Chinese government" since it "would be interpreted as a
confession of guilt." Better to have it published so that Chiang's supporters could contend squarely with its charges.[11]

Specifically titled *United States Relations with China, with a Special Reference to the Period 1944–1949* and more commonly referred
to as *The White Paper*, the collection of 1,054 pages of narrative and
documents was released to the public on August 5, 1949, with the intention of demonstrating that the collapse of the Guomindang was
beyond the control of the United States. In authorizing *The White Paper*, Truman hoped to "set the American public straight" on the
events there since the war, and according to one historian both he and
Acheson were "keen to publish."[12] A month before its release, presidential adviser Clark Clifford wrote Truman that he was "sure the
publication of a White Paper on China [would] be helpful to the American people in understanding the difficult and confused situation in
China."[13] Later in July, Secretary of State Acheson recorded that the
president expressed his belief that the publication of *The White Paper*
was not only desirable but necessary.[14] Finally, that the president
would attempt to defend his administration's policies through the
public disclosure of the diplomatic record is not surprising given his
earlier successes in selling such policies as the Truman Doctrine in
1947 and the European Recovery Program in 1947–48. The director of
the State Department's Office of Public Affairs made the remark that
both Truman and Acheson often emphasized the need of keeping the
American people informed on important matters—mostly when it
suited their purposes, of course.[15] And Bruce Russett has noted that
political leaders often "try to expand their freedom of action by persuading much of the public to shift its mixture of acceptable policy in
one direction or the other." "A great leader will actually do that," Russett says; "But the leader's ability to shift opinion is rarely great.
Rather, the maneuvering space is restricted chiefly to the range of actions already deemed acceptable."[16]

Not that the administration lacked entirely for supporters. Charles Collingwood of CBS News assessed *The White Paper* as "an admirable brief for the view that China is past saving, and has been for a long time." Although largely subscribing to the administration's position that events in China were beyond the United States' ability to control, even he lamented: was there "no moment where our influence might not have changed the incident at least, if not the pattern, no point where we could not have acted with decisive effect?"[17]

Overall, however, the Truman administration's attempt to gain some maneuvering room for its China policy by issuing *The White Paper* did not work out as hoped. In placing the blame for events squarely on the shoulders of Chiang Kai-shek, the administration found itself quickly penned in by two powerful constraints: the sentimental images of China and the belief that communism constituted an inexorable and monolithic force. Imputing the Nationalist government challenged the established view propagated by dedicated romantics, and withdrawing support for Chiang was quickly seized upon by Republicans as an act of international appeasement. Truman, who had initially developed and manipulated "American anticommunism for his own purposes," according to Richard Freeland, now found himself watching in frustration as "his political opponents attacked him, his administration, and his policies with an issue he had nurtured."[18] Thus, although the hostile press reaction to *The White Paper* came from predictable places, these attacks struck a responsive chord in part because of the success the Truman administration had had in convincing Americans of the imminent global threat posed by communism. *Time* quickly weighed in with its assessment: "China, the most important U.S. ally in the world outside Western Europe, was gone." That loss was the result of an American failure to work with what it found in China. Instead of fighting communism in Asia with the same vigor as it did in Europe, the Truman administration had "filed a petition in bankruptcy, [and] seemed desperate to be seeking solvency in platitudes and recriminations."[19] Under the title "China Whitewash," the *Wall Street Journal* blamed Truman, Acheson, and the appeasement at Yalta; and the *Chicago Daily Tribune* found yet another opportunity to condemn Roosevelt in addition to pointing a finger at the State Department.[20] For his part, Walter Judd denounced *The White Paper* for what it did not include as well as for what it did not admit: namely, that the Truman administration had made a series of disastrous mistakes by not applying containment to China. The following month, California Senator William Knowland used the nomination of W. Walton Butterworth as Assistant Secretary of State for Far Eastern Affairs to issue a lengthy speech on the Senate floor. He not only held Butterworth partly responsible for the collapse of the Nationalist government but also offered a counterattack upon the position advanced by the administration through *The White Paper.*[21]

Charles Collingwood commented that the explanation put forth by critics like Judd and Knowland belonged to "the dime novel school of diplomatic criticism," which was true enough, but that also accounted for the widespread acceptance accorded such a perspective; its conspiratorial simplicity made it easy to grasp.[22] One pro-Chiang American associated with the California College in China wrote Judd: "'Pinks,' in the government and out, have carried out a campaign of misrepresentation" against the Nationalist government. The broader endorsement of the notion that Communists, or at least Communist sympathizers, had infiltrated the State Department and that their infiltration had caused the United States to abandon its valued ally waxed as the year came to an end.[23] When Chinese Communists imprisoned the American consul general in Mukden, Angus Ward, and three of his staff in November, Judd received numerous angry letters urging him to continue his efforts to "clean out" or "clean up" the State Department, which was obviously filled with "Reds," "Pinks," or "Commies." One writer even suggested that Dean Acheson might "constitute . . . today one of the most important Fellow Travelers left in the once Communist ridden State Department."[24]

The distance from *The White Paper* to Senator Joseph McCarthy's claim in February 1950 that the State Department contained a number of security risks was not that far. Other events helped shape this perception, including the Soviet explosion of an atomic bomb the same month *The White Paper* was released, but the Chinese Communist revolution certainly made a significant contribution to the domestic political climate of the time. In fact, China provided opportunists like McCarthy with the justification they needed to pursue an anti–New Deal agenda domestically. As one historian put it, China and (later) Korea "were the blasting fuses for gunpowder that was very dry in domestic politics."[25]

As for United China Relief–United Service to China, the organization attempted to carry on its activities but declining revenues quickly made that impossible; by 1951, it discontinued fund-raising efforts altogether. Before that decision, however, USC made one last attempt to raise money for the Christian effort in China by sending encouraging letters to past contributors. Congressman Judd told of the Chinese who had written USC, saying "'Thank God, there are Americans who haven't sold us out to the Communists!'"²⁶ The same appeal letter, sent throughout 1950, also indicated that the Chinese people had been fighting communism for twenty-five years and would continue their battle in spite of present circumstances. Along the same line, B. A. Garside wrote to Charles Edison in 1950 that USC could serve an important function in a communist China. Kenaston Twitchell, Senator H. Alexander Smith's son-in-law, had suggested the establishment of a "beachhead for democracy in China" in 1949; Garside used the term bridgehead to suggest the same sort of outpost in hostile territory. If USC abandoned its institutions, he said, the organization would lose a valuable "re-entry into the life of the Chinese people" once the Communists were eventually defeated.²⁷ When their efforts proved futile in the face of Communist consolidation, Edison, Garside, Smith, and Judd became steering committee members for the Committee of One Million Against the Admission of Communist China to the United Nations, and Garside served as the assistant treasurer. Judd and Garside also maintained ties with the American Bureau for Medical Aid to (Free) China well into the 1980's, with the latter becoming the organization's executive director.²⁸

In early 1950, Senator Smith, at a Rutgers University forum, answered questions about his recent trip to Asia. He spoke of the ideological approach he felt would turn the tide in favor of the United States there. His comments reflected the highly moral (and sexual) overtones the Cold War had already acquired. He explained away communism's successes as literally stemming from its ability to seduce the naïve and uninitiated, much like the unsuspecting "Kelly" from *Life*. Offering his ideological approach as a countermeasure, he recounted a question he had once asked Chiang Kai-shek about why the Nationalist government had not produced the kind of program that would have prevented the Chinese people from being "*seduced* by these communist promises." Although he did not indicate what the generalissimo's answer was, Smith insisted that the "Western Christian tradition as opposed to this Marxian atheism that the Russians are putting over" had much to offer China in the long run.²⁹

Other UCR members continued to make the case for aiding Chiang and Madame Chiang even after they and the Nationalist government had withdrawn to Formosa. Geraldine Fitch wrote to her "Friends" in the spring of 1950 that once the American people were adequately informed about "how China has been sold down the Yangtze," they would organize on the generalissimo's behalf. Naturally, she made use of the appropriate historical analogies to clinch her argument:

"Had we deserted England after Dunkirk . . . England might have been finished."[30] She also commented that Madame Chiang had recently left the United States with a "stirring farewell radio speech" in order to return to Taiwan where she could "help her husband and cheer the troops," an activity Marguerite Atterbury decided to draw in cartoon form for her readers.[31] A year later, Fitch signed an open letter to President Truman, along with the Reverend William Johnson and others, in which the Chinese Nationalists' plight was compared to the one faced by Americans during their war for independence. Furthermore, the letter said in closing, "We know that, like Lincoln, [Chiang] has . . . persevered in devotion to his country."[32]

In the end, it was left to a Luce to advance what was perhaps the most poignant explanation for the American failure in China. This time, however, it was not Henry Luce; instead it was Clare Boothe Luce in speaking at a testimonial dinner in honor of the Archbishop of Nanjing. Talking on the theme "The Mystery of American Policy in China," she set out to debunk the various theories offered by the State Department for the nation's China policy since the war. Insisting that Americans were indeed interested in Asia and that the State Department had never bothered to take advantage of that latent support to push for increased aid to the Nationalists, she dismissed the notion that Guomindang corruption lay at the heart of the Nationalists' failure. She followed the well-worn path originally cut by others like Judd and Chennault when she pointed out that corruption was "not unknown in American politics, even in days of peace and prosperity." Corruption was a predictable part of any society under the twin strains of an enemy invasion and a civil war, and the Guomindang did not officially sanction corruption, but this particular preoccupation had led to a myopic view of conditions in China. She dismissed other theories too, including the one that it was too late or too expensive to do something for China.[33]

After discussing all the official explanations for the nation's postwar China policy to the satisfaction of herself and, presumably, her audience, Luce offered her own hypothesis as to why the United States had abandoned China. She was a relatively recent convert to Catholicism, so perhaps it is not surprising that she found the answer in the idea of Original Sin.[34] There are those who believe that "progress in the world is *not* irreversible or inevitable," she noted. The free will that human beings possess allows them to "be vain, greedy, avaricious, cruel, above all, proud." And it was pride that the Judaic-Christian belief posited lay at the root of Original Sin. Because the State Department was made up of a group of individuals—of human beings, that is—their collective human pride undoubtedly lay at the heart of the nation's foreign policy organization.

Pride and naïveté had combined to create the disastrous policies that caused the nation to turn its back on a country filled with a people so much like Americans. Young intellectuals who graduated from college during the 1930's, she argued, became seduced by Russian promises and prescriptions for world peace based on Marxian political ideology. With "warm hearts, but thick heads," these young people, many of whom gravitated to government service, became trapped in their initial intellectual immaturity. Once committed to this philosophy, which naturally led to certain concrete policies, members of the State Department could not reconsider their position, despite the obvious bankruptcy of Soviet political ideology in the postwar world: "The members of the State Department had a deeply vested interest in the tragic errors of Yalta, Teheran, and Potsdam. The Far East Desk's vested interest in the error of its recommended sellout to Stalin in the Pacific, is indeed, incalculable." The original error occurred at Yalta, and the mistake was compounded by the pride of Original Sin, which led to the devastating continuation of such flawed policies. To admit as much now, "in all *humility*," would cause State Department officials to lose face, to injure or weaken the ego. "The Christian says his *mea culpa, mea maxima culpa*, in the secrecy of the Confession and gets absolution from his priest," but no such privacy was accorded politicians and bureaucrats, she argued, and besides, such a confession would ultimately lead to professional disgrace, not to mention dismissal after the next election. Judd had once asked for a confession too, an admission of wrongdoing that was clearly not forthcoming with the publication of *The White Paper*. But another commentator saw *The White Paper* as just that: "A confession that we tried to do something about China and failed, and, that having failed, we'll try something else."[35]

Clare Boothe Luce wanted something different, however, something more specific and certainly more politically partisan than a broad admonition of national error and misunderstanding. Of the present collection of government employees, she declared, "The sacrifice of pride and post was too great a price for this lost generation of intellectuals to pay for a clear conscience and a clean balance sheet." Liberal naïveté and the pride of Original Sin combined to produce the truly American transgression of losing the opportunity to change China. "Your Excellency," she concluded in referring to the Archbishop, "has long contemplated the small inscrutable ways of State Departments with sorrow. But you also contemplate the vast inscrutable ways of God with joy." Finite man, infinite God: the former so miserable in his imperfection, the latter so sublime as a state of perfection. The mystery of America's China policy could be solved in time, she hoped, "by the big mystery of God's Loving Providence."[36]

Though she had converted to Catholicism, Luce's thinking clearly drew from the historical legacy of the Puritans. Evidently, they had been right in how they saw their relationship with God. The point at which human beings, in reaching up through faith despite their imperfection, met God's perfection was called regeneration. God initiated the process, producing a state of joy in the chosen ones. In traveling across the Pacific in a religious and secular version of this phenomenon, Americans had longed to bring the perfection of their society, in all its political, economic, and cultural manifestations, to the Chinese. This American-initiated attempt at regeneration ran aground on the shoals of State Department pride, Luce argued. But even she could not end on an entirely pessimistic note. She observed that those who had erred because they had succumbed to pride could find it within themselves to experience a change of heart: "Seeing their errors, they may . . . turn about and begin to make amends." A flicker of hope for the transformation of China, an opportunity for American redemption, then, continued to burn.[37]

In a sense, she was right. Certain Americans had committed a sin of sorts, but it was not the one she had in mind. In fact, the original sin came long before the Marshall mission, Potsdam, or Yalta. Americans had erred in thinking that China was made up of people who in their hearts wanted to become just like them. And it is a mistake that apparently continues to be made today.

In the decades since the Chinese Communist revolution, much has changed in the nature of Sino-American relations; more interestingly, however, much has remained the same. One of the apparent conundrums faced in considering the impact of the "loss of China" is how Richard Nixon could so readily and completely turn the entire matter around with his visit to the People's Republic in 1972. This is especially perplexing when one examines the polling data from the late 1960's, which indicated that Communist China had the lowest favorable rating of all countries Americans were asked about—lower than the Soviet Union, lower than Cuba, and even lower than North Vietnam. In 1968, the PRC's favorable rating was 5 percent; five years later it stood at 49 percent, fifteen points higher than that of the Soviet Union.[38] The remarkable turnaround mirrors, in reverse, the rapid plunge national attitudes toward China took from 1945 to 1950. But how could this inversion have come about so swiftly?

The long-standing malleability of American attitudes toward Asia must be considered first. If opinions about Japan could change so quickly after World War II, then opinions about China could change equally quickly a little over two decades later. In 1945, a Gallup poll showed that 13 percent of Americans queried felt that the Japanese people should be exterminated, and 82 percent thought the Japanese were more cruel than the Germans. By 1951, however, 51 percent of the American people indicated that they had "friendly feelings" toward the Japanese, and another 18 percent said that they were neutral.[39] The juxtaposition of Japan and China after the war and the reversal of American national attitudes toward them arose out of the Cold War circumstances in Asia, culminating with the outbreak of the Korean War.

A similar reversal became possible, almost necessary, by the late 1960's owing to a new set of exigencies. When Richard Nixon entered the White House, the war in Vietnam had already claimed tens of thousands of American lives and had cost the nation tens of billions of dollars. In addition, a decline in the economic climate had already begun to impinge on the living standard Americans had enjoyed in the two decades since the end of World War II, at the same time that West Germany and Japan had made significant strides toward competing in basic industries like textiles, steel, and automobile manufacturing. A further blow came when Nixon was forced to take the country off the gold standard in August 1971, a month after he had publicly announced his visit to the People's Republic. Nixon also imposed wage and price controls in an attempt to regulate the economic situation. The president needed a way out of this predicament, and China seemed to present, at the very least, a partial solution.

Nixon thus reopened the door that had closed in 1949. In the 1890's, certain Americans had viewed China as a continuation of the frontier, an extension of the safety valve that Frederick Jackson Turner argued had made Americans unique. By the early 1970's, China was again becoming part of a utilitarian perspective. First, China could be used as a diplomatic lever against the Soviets, or in the popular terminology of the day, Nixon could play the "China card." Presumably, this would be persuasive in getting the Soviets to negotiate, which, in turn, would help reduce some of the costs of containment. Second, Nixon hoped that the Chinese could use their influence with the North Vietnamese in the negotiations over the

United States' withdrawal from Southeast Asia. The United States sought a "decent interval" from the time it left until the time of South Vietnam's collapse—all in order to preserve the nation's international reputation. By pressuring Hanoi, China could help ease that interval. Third, the China market still beckoned, especially to a sluggish United States economy. Fourth, the Nixon administration could use China in its negotiations with the Japanese over trade issues. Reopening relations with China was in a sense Nixon's hint to Japan that its position was not quite as secure as it had been previously. Finally, and not the least, the trip to China was an election-year ploy. Nixon had used the "fall of China" to good political effect in the early 1950's, and he thought there might still be gold in that mine, in a reverse extraction process.[40]

Since 1973, American attitudes toward China have grown steadily more favorable except for certain unusual periods, particularly the immediate aftermath of the Tiananmen Square massacre, while attitudes toward Japan have consistently declined. The phenomenon of the juxtaposition of these two Asian nations and their peoples and the inverse relationship many American hold of them can be traced back to the nineteenth century, as Michael Hunt has noted. Negative attitudes toward Japan increased significantly during the 1980's, so much so that by 1989 more Americans viewed China favorably than Japan. In 1991, fifty years after Pearl Harbor, fewer Americans expressed "friendly" attitudes toward the Japanese people than in 1951. And a year later, overall favorable opinions toward Japan dropped to 47 percent, with 50 percent of those polled indicating that they held an unfavorable opinion.[41]

Perhaps nowhere has this sentiment been more stridently evidenced than in Michael Crichton's best-selling novel *Rising Sun*, published in 1991 and later made into a major motion picture. Although purportedly a work of fiction, *Rising Sun* included a bibliography that the author hoped would encourage interested Americans to read further on the nature of the Japanese threat to the United States. But the bibliography, as Robert Reich has pointed out, contained selected works, many of which envisioned a conspiratorial, omnipotent Japan strikingly similar to the superhuman image that was so popular immediately after Pearl Harbor.[42] According to one character in the novel, the present challenge is more than just one of friendly economic competition. As the seemingly lone member of the United States government who comprehends the true ramifications of recent Japanese acquisitions of American high-tech companies, the fictional Senator John Morton puts the matter this way: "We can't ignore the reality of *targeted,* adversarial trade as practiced by Japan—where business and government make a *planned attack* on some segment of the American economy."[43] But Crichton suggests that more than a simple business and government cabal has been at work, and that the other nations of Asia were in on the plan. As another character explains, the Japanese have "farmed out production to the little dragons, so the [U.S. trade] deficits appear in their columns, not Japan's." Such simple-mindedness posits that the independent governments in, presumably, South Korea, Singapore, and Taiwan (none is mentioned by name), are, in effect, working for Japan in some kind of economic resurrection of the greater East Asia Co-Prosperity Sphere.[44]

If recent attitudes toward Japan are at an all-time postwar low, it is not altogether surprising; indeed, it is quite logical, and perhaps even necessary, that images of China are on the rise in spite of the Tiananmen Square crackdown. From the American perspective, the link between the earlier period of Luce's American Century, with its emphasis on the applicability of American ways to the Chinese, and the present is best illustrated by an article first published in the *Christian Advocate* in 1951. This article, "Christianity and Capitalism," by Charles Crowe, offered the conclusion that "the free enterprise program of private ownership best supports and affords the chance to realize basic Christian ideals."[45] Although the article did not specifically mention China, Crowe's connection between what J. A. Hobson called "God and Mammon"—between religious worship and an economic system predicated upon acquiring private wealth—offers a link to the present set of assumptions in a number of salient ways.

Whereas during the 1930's and 1940's, a great deal of the American rhetoric about China focused on converting the Chinese to Christianity first (from which the transformation to political democracy and economic capitalism would naturally follow), the more recent public discourse has expressed a faith in the evolutionary powers of capitalism, largely bypassing the earlier concern with religious proselytization. In highlighting changes before the 1996 Chinese reacquisition of Hong Kong, *Forbes* noted that the Guangdong province "is firmly set on a road to capitalist prosperity."[46] One of *Forbes*'s covers even featured an artist's rendition of a young Chinese man with a Big Mac in his hand standing before a McDonald's restaurant in the Chinese architectural style. The notion of McDonald's as a symbol of America's growing importance for China was subsequently reinforced by a *New York Times* article on China's booming economy in which it was reported that McDonald's three best opening-day sales of foreign franchises were all located in China.[47] And in another recent story on a village just south and west of Hong Kong, the *New York Times* observed, "Almost everyone [there] is interested in America."[48]

Luce had once insisted that Christianity was completely familiar to the Chinese peasant. *Forbes* has similarly contended the same: the Chinese people, or at least some of them, are inherently predisposed toward capitalism. "Cantonese society," the writer claimed, "is deeply pragmatic, materialistic, *entrepreneurial*." In fact, "Once capitalism had its foot in the door" of Guangdong, "communism was doomed" since it was only a matter of time before a free market economy spread to the rest of the country. "Nearly four decades of communism did nothing to eradicate these deep impulses, which bubbled over once repression was lifted."[49] *Business Week*, appending its voice to the growing media chorus, argued that the "Western social views, free market theory and democratic principles" constitute the "seeds that could shape China's future."[50] The *New York Times* added that certain villages are "leaping toward capitalism and a modern Western way of living."[51] Were H. Alexander Smith, Ken Twitchell, and B. A. Garside on to something when they proposed creating and maintaining beachheads of western Christianity, democracy, and the American way of life within China? But instead of Christian enclaves, hasn't the real force for change become capitalism? Their suggestion of so long ago seemed to take on additional aptness given the subject of a *Reader's Digest* article on China's "underground" Christians that appeared at the same time as the *Forbes* piece.[52]

Other ideas have also resurfaced. As UCR had once sought to highlight China's medical needs during World War II by including "comely Chinese girls in nurses uniforms" in a parade through New York City's Chinatown, *Forbes* noted that a new generation of "comely [Chinese] girls from Shanghai and farther north" work as prostitutes and "lure Hong Kong businessmen in the city's sleek new hotels and Japanese-style karaoke bars."[53]

The main purpose of the *Forbes* article was to offer support for President Bush's decision not to impose economic sanctions as a result of the political crackdown on the Tiananmen protestors in June 1989. Such punitive policies would only retard the growth of capitalism and prove to be counterproductive in the larger effort to transform China through capitalism. In fact, *Forbes* insisted, punishing China would simply play "right into the hands of the reactionary, nationalistic rulers in Beijing." Communism there might not collapse with the same dramatic swiftness as it did in Eastern Europe and the Soviet Union, but nonetheless, the Asian giant's future was "equally irreversible."

The *National Review* also concurred with the administration's policies, recommending that "the most subversive thing [Americans] can do to China's Neanderthal political system is to maintain—not curtail—China's exposure to the pressures of economic growth and the influences of the outside world."[54]

Bush's political demise has not stemmed the tide of advice progressing along these lines. The responsibility has simply switched to the Clinton administration to adopt a set of policies appropriate for facilitating the transformation of China. Writing in *Foreign Affairs* immediately after the 1992 election, two authors insisted that Asia's regional economic growth "promises a more stable East Asia," one that "will gradually create the conditions for a more pluralistic and humanely governed society in China's mainland."[55]

This is not to insist that *Forbes*, the *New York Times*, and other observers are wrong in their assessments of the changes that are occurring inside China today. These assessments of the developments there are not necessarily exaggerated. But the projections for the future as a result of these changes make about as much sense as arguing that because Japan sells so many automobiles, television sets, and electronic devices in the United States, Americans will soon begin practicing Shintoism and observing other manifestations of Japanese culture. Although obviously far-fetched, the notion is not altogether different from what many Americans have come to expect from China. A more ominous perspective could well be that the economic reforms applauded by most Western commentators have largely served the very groups bent on maintaining political control in China. The principal beneficiaries of increasing trade between the United States and China, Lynn Chu wrote in the *Atlantic*, "have been the military and security police, whose resources have been modernized at a far faster pace than those of the Chinese people at large."[56]

Other commentators on Sino-American relations in the 1990's have urged caution in evaluating the direction of future changes in China. One scholar, Nancy Tucker, has recently warned against advancing such sentimental ideas as the ones propagated by *Forbes*: "Americans should . . . dispense with the hoary notion that a hugely profitable China market waits to be exploited." She added that a Soviet-style collapse there is unlikely.[57] And another observer has noted that China may not be nearly so amenable to outside influence as many people wish to believe.[58]

A little over one hundred years ago, Geraldine Guiness selected China as first in line, "amongst all the heathen countries of the world," for an infusion of the Christian gospel. China's "vast extent," its "overwhelming population," and its "leading position in the scale of nations" had drawn missionaries to the area, and their recent successes in distributing "Bibles, Testaments, and Scripture portions" led her to conclude that the transformation of China was well in hand.[59] Today, in spite of all the changes in the Asian world, Americans persist in gazing across the Pacific in search of a China to suit their immediate needs. Although Luce's vision for China appeared to last only eighteen years, the emotions and sentiments behind the American Century have easily spanned the time period it demarcates.

Images and conceptions of China have been, and continue to be, more the product of domestic forces than the result of anything else. The very resilience of the notion that China can and should be changed to fit into an American model bespeaks the fact that, although China certainly has changed over the past one hundred years, the basis for Americans' understanding of that nation and its people has not. It is through relations with China that Americans persist in seeing the opportunity to achieve success on a scale unmatched elsewhere. The tenacity of this desire by many to change China reflects, in the words of Jonathan Spence, their hope "to influence history by the force of personality" and in the process "to prove their own significance."[60] Or as the newspaper columnist Joseph Kraft phrased it at the time of Richard Nixon's visit in 1972, "China has been for American opinion a focus of narcissism, an occasion for striking self-adoring poses."[61]

In the aftermath of the Chinese Communist revolution, the Truman administration's Assistant Secretary of State, W. Walton Butterworth, made a particularly thoughtful statement in discussing China with students at the Lawrenceville School in Lawrenceville, New Jersey. He noted:

> It is not surprising that we tend to think [of] foreign people like ourselves, with very much the same standards of values, the same motivations and objectives in life, and the same capabilities and accomplishments. This tendency to clothe peoples in other lands with our own characteristics and circumstances increases our difficulty in understanding even those peoples who share with us a common cultural and political heritage; we must be especially wary of it in thinking of the Chinese whose roots go far back into a past totally different from our own.[62]

He went on to discuss the nature of Chinese society, the history of the country, and the problems facing the new Communist government. American attempts to influence events in China must take into account the most obvious of all factors, he observed: the Chinese people. "We cannot remake China nor can we remold the Chinese people in our image."

As Americans confront the international issues facing them in a post–Cold War world, they would do well to keep Butterworth's simple truism in mind. The danger lies not so much in the nature of paternalistic expectations, such as they are; rather, it resides in the wild and drastic swing of the emotional pendulum that will follow the inevitable disappointment to those profoundly misguided aspirations. China is indeed changing, and tremendous economic development has certainly been a significant part of that process, but that does not necessarily translate into China's becoming more of a Christian, capitalist, or democratic nation. As obvious as it may seem, it is often overlooked: that remains for the Chinese to determine themselves.

REFERENCE MATTER

Notes

Complete authors' names and publication data for works cited in short form are given in the Bibliography, pp. 235–47. The following abbreviations are used in the Notes.

ABMAC	American Bureau for Medical Aid to China
FDRL	Franklin D. Roosevelt Library
FRUS	*Foreign Relations of the United States*
HSTL	Harry S. Truman Library
MPC	Missions Pamphlet Collection
NYHT	*New York Herald Tribune*
NYT	*New York Times*
OF	Office Files
PPF	President's Personal File
PPP:GB	*Public Papers of the Presidents: George Bush*
SVM	Student Volunteer Movement
UBCHEA	United Board for Christian Higher Education in Asia
UCR-USC	United China Relief–United Service to China
WP	*Washington Post*

Preface

1. *PPP:GB* (1989, book I), p. 143.
2. Ibid., p. 290. The Bushes had waited to christen their daughter in an effort to get the entire family together. Dorothy was christened on Aug. 18, 1975, by three Chinese clergymen: one Episcopalian, one Presbyterian, and one Baptist, in the church used by the diplomatic community in Beijing. See Bush with Gold, *Looking Forward*, p. 144.
3. *PPP:GB* (1989, book 1), p. 699.

4. Ibid., pp. 672–73.

5. As quoted in Blumenthal, *Pledging Allegiance*, pp. 334–35.

6. *Sino-American Relations: One Year After the Massacre at Tiananmen Square*, June 6, 1990, Senate, Foreign Relations, Subcommittee on East Asian and Pacific Affairs, 101st Cong. 2d sess., p. 20.

7. Kaplan, "'Left Alone with America,'" in Kaplan and Pease, eds., *Cultures of United States Imperialism*, p. 16.

8. In addition to the works already cited, see Iriye "The Internationalization of History," and Hunt, "Internationalizing U.S. Diplomatic History." Hunt observes (p. 10), "Perceptions, which serve as the basis for policy, are profoundly conditioned by cultural values." The intent here is to place U.S.-China relations within that set of cultural values from the American perspective. Americans were generally ignorant about China, and their perceptions, far from being based on a clear understanding of Chinese history and culture, were determined by various assumptions about the applicability of American ideals to the situation in Asia.

9. Henry R. Luce, "The American Century," *Life*, Feb. 17, 1941; reprinted in Jessup, ed., *The Ideas of Henry Luce*, p. 120.

10. Even more specific investigations into Sino-American relations customarily fail to take into account Luce's significance in shaping American perceptions of China. Luce (or one of his magazines) is mentioned briefly in Borg and Heinrichs, eds., *Uncertain Years*; Schaller, *The United States and China in the Twentieth Century*, especially chap. 1; Thomson, Jr., Stanley, and Perry, *Sentimental Imperialists*; Tsou, *America's Failure in China, 1941–1950*; Tuchman, *Stilwell and the American Experience in China, 1911–1945*. Accounts that discuss Luce and his publications in greater detail include Purifoy, *Harry Truman's China Policy*, and Tucker, *Patterns in the Dust*. Tucker also has useful chapters on the Guomindang, the China Lobby, and missionaries, all of which involved Luce to some extent. Three exceptions to the general lack of interest in Luce need to be noted. The first is Neils, *China Images in the Life and Times of Henry Luce* (1990), essentially an attempt to rehabilitate Luce's image, which was tarnished with the publication of Swanberg's *Luce and His Empire* (1972). Neils argues that Luce was right about China, Chiang Kai-shek, and Mao Zedong—a visionary ahead of his time. "From the perspective of the 1990s," she concludes, "it appears that Henry Luce's assessment of the China situation was not so far wrong; that he understood the Chinese people, the dilemma of Chiang and the motivations of Mao far more clearly than did [Theodore] White, W. A. Swanberg, and the countless other critics who have denounced his China views and editorial policies" (p. 292). This view does not reflect any better understanding of China now than it did fifty years ago, and it is in fact part of a long-standing American way of thinking about China and the Chinese that has far more to do with domestic political and cultural mores than with any accurate reading of the Chinese situation. Neils's conclusion is simply further evidence of the persistence of this blindness. The more recent book by Robert E. Herzstein, *Henry R. Luce* (1994), is a well-researched political biography of Luce up to the year 1945.

My focus extends beyond the war to the proclamation of the People's Republic of China in 1949, and rather than concentrating solely on Luce, I examine his career as part of a larger American perspective on China, one that encompassed many other people and both pre- and postdates Luce's involvement.

11. Rosenberg, *Spreading the American Dream*, p. 7; Williams, *The Tragedy of American Diplomacy*, p. 11.

12. Guimond, *American Photography and the American Dream*, pp. 160–61.

13. Peck, *Two Kinds of Time*, p. 181.

14. Feinberg, *Harm to Self*, pp. 3–8.

15. Japan and Vietnam have, at various times, been placed within a similar context and specifically denoted as children in the American way of thinking about the region. For Japan, see Dower, *War Without Mercy*, p. 303; for Vietnam, see the comments by General William C. Westmoreland in the film *Hearts and Minds*, USA 1974, Touchstone/Warner Bros.

16. For an assessment of a similar phenomenon, but one relating to American contacts with the Chinese Communists for roughly the same period, see Shewmaker, *Americans and Chinese Communists*.

17. Kaplan, "'Left Alone with America,'" in Kaplan and Pease, eds., p. 16.

18. Joseph Kraft, "America's China Myths," Feb. 22, 1972, Judd Papers, box 196.

19. Swidler, "Culture in Action," p. 283.

20. Marchand, *Advertising the American Dream*, pp. xvi–xvii.

21. Gamson and Modigliani, "Media Discourse and Public Opinion," p. 3.

22. Ninkovich, "Interests and Discourse in Diplomatic History," p. 159.

23. Hunt, *Ideology and U.S. Foreign Policy*, p. 15.

Prologue

1. D. Z. Sheffield as quoted in McClellan, *The Heathen Chinee*, p. 223.

2. *FRUS*, 1895, p. 197.

3. For more on the interest expressed by American businesses in China and other parts of the globe, see Rosenberg, *Spreading the American Dream*, pp. 15–28, and Wiebe, *The Search for Order, 1877–1920*, pp. 249–55. For more on China specifically, see McCormick, *China Market*, and LaFeber, *The New Empire*, pp. 300–311, 352–62.

4. For more on the Open Door notes, in addition to Rosenberg and McCormick, see the following: Hunt, *The Making of a Special Relationship*, chap. 6; Thomson, Jr., Stanley, and Perry, *Sentimental Imperialists*, chap. 9; Young, *The Rhetoric of Empire*, chap. 6; Williams, *The Tragedy of American Diplomacy*, pp. 50–57; and Williams, *The Contours of American History*, pp. 414–20.

5. Samuel Gompers, for example, supported the renewal of the exclusionary legislation in 1902 and testified that other leaders of the American Federation of Labor did so too. See McClellan, *Heathen Chinee*, p. 199.

6. The pressure to pass an exclusionary bill dated from the 1860's, when

the first Chinese laborers were brought in to work on the railroads. President Rutherford B. Hayes vetoed two measures, but Chester A. Arthur finally signed a bill in 1882 that forbade Chinese immigration for a period of ten years. A new treaty with China in 1894 extended the ban on laborers for another ten years, but the United States continued the ban unilaterally until 1924. For more on this subject, see W. Cohen, *America's Response to China*, pp. 30–32. Cohen also comments on the economic interests of the United States in China; see table on p. 37. For another discussion of the exclusionary legislation, see McClellan, *Heathen Chinee*, pp. 112–13, 198–200. For both an American and a Chinese perspective on the exclusionary legislation, see Hunt, *Making of a Special Relationship*, chaps. 3 and 7. See also, Hunt's *Ideology and U.S. Foreign Policy*, p. 71, where he argues that the uneasy coexistence between anti-Chinese xenophobia and the lure of economic opportunity eased after 1910 when it became clear that the former had been eliminated as a political issue on account of the exclusionary legislation.

7. Varg, *Missionaries, Chinese, and Diplomats*, p. 153.

8. *FRUS*, 1895, p. 198.

9. Eddy, *Pathfinders of the World Missionary Crusade*, p. 50.

10. Hunter, *The Gospel of Gentility*, pp. 49–51. She points out that these women expressed "their desire for self-liberation in the language of self-sacrifice" (p. 51).

11. Letter, Henry W. Luce to Willard, Feb. 2, 1895, SVM Papers, box 362.

12. H. W. Luce to H. R. Luce, Nov. 4 and 14, 1914, Garside Papers, box 2.

13. McClellan, *Heathen Chinee*, p. 176.

14. *North Carolina's "China Connection," 1840–1949: A Record*, p. 95. Louisa Kilgroe of the North Carolina China Council brought this picture to my attention. In addition to preserving their frontier heritage, many missionaries to China sought to recreate their former surroundings as much as possible. Hunter, *Gospel of Gentility*, notes how women, particularly married ones, used gardening as a means of achieving some connection with America; see chap. 5.

15. Geraldine Guiness, May 2, 1890, pp. 4–5, SVM Papers, box 554.

16. John R. Mott, "Urgency and Crisis in the Far East," Jan. 2–7 1908, pp. 12–13, SVM Papers, box 557.

17. Buck, *My Several Worlds*.

18. Letter, H. R. Luce to John Shaw Billings, Nov. 12, 1945, p. 5, Swanberg Papers, box 17. Because Swanberg's notes were taken in shorthand, I have made spelling changes without noting them in the text.

19. Alice Berry-Hart, draft of her memoirs, "Shanghai and the China We Knew," p. 60, China Records Project, box 24.

20. Buck, *My Several Worlds*, p. 5.

21. Elson, *Time Inc.*, p. 23.

22. Baughman, *Henry R. Luce and the Rise of the American News Media*, p. 11.

23. Luce as quoted in Elson, *Time Inc.*, p. 27.

24. Varg, *Missionaries, Chinese, and Diplomats*, pp. 148, 151. Political

turmoil and anti-foreign activities led a significant number of missionaries to leave China after March 1927. Heininger, "Private Positions Versus Public Policy," pp. 290–91, cites a figure of a 40 percent decline in the Protestant missionary force from early 1927 until the middle of 1928. Hunter, *Gospel of Gentility*, p. 5, also notes the creation of the Anti-Christian Student Federation in 1922.

25. Varg, *Missionaries*, p. 215. See also, Rosenberg, *Spreading the American Dream*, p. 79.

26. Rosenberg, *American Dream*, p. 111.

27. Letter, Johnson to Dr. Joy, Nov. 19, 1927, pp. 3, 4, Johnson Papers, box 13.

28. Judd interview, Columbia Oral History Collection. For the comment about Judd's importance in building up Chiang's following in the United States, see Varg, *Missionaries*, p. 294.

29. Letter, Judd to Strong, Mar. 24, 1927, p. 6, China Records Project, box 107. The letter is impressive for other reasons besides its length. Judd analyzed the situation in China in considerable detail. Although he was highly critical of the missionary activity in China, he felt that his remarks might spur constructive action.

30. Ibid., p. 3.

31. Acheson, *Present at the Creation*, p. 8.

32. John Foster Dulles, May 18, 1951, Smith Papers, box 105. The speech was broadcast by NBC.

33. Epstein, "Henry Luce and His Time," p. 38.

34. Eric Hodgins interview, p. 40, Eisenhower Project, Columbia Oral History Collection.

Chapter One

1. Gamson and Modigliani, "Media Discourse and Public Opinion," p. 9.

2. Time Inc. guaranteed advertisers a circulation of 250,000 for the first twelve months and had set rates accordingly. Moreover, because Luce insisted on using a better-quality paper for the photographs, production costs for *Life* were high. The problem arose when *Life* became an immediate sensation, and demand exceeded Time Inc.'s estimations. The first issue sold 435,000. By January 1937, *Life* had a circulation of 760,000, and production costs exceeded the revenues from the advertising. Luce's gamble paid handsome dividends later on, however. For more, see Baughman, *Henry R. Luce and the Rise of the American News Media*, pp. 92–94, and Elson, *Time Inc.*, pp. 274–77, 281–82, 297–303, 309, 328–31. Dwight Macdonald reported that advertising for the early issues of *Life* was conservatively valued at $7 million but was sold for only $2.5 million. See Macdonald's article, "*Time, Fortune, Life*," *Nation*, May 22, 1937, p. 585.

3. Letter, Luce to Macdonald, July 31, 1934, Macdonald Papers, box 29.

4. Thomas S. Matthews interview, p. 93, Eisenhower Project, Columbia Oral History Collection.

5. As quoted in Jessup, ed., *The Ideas of Henry Luce*, p. 3.

6. Letter, Van Meter to R. D. Miller, July 20, 1937, Macdonald Papers, box 52.

7. Letter to *Time* subscribers, Mar. 2, 1935, OF 2442, FDRL. One Time Inc. editor, Eric Hodgins, commented that *Time* was designed to meet the "growing need of the busy person, to present things in capsule form." Eric Hodgins interview, p. 96, Eisenhower Project, Columbia Oral History Collection.

8. Letter to *Time* subscribers, n.d., but sometime in either Jan. or Feb. 1938, PPF 3338, FDRL.

9. Letter to Time Inc. magazine subscribers, Sept. 29, 1941, OF 2442, FDRL. "The March of Time" radio program had run from 1931 until 1939. It was brought back in 1941 and ran until 1945.

10. Luce, from a speech entitled "Causes, Causes!" given to *Life* advertising salesmen, May 27, 1939, quoted in Jessup, ed., *The Ideas of Henry Luce*, pp. 56–57.

11. The ideas and quotation are from a speech at a dinner for *Time* editors, Nov. 14, 1952, quoted in ibid., pp. 70–71.

12. Letter, Macdonald to Luce, n.d., but sometime in late Jan. or Feb. 1936, Macdonald Papers, box 29. See also Elson, *Time Inc.*, pp. 250–52.

13. Letter, Macdonald to Luce, n.d., but sometime in late Jan. or Feb. 1936, Macdonald Papers, box 29.

14. Letter, Luce to Macdonald, Feb. 24, 1936, Macdonald Papers, box 29. See also Elson, *Time Inc.*, p. 252.

15. Macdonald, "'Time' and Henry Luce," *Nation*, May 1, 1937, pp. 501, 502.

16. Letter, Miller to Roland Toms, Oct. 16, 1937, Macdonald Papers, box 52. Emphasis mine.

17. Letter, Luce to Macdonald, July 31, 1934, Macdonald Papers, box 29.

18. Letter, Van Meter to R. D. Miller, July 20, 1937, Macdonald Papers, box 52.

19. Letter, Toms to Miller, Aug. 30, 1937, Macdonald Papers, box 52.

20. For more on the relationship between Roosevelt and Luce, see Winfield, *FDR and the News Media*. See also, Baughman, *Henry Luce and the Rise of the American News Media*; and Elson, *Time Inc.* and *The World of Time Inc.*

21. Memo, Roosevelt to Early, Dec. 3, 1940, PPF 3338, FDRL.

22. Letter, Mellet to Luce, Dec. 7, 1940, p. 3. PPF 3338, FDRL.

23. Ibid., p. 4.

24. Letter, Luce to Mellet, Dec. 24, 1940, PPF 3338, FDRL. See also, Winfield, *FDR and the News Media*, pp. 145–46.

25. Memo, Roosevelt to Mellet, Dec. 31, 1940, PPF 3338, FDRL. FDR crossed out "lie" and wrote "sin" underneath it on the original.

26. Elson, *Time Inc.*, p. 178. For a general discussion of "The March of Time" radio program see Fielding, *The March of Time*, pp. 3–20.

27. Fielding, *The March of Time*, p. 12.

28. Elson, *Time Inc.*, pp. 184–85; Fielding, *The March of Time*, p. 15.

29. Letter, Butler to Early, Jan. 16, 1934, OF 2442, FDRL.
30. Letter, Walter Volckhausen to Early, Jan. 23, 1934, OF 2442, FDRL.
31. Letter, Butler to Early, Jan. 16, 1934, OF 2442, FDRL.
32. Letter, W. T. Baldwin, Jr., to the White House, Jan. 15, 1934, OF 2442, FDRL.
33. Letter, Volckhausen to Early, Jan. 23, 1934, OF 2442, FDRL.
34. Letter, Duryee Crooks to Roosevelt, Jan. 26, 1934, OF 2442, FDRL.
35. Elson, *Time Inc.*, p. 183; Fielding, *The March of Time*, p. 19.
36. Fielding, *March of Time*, pp. 139, 154.
37. Elson, *Time Inc.*, p. 237.
38. Fielding, *March of Time*, pp. 154–55, 208–9; Elson, *Time Inc.*, p. 235.
39. Thomas S. Matthews interview, pp. 89, 93, Columbia Oral History Collection. It should be kept in mind that Matthews thought Luce knew more about China than anyone else though his feelings may have been misguided. Thus, Matthews was not really critical of Luce here in his overall assessment.
40. Kopkind, "Serving Time," p. 28.
41. Ibid., p. 26.

Chapter Two

1. For more on these events, see Spence, *The Search for Modern China*, pp. 341–70; Sheridan, *China in Disintegration*, pp. 156–82; Van Slyke, *Enemies and Friends*, pp. 14–30; Gasster, *China's Struggle to Modernize*, pp. 43–46.
2. Chiang was baptized in October 1930. *Time* made note of Chiang's conversion in its issue of Nov. 3, 1930, p. 25: "Chiang is as much a Conqueror as was Constantine I (288–337 A.D.), the Roman general who espoused Christianity when convinced that by the Sign of the Cross he would conquer, and who did conquer Rome itself, became emperor [*sic*]."
3. Spence, *Search for Modern China*, p. 387.
4. *NYT*, Feb. 3, 1937, p. 27.
5. Spence, *Search for Modern China*, p. 387. Spence points out that Buck's novel sold 1.5 million copies, and that the movie was seen by an estimated 23 million Americans, but not because it presented a picture of an exotic China: "Perhaps, as the United States began to confront the Great Depression in all its complexity, it was comforting to know that in China things were even worse" (p. 388).
6. For more on the relationship between Germany and China during this period, see Kirby, *Germany and Republican China*, especially pp. 113–26; see also, Spence, *Search for Modern China*, pp. 396–402.
7. Kirby, p. 159.
8. For much more on the New Life Movement and the involvement of American missionaries in it, see Thomson, Jr., *While China Faced West*, chap. 7. On the influence of Germany in the creation of the New Life Movement, see Kirby, pp. 176–85.
9. The first of Chiang's many *Time* cover appearances was the issue of Oct.

26, 1931. The photograph shows him with his wife, Soong Meiling. The legend reads: "President of China & Wife. He Threatened to Whampoa Japan"—a word play on Chiang's former position as head of the Whampoa Military Academy. In their early years, Time Inc.'s magazines, especially *Time*, were known for their sophomoric writing. The quote in the text is from the *Time* issue of Dec. 11, 1933 (pp. 20–22), Chiang's second cover appearance.

10. The previous February, Chiang shared the cover with Joseph Stalin, Emperor Hirohito, and Puyi.

11. *Time*, Nov. 9, 1936, pp. 18–19.

12. The line of pillboxes from Shanghai to Nanjing became known as the Hindenberg Line. See Kirby, p. 123.

13. *Time*, Nov. 9, 1936, p. 19.

14. The planes were bought with funds raised by popular subscription, with many provinces and cities exceeding their quotas. See Thomson, *While China Faced West*, p. 33; and *FRUS*, 1936, 4:455.

15. Thomson, *While China Faced West*, p. 20.

16. Associated Press Biographical Service, Sketch 2889, issued May 1, 1941, p. 2, UCR-USC Papers, box 91.

17. For a more detailed account of the events surrounding the kidnapping, see Spence, *Search for Modern China*, pp. 420–24, and Van Slyke, *Enemies and Friends*, pp. 75–91.

18. The phrase "most powerful man in Eastern Asia" was used again in the issue of Jan. 4, 1937, p. 18.

19. *Time*, Dec. 28, 1936, p. 14. Spence, *Search for Modern China*, p. 420, says that Zhang had been cured of his opium addiction.

20. In addition to Spence's balanced historical account of the Xi'an incident, one of the best descriptions of the events immediately before and during Chiang's capture is still Snow's *Red Star Over China*, pp. 395–422. Snow has strong biases, to be sure, but his narrative is packed with details. On Moscow's criticism of the incident, see Schram, *Mao Tse-tung*, p. 199. For the growing tensions on account of Chiang's policies, see Sheridan, *China in Disintegration*, p. 254.

21. As quoted in Snow, p. 403.

22. As quoted in Snow, p. 403.

23. Snow, pp. 414–15.

24. Snow, 415–17; Spence, *Search for Modern China*, pp. 423–24; Sheridan, pp. 254–55.

25. Quoted in Fielding, *The March of Time*, p. 134.

26. "The Far East!" "The March of Time," vol. 3, no. 5, RKO Radio Pictures Distributors, 1936.

27. One consistent aspect of Time Inc.'s coverage of the personalities in China throughout the 1930's and 1940's was its proclivity to point out differences in dress. Chiang was always smartly attired while his opponents usually came across as slobs.

28. All quotations are from a copy of the sermon in China Records Project, box 201.

29. Chiang Kai-shek, "What the Sufferings of Jesus Mean to Me," *Chris-

tian Century, May 12, 1937, p. 612. This two-page article is virtually identical to Chiang's Easter Sunday sermon.

30. Chiang Kai-shek, "Why I Believe in Jesus," printed in *Christian Century*, June 8, 1938, pp. 723–24. The speech was broadcast on the "March of Time" in the United States. See letter, Reginald Wheeler to General and Madame Chiang Kai-shek, Apr. 25, 1938, UBCHEA Papers, box 4.

31. China Records Project, box 201.

32. Lancelot Foster, "The Generalissimo and Madame Chiang Kai-shek," *Hibbert Journal*, Oct. 1937, p. 100.

33. Varg, *Missionaries, Chinese, Diplomats*, p. 153.

34. Luce, "The Human Situation," address delivered at the fifty-third commencement, Stanford University, July 2, 1944, UCR-USC Papers, box 48.

35. Letter, Luce to Winthrop Aldrich, May 6, 1944, UCR-USC Papers, box 48.

36. Address given by Luce at a special United Nations service in tribute to China, Dec. 13, 1942, UCR-USC Papers, box 48. All subsequent quotations are from this source.

37. "U.S. Foreign Policy," *Fortune*, Dec. 1940, p. 153.

38. "The China Trade," *Fortune*, May 1941, pp. 69–120.

39. "U.S. Foreign Policy," *Fortune*, Dec. 1940, p. 153.

40. *Time*, June 13, 1938. For similar remarks, see also issues of Jan. 3, 1938, p. 14; Feb. 21, 1938, p. 23; Nov. 7, 1938, pp. 12–13; and *Life*, May 16, 1938, p. 12.

41. *Time*, Oct. 4, 1937, p. 19.

42. For "China's Pacific Northwest," see *Time*, June 13, 1938, p. 18. For "China's potential Pennsylvania," see *Time*, Dec. 18, 1939, p. 23.

43. See "The New China, " *Fortune*, Apr. 1941, p. 121. The article remarked, "When you look at the Kuomintang, you think of the democratic party; when you consider Ch'ung King's industry, you think of Pittsburgh." The paragraph actually warned against making such simplistic comparisons but in the process did exactly that.

44. *Time*, Nov. 7, 1938, p. 13.

45. *Time*, June 26, 1939, p. 30.

46. "The New China," *Fortune*, Apr. 1941, p. 120. The article describes Dr. Kung as so sophisticated "that though he is one of the most Western-minded of the big men of China, he has the sense to hide his Oberlin and Yale training under a facade of charming old-style manners"; T. V. Soong is described as "brilliant."

47. *Time*, June 16, 1941, pp. 23–25.

48. "The Army of the Republic of China," *Fortune*, Sept. 1941, p. 50.

49. *Time*, June 16, 1941.

50. *Time*, Dec. 5, 1938, p. 17, and *Time*, Nov. 28, 1938, pp. 15–16.

51. "The Army of the Republic of China," *Fortune*, Sept. 1941, p. 49.

52. *Time*, June 26, 1939, p. 29. For a detailed discussion of American impressions of the Chinese Communists, see Shewmaker, *Americans and Chinese Communists*.

53. See issues of Feb. 3, 1941, p. 23, and Feb. 10, 1941, p. 14. See also, "The

New China," *Fortune*, Apr. 1941, p. 116. The mutual maneuverings between the Nationalists and Communists for control of important strategic areas during the second united front led to the clash of forces in what became known as the New Fourth Army Incident. For more on this, see Spence, *Search for Modern China*, pp. 463–66; and Johnson, *Peasant Nationalism and Communist Power*, pp. 136–40. See also, Tsou, *America's Failure in China, 1941–1950*, pp. 138–41. More critical accounts of the Guomindang's responsibility in constructing the whole scenario are in White and Jacoby, *Thunder Out of China*, pp. 75–76, 211–12. See also, White's *In Search of History*, pp. 110–16.

54. *Time*, Jan. 3, 1938, pp. 13–16.

55. *Time*, June 26, 1939, p. 30.

56. *Time*, Jan. 3, 1938, p. 15. For other comments that the New Life Movement was a "form of Christian Chinese Puritanism," see *Time*, Mar. 1, 1937, p. 21.

57. "The Army of the Republic of China," *Fortune*, Sept. 1941, p. 47.

58. Peck, *Two Kinds of Time*, p. 35.

59. Halberstam, *The Powers That Be*, p. 49.

Chapter Three

1. Iriye, *Across the Pacific*, p. 220.

2. Gallup, *The Gallup Poll: Public Opinion, 1935–1971*, 1:72. For additional information on American sympathy for China at this time, see also Steele, *The American People and China*, pp. 20–22. The Ohio floods received a 28.3 percent response; the events in China were next with 27.8 percent.

3. Gallup, *The Gallup Poll, 1935–1971*, 1:69, 159.

4. *Fortune*, July 1938, p. 80. The figures were 29.4 percent for Japan's attack upon China and 22.8 percent for Germany's *anschluss* in Austria.

5. Schaller, *The U.S. Crusade in China, 1938–1945*, p. 14.

6. For general information on United China Relief (which changed its name after World War II to United Service to China), see UCR-USC Papers, ABMAC Papers, and Indusco Papers.

7. *United China Relief, Inc., Statement by the Board of Directors*, p. 1, Indusco Papers, box 167.

8. All information is from *Basic Facts Concerning United China Relief, Inc.*, UCR-USC Papers, box 68. See also, *Five Years of United China Relief*, especially p. 2 for quote, UCR-USC Papers, box 48. A 1941 statement by the Board of Directors is available in Indusco Papers, box 167. For another account of Luce's role in assisting in the creation of UCR, see Swanberg, *Luce and His Empire*, pp. 183–84; Herzstein, *Henry R. Luce*, pp. 207–16.

9. *Basic Facts Concerning United China Relief, Inc.*, pp. 1–6.

10. Figures from *Five Years of United China Relief*, pp. 3–4; the quote is from p. 3. UCR-USC Papers, box 48.

11. UCR-USC Papers, box 48. For the years 1939–49, Luce himself contributed a total of over $93,000 to UCR. In addition, he also donated $25,000 over two years, 1937–38, to the National Emergency Committee for Chris-

tian Colleges in China. He contributed another $50,000 in the name of his father to the Luce Scholarship Fund for Yanjing University. The last two donations are documented in two letters: Allen Grover to B. A. Garside, Dec. 20, 1937; and Garside to Grover, Dec. 30, 1937, UBCHEA, box 14.

12. A list of New York donors to UCR as of Sept. 15, 1941, indicates that UCR's board of directors contributed a little under $150,000. Indusco Papers, box 168.

13. Letter, Luce to Secretary of State Hull, Aug. 5, 1941. Included with Luce's letter was a suggested draft for a letter from the Secretary of State to James G. Blaine of UCR. National Archives, 893.48/2138.

14. Letter, Hull to Luce, Sept. 5, 1941, National Archives, 893.48/2138. The last paragraph of Hull's response came directly from the tentative draft suggested by Luce in his earlier letter. Hull closed with the remark, "The kind sentiment which you were so good as to express in your last paragraph is much appreciated."

15. *Informal Report of Chairman James G. Blaine*, May 16, 1941, p. 8, Garside Papers, box 3.

16. *Five Years of United China Relief*, p. 6, UCR-USC Papers, box 48.

17. Maud Russell, "Encouraging Democracy in China," in "The Growth of Culture," pamphlet no. 15, reprint of a broadcast by Maud Russell, June 1941, MPC, box 401.

18. Peck, *Two Kinds of Time*, p. 166.

19. Press release of a statement made by John Garfield on behalf of Indusco, May 1, 1941, Indusco Papers, box 174.

20. For a more extensive discussion of the intentions and results of the Chinese Industrial Cooperative Association, see Peck, chaps. 7 and 8. See also, Eastman, *Seeds of Destruction*, p. 220. For a brief but positive and contemporaneous American account of the CIC, see Willkie, *One World*, p. 120.

21. *Time*, Apr. 22, 1940, p. 32.

22. Peck, pp. 163–70, 176–83.

23. No author, "Education in Wartorn China," pp. 11–15 in "The Growth of Culture," MPC, box 401.

24. "The New China," *Fortune*, Apr. 1941, p. 122.

25. Lewis S. C. Smythe, "Building for the Future," May 1941, MPC, box 401.

26. Hubert Freyn, "A Miniature Democracy: The Shanghai Boy Scouts Vocational School in Chongqing," MPC, box 401.

27. Dr. William P. Fenn, "Help China in Her Struggle," May 1941, pp. 5, 7, MPC, box 401.

28. J. A. Endicott, "Social Conditions in Wartime China," May 1941, p. 4, MPC, box 401.

29. Guest list obtained from an invitation to Walter Lippmann, Lippmann Papers, box 106.

30. Talk delivered by Clare Boothe Luce at United China Relief dinner, June 18, 1941, p. 4, UCR-USC Papers, box 95.

31. Ibid., p. 6.

32. "Part American rose" and "girl of the Golden West" would seem to be

a clear allusion to Belasco's play, and perhaps also to the Puccini opera, *La Fanciulla del West.* "Dreamy lotus flower" and "sullen tiger lily" could be allusions to two other Puccini heroines, Madama Butterfly and the Princess Turandot, both of whom, like Minnie in *La Fanciulla del West,* would no doubt have been recognized by Luce's audience. *Butterfly* had recently been performed by the Metropolitan Opera (Dec. 5, 1940); *Fanciulla del West's* most recent performance had been in 1931; *Turandot's* in 1929. See *Annals of the Metropolitan Opera, Chronology 1883–1985* (New York, 1985). I thank Shirley Taylor, Jane Adas, Lynn Berretoni, and Roy Domenico for their help in research on this interesting matter.

33. Letter, Swift to Luce, Apr. 14, 1941, p. 1, UCR-USC Papers, box 48.
34. MPC, box 231.
35. Ibid.
36. One figure estimates that over 136 million people saw the motion picture or print photograph of Ping Mei. See Fielding, *The American Newsreel, 1911–1967,* p. 260.
37. As quoted in Tuchman, *Stilwell and the American Experience in China,* p. 349.
38. Garside, "China Must Have Our Help—Now," Autumn 1941, UCR-USC Papers, box 41.
39. Charles H. Corbett, "A Vital Factor," Oct. 1941, UCR-USC Papers, box 52.
40. Garside, "China Must Have Our Help—Now," Autumn 1941, UCR-USC Papers, box 41.
41. Memorandum, Garside to Luce, Nov. 6, 1941, UCR-USC Papers, box 48.
42. The *Time* subscription letter was dated Nov. 8, 1941. The detail about getting behind on acknowledgments is taken from a Jan. 17, 1942, memo from Douglas Auchincloss to Garside, UCR-USC Papers, box 45. Swanberg, *Luce and His Empire,* p. 184, notes that Luce's appeal brought in some $240,000.
43. *Five Years of United China Relief,* p. 4, UCR-USC Papers, box 48.
44. Ibid., p. 6. International General Electric contributed $2,500 for 1941.
45. Iriye, *Across the Pacific,* pp. 185, 220.

Chapter Four

1. White, *In Search of History,* p. 130. See also Swanberg, *Luce and His Empire,* p. 189.
2. Dower, *War Without Mercy,* pp. 94–117, especially p. 98.
3. Ibid., p. 116.
4. Memo, Jan. 26, 1942, UCR-USC Papers, box 45.
5. Letter, Swift to W. R. Herod, Jan. 22, 1942, UCR-USC Papers, box 45.
6. See "China Week" memo, n.d. but sometime in the spring of 1942, UCR-USC Papers, box 52.
7. See Herod's letters to Davis, Mar. 9 and 25, 1942, UCR-USC Papers, box 63.

8. Letter, Davis to the President and Secretary of Each Rotary Club in the U.S.A., Feb. 2, 1942, UCR-USC Papers, box 63.

9. Letter, Davis to Herod, Feb. 21, 1942, UCR-USC Papers, box 63.

10. Telegram, Selznick to Bailey, Feb. 28, 1942, UCR-USC Papers, box 64.

11. The list of names is compiled from two memoranda, both dated Mar. 12, 1942, UCR-USC Papers, box 45. In its mention of Charlie Chaplin, the memo from Russell Whelan to Swift, Fletcher, Bailey, and Romily says that he would "make his first (or almost) radio appearance." The other memo, O. P. Swift to W. R. Herod, discusses how the show would be carried on the NBC Blue Network, which covered 100 stations throughout the country.

12. Mickey Rooney is mentioned in a memo from Whelan to Herod, Swift, Garside, Bailey, Fletcher, and Romily, Apr. 7, 1942, UCR-USC Papers, box 62. Whelan notes that Mickey Rooney is "the biggest box-office draw in the movies."

13. Memo from Swift, Mar. 27, 1942, UCR-USC Papers, box 62.

14. Letter, Luce to Swift, n.d. but sometime early in 1942, UCR-USC Papers, box 48.

15. All quotes from Whelan's memo to various UCR officers, Apr. 7, 1942, UCR-USC Papers, box 62.

16. Memo, Whelan to UCR officers, Mar. 12, 1942, UCR-USC Papers, box 45. Bailey also noted that the Chrysler Corporation agreed to publicize UCR's message during its advertising time on Major Bowes's program.

17. Letter, Bailey to Swift, Mar. 12, 1942, UCR-USC Papers, box 66. The circulation of the *Saturday Evening Post* in 1941 was slightly larger than *Life*'s—3.2 million compared with 2.9 million; *Reader's Digest* had the largest circulation.

18. ABMAC Papers, box 86.

19. Letter, Bailey to Swift, Mar. 12, 1942, UCR-USC Papers, box 66.

20. *NYT*, Apr. 12, 1942, p. 8E, and p. 34.

21. *WP*, Apr. 17, 1942, p. 3. See also issues of Apr. 14, p. 9, and Apr. 16, p. 16X.

22. Net sales and the net profit for the merchandising division break down as follows: for 1943, net sales were $117,285 with profits of $36,356; for 1944, net sales were $112,029 with profits of $43,441; for 1945, net sales were $116,482 with profits of $40,043. All figures are from UCR-USC Papers, box 38.

23. All quotes are taken from a kit of sample letters sent by UCR to local chairpersons, UCR-USC Papers, box 64.

24. From a pamphlet entitled *Studying China in American Elementary Schools*, prepared by Edna Ambrose and Kay Grimshaw at the Harvard Workshop in Social Studies, UCR-USC Papers, box 93. The pamphlet was issued by the Committee on Asiatic Studies of the American Council on Education, which included such noted historians as Dorothy Borg and John K. Fairbank, and was reprinted by UCR "to encourage greater attention on China in the American elementary schools."

25. *China Primer*, "Especially Prepared for Young America," reprinted and distributed by UCR, UCR-USC Papers, box 93.
26. "American Attitudes Towards China," n.d., UCR-USC Papers, box 65.
27. Text of the movie *Western Front*, UCR-USC Papers, box 50, especially pp. 10, 12, 13.
28. *Time*, Feb. 23, 1942, p. 19.
29. *Time*, June 1, 1942, pp. 18–21.
30. William E. Hocking, "A New East in a New World," *Fortune*, Aug. 1942, p. 124.
31. Theodore H. White, "Chiang Kai-shek," *Life*, Mar. 2, 1942, p. 80.
32. *Time*, June 22, 1942, p. 4.
33. *Time*, Dec. 28, 1942, p. 2.
34. *Time*, Jan. 5, 1943, p. 13.
35. *Time*, Jan. 26, 1942, p. 18. George Washington was, of course, as many readers of *Time* surely knew, childless. For another reference to Sun as "China's George Washington," see White, "Chiang Kai-shek," *Life*, Mar. 2, 1942, p. 72. *Time* in its issue of Dec. 7, 1942, called Sun Yat-sen "great."
36. *Life*, Mar. 2, 1942, p. 72. The legend below the last photograph takes special note of Roosevelt's picture.
37. "What Li Wen Saw," p. 18, MPC, box 231.
38. Ernest O. Hauser, "'Old Chiang' China's Strong Man," *Saturday Evening Post*, Aug. 28, 1943, p. 20.
39. *Time*, Mar. 2, 1942, p. 24.
40. *Time*, June 1, 1942, p. 20.
41. "We Are Still Taking 'A Hell of a Beating,'" *Fortune*, Aug. 1942, pp. 112–16.
42. "War in the East," *Fortune*, Dec. 1942, p. 100.
43. *Fortune*, Aug. 1942, p. 114.
44. See "China's Postwar Plans," *Fortune*, Oct. 1943, pp. 151–64. The figures presented for other industries were equally impressive: 20 million kilowatts of electricity, half generated by hydroelectric plants, the other half by fuel-burning plants; 80 million telephones; 12 million miles of telephone cable, which would require 1.5 million tons of copper; one million new homes as well as a precision industry that would need 90,000 tools from the West. All figures are from p. 154.
45. Garside, "What the Chinese Revolution Means to America," speech broadcast Oct. 10, 1944, pp. 1–4, UCR-USC Papers, box 65.
46. Memo by Pearl S. Buck attached to a letter from Buck to Mrs. Stimson, June 23, 1941, Stimson Papers, reel 104, plates 147–49.
47. "The People of China," created and distributed by the East and West Association, Mar. 1943, UCR-USC Papers, box 69. See also, Dr. Lin Mousheng, "The Meaning of the Chinese Revolution," Oct. 10, 1943, UCR-USC Papers, box 61.
48. For a brief description of the examination system, see Spence, *The Search for Modern China*, pp. 10–11. For a more detailed discussion of the broader social impact of the examination system in China and Vietnam, see

Woodside, *Vietnam and the Chinese Model*. Naquin and Rawski, in *Chinese Society in the Eighteenth Century* (p. 123), conclude that even though advancement in the Chinese examination system was ostensibly predicated upon merit, "the majority of degree-holders had degree-holding relatives." Many thanks to Jim Millward for bringing this last citation to my attention.

49. *China Fights Democracy*, speech given to the Indiana War Fund and the United War Fund of Indianapolis, n.d., but from the context, sometime during the summer of 1944, UCR-USC Papers, box 65. The speaker was probably Charles Edison or B. A. Garside, but there is no indication in the text. See also, "The People of China," a speech prepared for radio broadcast, n.d., UCR-USC Papers, box 65.

50. Letter, Edison to UCR state and local leaders, May 4, 1944, p. 2, UCR-USC Papers, box 34, and speech on behalf of National War Fund and UCR, Detroit Symphony Orchestra Program, Station WWJ, Oct. 8, 1944, p. 1, UCR-USC Papers, box 65.

51. "How to Spot a Jap," from *China Primer*, p. 16, UCR-USC Papers, box 93. The illustrations were drawn by cartoonist Milton Caniff of "Terry and the Pirates" fame and appeared in the Army's *Pocket Guide to China*. Caniff later drew another of his characters, Miss Lace, in an appeal for UCR.

52. *Life*, Mar. 1, 1943, p. 12. (*Time* that same week had Madame Chiang on the cover.) Even before Pearl Harbor, *Time* had commented disparagingly on the physical characteristics of Japanese soldiers. The Nov. 28, 1938 issue, p. 15, said, "The Chinese claim it is easy to spot a Japanese in Chinese uniform because the Japanese have a characteristic shuffle acquired in childhood as a result of wearing wooden sandals." A map in the Jan. 5, 1942, issue, p. 22, tracing the Japanese drive on the island of Borneo, showed a monkey hanging from the letters B and N.

53. Two points need to be made in connection with the twin issues of racism and paternalism. First, Dower in his study of racism and the Pacific War, has noted that after 1945, the wartime images of the Japanese were quickly replaced with paternalistic ones of the Japanese as children or domesticated pets; see *War Without Mercy*, pp. 302–3. The very change of these images from a racist to a paternalistic framework illustrates the close connection between the two concepts. Second, in his study of race and American society in the nineteenth century, Horsman has discussed the two views white Americans had of Indians. The first conception viewed them as Noble Savages and people worthy of preserving through assimilation. The second viewed them simply as savages, for whom extermination was the only realistic solution. The same sort of assimilationist-exterminationist dichotomy was part of the American view of the Chinese and Japanese during the war. See Horsman, *Race and Manifest Destiny*.

54. *The People of China*, from the East and West Association, p. 1, UCR-USC Papers, box 69.

55. "*China Fights for Democracy*," p. 1, n.d., UCR-USC Papers, box 65.

56. "The Future of Chinese-American Relations," n.d., but sometime after August 1945, p. 2, UCR-USC Papers, box 65.

57. Nathaniel Peffer, "Our Distorted View of China," *New York Times Magazine*, Nov. 7, 1943. Reprint of original article in MPC, box 230.

58. Memo by Garside, "Have We 'Over-Sold' China," Nov. 8, 1943, UCR-USC Papers, box 41.

59. Letter, McConaughy to UCR personnel, Oct. 1944, MPC, box 230. One wonders, however, how many Chinese could read and had radios with which to be "heartened" by Americans' celebrations.

60. Letter, Garside to Edison, Oct. 26, 1944, UCR-USC Papers, box 34.

61. Dr. T. F. Tsiang, "China at War," Dec. 13, 1943, MPC, box 231.

62. English translation of a four-minute recording made by UCR, n.d., but apparently after 1944 but before the end of the war, UCR-USC Papers, box 34.

63. The first figure is from a UCR memo, Mr. Hedrick to McConaughy, Oct. 16, 1943, UCR-USC Papers, box 66. The second figure is from a letter, Edison to governors in the U.S., May 31, 1944, Winslow Papers, box 28.

64. Report on Activities of the Speakers Bureau, 1944, Dec. 29, 1944, UCR-USC Papers, box 45.

65. All figures are from memo, Mary Ferguson to Garside, Mar. 12, 1945, pp. 1–6, UCR-USC Papers, box 45.

66. The total figure comes from financial statements in UCR-USC Papers, boxes 36, 37, and 52. The figures are for the years 1942, 1943, 1944, and 1945. The $3.25 million raised in 1941 is not included in the total figure since most of that occurred before Pearl Harbor. All figures are in U.S. dollars. The breakdown by year is as follows: 1942–$9.3; 1943–$6.6; 1944–$9.9; 1945–$11.8 (in millions of dollars).

67. This figure comes from UCR's monthly newspaper, *News of China* 4, no. 12 (Dec. 1945): 6. To ensure a favorable balance for next year's activities, UCR did not distribute all the money it raised every year; moreover, the funds made available do not include the last three months of 1945.

68. Speech of Thomas Hart Benton reprinted in Williams et al., eds., *America in Vietnam*, p. 11. Willkie also makes note of the seemingly endless possibilities in his *One World*, pp. 128, 130, 133, 145.

69. "The Future of Chinese-American Relations," p. 1, UCR-USC Papers, box 65.

70. Eric Johnston, "America's World Chance," *Reader's Digest*, June 1945, pp. 5–9.

71. Donald M. Nelson, "China Can Also Help Us," *Collier's*, May 12, 1945, pp. 13, 47.

72. As quoted in Koppes and Black, *Hollywood Goes to War*, pp. 68, 236. Emphasis mine.

73. *The Battle of China*, no. 6 in the series of seven information films titled "Why We Fight," directed by Frank Capra and produced by the War Department Signal Corps for the Morale Services Division. For more on how Capra was influenced by earlier documentaries, especially "The March of Time" series, see Culbert, "'Why We Fight': Social Engineering for a Democratic Society at War," in Short, ed., *Film and Radio Propaganda in World*

War II, pp. 173–91; and Bohn, *An Historical and Descriptive Analysis of the "Why We Fight" Series*, p. 239.

74. Dower, *War Without Mercy*, p. 17.

75. Culbert, p. 184. He cites a figure of "at least 3.75 million" by July 1, 1945.

76. *Chinese in America*, filmstrip no. 10, n.d., but probably 1942, Hutchinson Papers, box 1. Of the 121 frames, over 20 had pictures of or references to children.

77. *Tale of Two Cities*, filmstrip no. 135, June 26, 1945, p. 7, scene 124, Hutchinson Papers, box 1. These short films were distributed variously for public education.

78. Judd, "What Is the Truth About China?" Mar. 15, 1945, pp. 1–20, UCR-USC Papers, box 91.

79. "How Can Unity Be Achieved in China?" Feb. 22, 1945, broadcast over the Blue Network as part of Town Meeting, the Bulletin of America's Town Meeting of the Air, sponsored by the *Reader's Digest*, Judd Papers, box 34. Judd, who was chairman of the Board of the East and West Association, was always called upon to participate in these structured debates whenever the topic was China.

80. "What Is the Truth About China?" Mar. 15, 1945, UCR-USC Papers, box 91.

81. Judd, "What Goes On in China," address before the Economic Club of Detroit, Feb. 12, 1945, p. 2, Judd Papers, box 34.

82. Letter, Judd to Luce, May 22, 1944, Judd Papers, box 31.

83. Judd, "What Is the Truth About China?" Mar. 15, 1945, UCR-USC Papers, box 91.

Chapter Five

1. Quoted in Seagrave, *The Soong Dynasty*, p. 285. See also Hahn, *The Soong Sisters*.

2. Crow, *China Takes Her Place*, p. 149. Crow wrote numerous books on China and Sino-American relations, all with a determinedly optimistic view. The titles display the sentiment well: *Four Hundred Million Customers, I Speak for the Chinese*, and *The Chinese Are Like That*.

3. Scott, "Gender: A Useful Category of Historical Analysis," p. 1056.

4. Billington et al., *Culture and Society*, p. 125.

5. For much of the theoretical framework in this chapter, see Rosenberg, "Gender," in "A Round Table: Explaining the History of American Foreign Relations," pp. 116–24; Chafe, *The American Woman*; Hartmann, *The Home Front and Beyond*; Rupp, *Mobilizing Women for War*; Kaplan, "Left Alone with America," in Kaplan and Pease, eds.; and especially May, *Homeward Bound*.

6. For a detailed account of Charles Jones Soong's early life, see Seagrave, *The Soong Dynasty*, pp. 15–95; see also Hahn, *The Soong Sisters*, chaps. 1, 3, 5, 11. For a traditional, and inaccurate, account of Soong's early life, one re-

peated numerous times and the one used by Time Inc., see Burke, *My Father in China*, pp. 11–17, 29–35, 42–45. For the material on Meiling's early education, see Seagrave, pp. 109–15; Hahn, pp. 49–55.

7. Crow, *China Takes Her Place*, pp. 140–42; Hahn, p. 105.

8. Hahn, chap. 14. The events leading up to and including the marriage are also recounted in Berkov, *Strong Man of China*, chap. 13.

9. Schaller, *The United States and China in the Twentieth Century*, p. 44.

10. Letter, L. J. Birney to Johnson, Nov. 8, 1927, Johnson Papers, box 13. For more on American missionaries in China, see Thomson, Jr., *While China Faced West*, especially pp. 59–65 for more on William Johnson.

11. Johnson to Arlo (no last name given), Nov. 6, 1933, Johnson Papers, box 14. See also, Thomson, *While China Faced West*, pp. 61–63, 71–72, and 104, where he notes that the Nationalist government was especially interested in the missionaries administering former Communist-held areas. Lutz's *China and the Christian Colleges, 1850–1950*, chap. 8, deals with the issue of Christian missionaries and reform more generally.

12. Letter, Madame Chiang Kai-shek to Elizabeth Moore, Nov. 2, 1939, UBCHEA Papers, box 4. See also, Lutz, pp. 313–16; West, *Yenching University and Sino-Western Relations, 1916–1952*.

13. Thomson, *While China Faced West*, p. 185.

14. Of particular interest here is Time Inc. See, for example, *Time*, Dec. 21 and 28, 1936, and Jan. 4, 1937. See also, "The March of Time" newsreel "The Far East!" vol. 3 no. 5, RKO Radio Pictures Distributors, 1936.

15. The story ran in *NYT*, Apr. 16–24, 1937. One headline proclaimed, "Mme. Kai-shek [*sic*] Declares Future of China Hinged on Outcome of Rebellion at Sian." A good deal can be said to support such an assertion. But the story contained another subheading that was far more dubious: "Chiang's Mystery Cleared by Chiang's 'Diary of My Captivity in Si'an' and *His Wife's Own Story of How Her Diplomacy Saved His Life*."

16. Carnegie, *Dale Carnegie's Biographical Roundup*, p. 137. Many thanks go to John Krueckeberg for bringing this to my attention. Carnegie's account does mention that Madame Chiang's real accomplishment came in preventing Guomindang generals from attempting to use force to secure Chiang's release.

17. For more on this incident, see Thomson, *While China Faced West*, pp. 184–86; see also, Spence, *The Search for Modern China*, pp. 420–24, which mentions a telegram from Joseph Stalin that advocated saving Chiang's life; Van Slyke, *Enemies and Friends*, pp. 77–90; and Snow, *Red Star Over China*, pp. 411–12. Snow describes how Madame Chiang specifically thwarted efforts by Minister of War Ho Ying-chin to launch an expedition. For other contemporaneous accounts that emphasize Madame Chiang's role in securing her husband's release, see Hahn, *The Soong Sisters*, pp. 205–33, especially pp. 224–33; Bertram, *First Act in China*.

18. Mayling Soong Chiang, "Mme. Kai-shek [*sic*] Declares Future of China Hinged on Outcome of Rebellion at Sian," *New Haven Evening Register*, Apr. 16, 1937, p. 26, Yale-China Records, box 23. Madame Chiang's account of the

incident does, I believe, bear out my thesis that her image in the United States depended greatly upon promoting gender-defined characteristics—in this case, a cross between her duties as wife and mother.

19. Ibid., Madame Chiang wrote, "To calm him I opened the psalms and read to him until he drifted off to quiet sleep." Mayling Soong Chiang, "Mme. Chiang Braves Death Among Rebels Only to Find Them Penitent and Ashamed."

20. Hartmann, *The Home Front and Beyond*, p. 189.

21. May, *Homeward Bound*, pp. 61–62.

22. Rosenberg, "Gender," in "A Round Table;" p. 119. For the examples on Latin America, see Hunt, *Ideology and U.S. Foreign Policy*. The other image projected is one of other nations as children in need of American guidance and tutelage. Hunt discusses this attitude as well, and it is also pertinent for Sino-American relations.

23. As quoted by John Cournos in a review of a new novel by Preston Shoyer, " 'The Foreigners' and Other New Works of Fiction," *New York Times Book Review*, Mar. 15, 1942, p. 6.

24. In addition to Hartmann and May, see Rupp, *Mobilizing Women for War*, chap. 6.

25. Associated Press Biographical Service Sketch no. 2996, Nov. 1, 1942, UCR-USC Papers, box 91. Emphasis mine.

26. Mayling Soong Chiang, "First Lady of the East Speaks to the West," *New York Times Magazine*, Apr. 18, 1942, pp. 5, 36.

27. Letter, Madame Chiang Kai-shek to L. Currie, May 18, 1942, Currie Papers, box 1.

28. "China Emergent," *Atlantic Monthly*, May 1942, pp. 533–37.

29. For one invitation, see letter from United Board for Christian Higher Education in Asia to Madame Chiang Kai-shek, Feb. 25, 1937, UBCHEA Papers, box 4.

30. Stilwell, *The Stilwell Papers*, ed. White, p. 36. See also, Thorne, *Allies of a Kind*, p. 156. White House thinking obviously changed by the following September, however, when Eleanor Roosevelt sent an official invitation to Madame Chiang to visit. Lauchlin Currie played a role in the turnaround, since Roosevelt indicated that Madame Chiang's presence in the U.S. would "not only enable us to get to know you better and to secure a better appreciation of China's problems, but would also, in large measure, serve the ends of publicity." Letter, Eleanor Roosevelt to Madame Chiang Kai-shek, Sept. 16, 1942, Currie Papers, box 3.

31. Stilwell noted on July 1, 1942, that Madame Chiang had indicated to him that "she wanted to go the States soon," never mentioning medical treatment as the reason. See *Stilwell Papers*, p. 120. In her May 18, 1942, letter to Lauchlin Currie, Madame Chiang specifically mentioned a possible trip because of her gums and gastritis.

32. Letter, Price to Madame Chiang, Oct. 10, 1942, Price Papers, box 1. Emphasis mine.

33. For other examples of Madame Chiang's urgings for greater numbers

of American aircraft, dating back to July 1, 1942, see *Stilwell Papers*, pp. 120–23.

34. Sherwood, *Roosevelt and Hopkins*, pp. 660–61.

35. Edward T. Folliard, "Wife of China's Warrior Chieftain Roosevelts' Guest," *WP*, Feb. 18, 1943, p. 1.

36. "Missimo," editorial *WP*, Feb. 18, 1943, p. 8. Madame Chiang was always defined according to the relationship she had with her husband, and her service to him helped determine who she was. Joan Scott in her discussion of earlier approaches to gender notes, "This usage insists that the world of women is part of the world of men, created in and by it." See Scott, "Gender: A Useful Category of Historical Analysis," p. 1056.

37. This is a perfect example of Soong Meiling's versatility. As the dutiful wife, she fulfilled masculine ideas about women and women's roles; as a partner in the governing of China, she fulfilled ideas about women assuming positions of equality.

38. As quoted in Susman, *Culture as History*, p. 279. In compelling others to like her, as Marden instructed people to do, Madame Chiang clearly fitted within the changing nature of personality over character that Susman outlines. One notes that Madame Chiang's schooling in America occurred at the time of this transformation, which Susman places within the period from roughly 1900 to 1920.

39. The first woman to address Congress was Queen Wilhelmina of the Netherlands.

40. *Time*, Mar. 1, 1943, p. 23.

41. For the text of Madame Chiang's addresses before both the Senate and the House, see *NYT*, Feb. 19, 1943, p. 4.

42. Emphasis mine.

43. For a short analysis of *Thirty Seconds Over Tokyo*, see Koppes and Black, *Hollywood Goes to War*, pp. 266–67; May, *Homeward Bound*, chap. 3, is especially useful for the home front mentality.

44. *NYT*, Feb. 19, 1943.

45. In the official reprint of Madame Chiang's speech, the words Democracy and Democratic are capitalized; newspaper reprints used lower case.

46. Wendell Willkie expressed many of the same sentiments about the strength of the Japanese empire in his book *One World* (1943), pp. 105–8. Certain members of the American military also favored a Pacific-first strategy, namely, General Douglas MacArthur, Admiral Ernest King, and Admiral William D. Leahy. For more on this sentiment, see Thorne, *Allies of a Kind*, pp. 156–57, 163. Thorne points out (p. 156) that public opinion polls in February 1943 indicated that 53 percent viewed Japan as "the major foe."

47. W. H. Lawrence, "Mme. Chiang Asks Defeat of Japan, and House Cheers," *NYT*, Feb. 19, 1943, p. 1.

48. Nancy MacLennan, "Mme. Chiang Charms Congress," *NYT*, Feb. 19, 1943, p. 4.

49. "Lady from China," *NYT*, Feb. 19, 1943, p. 18.

50. Edward T. Folliard, "Congress Cheers Madame Chiang as Foe Drives to Crush China," *WP*, Feb. 19, 1943, pp. 1–2.

51. This type of prediction coincided with claims made consistently during the war by Major General Claire Chennault, the American commander of the U.S. Air Task Force in China, which grew out of the American Volunteer Group (AVG), more commonly referred to as the Flying Tigers. Among the numerous accounts available, see Feis, *China Tangle*, pp. 37–40, 51–52, 63–64, 133–34; Tuchman, *Stilwell and the American Experience in China*, pp. 215–20, 335–39, 356–57; and Chennault, *Way of a Fighter*.

52. "Speech to Congress," *Life*, Mar. 1, 1943, p. 26.

53. See Sherwood, *Hopkins and Roosevelt*, p. 706; Feis, *China Tangle*, p. 59; Tuchman, *Stilwell and the American Experience*, p. 352; and *Stilwell Papers*, p. 217. According to Stilwell, a defect in the plane's carburetor that caused it to ice up too easily had resulted in the loss of six planes by the middle of July.

54. See Roosevelt, *Public Papers and Addresses*, 1943, pp. 100–108. Quotes are from pp. 101, 103–4.

55. Ibid., p. 106.

56. Edward T. Folliard, "President Sees Blow at Japs Based in China," *WP*, Feb. 20, 1943, pp. 1, 3. For additional coverage, see Eliot Janeway, "Trials and Errors," *Fortune*, Apr. 1943, p. 62; and *Time*, Mar. 1, 1943, p. 10.

57. Hope Ridings Miller, "In the Capital Spotlight," *WP*, Feb. 25, 1943, p. 5B.

58. Harrison Forman, "In Chunking with China's Leaders," *New York Times Magazine*, Mar. 15, 1942, p. 6.

59. Anne O'Hare McCormick, "The Voice of China in the Lend-Lease Debate," *NYT*, Mar. 8, 1943, p. 14.

60. "Madame Chiang," *San Francisco Chronicle*, Mar. 25, 1943, p. 16.

61. Ruth A. Greene, "Chinese Women and the War," *The Bulletin*, Jan. 1944, pp. 5, 10, Greene Papers, box 6. This publication is obviously less important in many ways than the leading newspapers and widely circulated periodicals mentioned so far, but because it was for women only, Greene's analysis has particular significance; it indicates some of the fundamental assumptions that prevailed in discussions of Sino-American relations and Madame Chiang.

62. Claire M. Flanagan, "Service," letter to the editor, *San Francisco Chronicle*, Mar. 30, 1943, p. 12.

63. Sues, *Shark's Fins and Millet*, p. 64. Sues's account, though generally critical of the Guomindang and Madame Chiang, notes some of her many activities on behalf of China and the Nationalist government. Interestingly, Secretary of the Treasury Henry Morgenthau, Jr., mentioned this book early in 1944 when the Nationalist government was trying to secure another loan from the United States. See Committee on the Judiciary, *Morgenthau Diary (China)*, 89th Cong., 1st sess., Feb. 2, 1965, p. 1022. For Madame Chiang's role in the New Life Movement, see Thomson, *While China Faced West*, chap. 7.

64. More than one American observer noted Madame Chiang's habit of frequently interrupting while translating to offer her own opinions. For examples, see *Stilwell Papers*, pp. 120–21; *Morgenthau Dairy (China)*, pp. 460–61. During one period in the war, she served as liaison between the generalissimo and the American Army in China, passing along messages between the two. Of this practice, one observer noted, "This is extraordinarily stupid as Madame Chiang will, if she feels it expedient, hold up messages." Letter from Sol Adler in *Morgenthau Dairy*, p. 1134.

65. Crow, *China Takes Her Place*, pp. 148–49. Crow's explanation of Madame Chiang's duties in terms related to traditional women's responsibilities is consistent with William Chafe's findings on how certain American manufacturers came to understand women workers' abilities to handle various industrial tasks: "The ease with which women assumed their new responsibilities challenged many of the conventional stereotypes of women's work. Employers resorted to traditional imagery to explain women's success, claiming that an overhead crane operated 'just like a gigantic wringer,' and that the winding of wire spools in electrical factories was very much like crocheting." See Chafe, *The American Woman*, pp. 138–39; Rupp makes mention of this as well, p. 152. Minutes of meetings that Madame Chiang chaired do not support Crow's gendered reading. A memo put together by Brigadier General Clayton Bissell of a meeting held on July 2, 1942, clearly indicates that Madame Chiang took charge of the discussion in much the same way that any officer would have done, requesting information on certain types of aircraft, raising pertinent questions and so forth, all in an effort to outline a plan for a 500-airplane program for China. Currie Papers, box 4.

66. May-ling Soong Chiang, *China Shall Rise Again*, p. 59.

67. Swanberg, *Luce and His Empire*, pp. 200–203. He notes especially the arrangements made by UCR for Chicago. Although the organization had secured a floor of the Palmer House free of charge, Madame Chiang's nephew insisted that she have the best, which he understood to be the Drake. For this, UCR had to pay.

68. The crowd figure for City Hall is from *NYT*, Mar. 2, 1943, p. 1. The Chinatown figure is from *NYHT*, Mar. 2, 1943, p. 12, and *NYT*, same date, p. 3.

69. "The First Lady of China," *NYHT*, Mar. 2, 1943, p. 18.

70. "At Stake—China's Confidence," *NYHT*, Mar. 2, 1943, p. 18.

71. The list of guests is compiled from an account by *New York Herald-Tribune* reporter Marguerite Higgins, who was part of the select group that saw Madame Chiang. See "Nine Governors Pay Brief Call on Mrs. Chiang," *NYHT*, Mar. 3, 1943, p. 13. For another account of the evening, that is far less charitable toward Madame Chiang, see Swanberg, *Luce and His Empire*, pp. 201–2. Willkie in *One World* speaks of Madame Chiang's "pleasant but firm authority" (p. 132); see also pp. 139–41. According to Willkie's account, it was his suggestion while visiting China in 1942 that led to Madame Chiang's tour of the United States a year later: "We would listen to her as to no one else. With wit and charm, a generous and understanding heart, a gracious and

beautiful manner and appearance, and a burning conviction, she is just what we need as a visitor."

72. Madame Chiang's refusal to attend the dinner has been described by some commentators as one episode, among many, of her haughty and condescending manner; see Swanberg, pp. 200–201, and Tuchman, pp. 351–53, for more on this and other incidents. In this context, one example should be mentioned. Madame Chiang traveled with her own silk sheets, which were changed daily, twice if she napped in the afternoon. Some observers have commented that the sheets were an example of her insistence on being treated like royalty, but supporters argued that Madame Chiang's skin condition (which she did in fact have) necessitated frequent applications of an oily lotion that stained the sheets. According to the latter accounts, Madame Chiang brought her own sheets for convenience (silk ones did not stick to her skin as readily), silk was cheaper in China so expense was another concern, and she also did this out of courtesy to her hosts (so as not to ruin their sheets). These sorts of niggling criticism rarely got into public print at the time, and though they have been discussed in more recent historical accounts, they seem quite insignificant within the larger context of Sino-American relations. For a response to some of these criticisms, see Garside, "Madame Chiang Kai-shek as a Human Being," especially p. 5, ABMAC Papers, box 5.

73. The figure of 17,000 is from "Mme. Chiang Voices China's Resolution to Continue Fight," *NYT*, Mar. 3, 1943, p. 1. The 20,000 figure is from John G. Rogers, "Mrs. Chiang Asks for Victory Without Hate," *NYHT*, Mar. 3, 1943, p. 1. The event was also broadcast over the Columbia and Mutual radio networks.

74. "Mme. Chiang Voices China's Resolution to Continue to Fight," *NYT*, Mar. 3, 1943, p. 13.

75. "Our Neighbor China," *NYT*, Mar. 3, 1943, p. 22.

76. *Time*, Mar. 15, 1943, p. 17.

77. "May Ling Soong Chiang," *Vogue*, Apr. 15, 1943. This article, not surprisingly, discussed her choice of clothing, but also proclaimed her speech before Congress: "So deep ran the heroine worship, so important was her mission, so stirring was her appeal, both intellectually and as a woman, that there were moments when it was necessary to remind Americans of her program." See p. 36. For other *Vogue* coverage, see "Chinese Women in America," *Vogue*, June 1, 1942; Helen Kuo, "The China You Don't Know," *Vogue*, Sept. 1, 1942: "The truth is that China has a large percentage of middle-class people just as has America and France," p. 83; "Mme. Wellington Koo," *Vogue*, Jan. 1, 1943.

78. "'There Must Be No Bitterness,'" *NYHT*, Mar. 4, 1943, p. 18.

79. Martha Murphy, "Mme. Chiang Receives $68,087 War Aid Fund in Chinatown," *Chicago Daily Tribune*, Mar. 22, 1943, p. 1. This article mentioned that although Madame Chiang spoke in Mandarin whereas most of her audience spoke Cantonese, "no one seemed to have difficulty understanding her."

80. Letter, Yu Zunji to Madame Chiang Kai-shek, Mar. 23, 1943, Koo Papers, box 156.

81. Gene Sherman, "Mme. Chiang 'Captures' City," *Los Angeles Times*, Apr. 1, 1943, p.1.

82. See *Life*, Apr. 19, 1943, pp. 36–37.

83. "Madame Chiang in Hollywood," ibid., pp. 34–35.

84. Kimmis Hendrick, "The Country Speaks: California," newspaper and exact date unknown, UCR-USC Papers, box 100.

85. Letter, Price to Madame Chiang Kai-shek, Aug. 27, 1943, Price Papers, box 1.

86. See Elizabeth Green and Craighill Handy, "Two Great Ambassadors of the New Order: Anson Burlingame and Mei-ling Chiang," *South Atlantic Quarterly*, Oct. 1943, pp. 391–400.

87. Tuchman, pp. 375–81; *Stilwell Papers*, pp. 211–12, 215.

88. Proposed Message for General Stilwell's Eyes Only from General Marshall, Oct. 19, 1943, Marshall Papers, box 60.

89. For more on this, see Tuchman, chap. 15, and *Stilwell Papers*, pp. 223–36. On the subject of T. V. Soong, Lt. General Brehon Somervell wrote to Marshall, "I was quite unprepared for T. V. Soong's flat statement in Delhi that the Generalissimo would have no more of Stilwell and that he would demand his release." Somervell to Marshall, Oct. 24, 1943, Marshall Papers, box 60.

90. *Stilwell Papers*, pp. 224, 226. Stilwell quoted Madame Chiang as saying, "We should put everything aside and concentrate on the Army. What good will politics and the youth movement do us if we lose?"

91. Ibid., p. 231.

92. Ibid., pp. 228, 232–33. Feis comes to the same conclusion: "It seems to have been the animated opposition of [Madame Chiang] and her sister, Madame Kung, that drove the Generalissimo to cancel at the last moment the message he had asked Somervell to send to Washington asking for Stilwell's recall." See *China Tangle*, p. 78.

93. Madame Chiang was perceived by some Americans as the cogovernor of China with her husband even before the war. As early as 1937, the *New York Times Magazine* noted that she had been "termed his unofficial Foreign Minister. When he receives foreigners she translates for him into English with a clipped London accent, although she is a graduate of Wellesley. Whenever possible, visitors are persuaded to see her instead of him." See Paula Lecler, "Chiang Adds to His Exploits," *New York Times Magazine*, Jan. 3, 1937, p. 6.

94. For a listing of the meetings, see *FRUS: The Conferences at Cairo and Teheran, 1943*, pp. 307, 322–23, 349, 366, 367. It is clear from the list of the participants that Madame Chiang was the only person there who spoke both Chinese and English.

95. *Stilwell Papers*, p. 263.

96. Memorandum of Conversation, by the Secretary of State, June 28, 1943, *FRUS: China*, 1943, pp. 65–67.

97. Christmas Eve Fireside Chat on Teheran and Cairo Conferences, Dec. 24, 1943, Roosevelt, *Public Papers and Addresses*, 1943, p. 556.

98. I arrived at my estimate—certainly a conservative one—by adding the

estimates from the various parades and speaking engagements Madame Chiang attended during her tour.

99. May, *Homeward Bound*, p. 90.

100. I am combining May's work with Rosenberg, *Spreading the American Dream*, especially chap. 10, to show how domestic notions radiated outward during the war.

101. On Guomindang deficiencies, see Isaacs, *No Peace for Asia*, especially pp. 43–80; and White and Jacoby, *Thunder Out of China*. Some of the unflattering, but accurate, accounts of conditions in China began to appear during the war, particularly after Stilwell's dismissal in the fall of 1944; Isaacs's articles in *Newsweek* in November 1944 were especially effective in offering a far more honest portrait. On the whole, however, Chiang's China still received considerable support from various American media organizations, most notably Henry Luce's Time Inc.

102. Gallup, *The Gallup Poll: Public Opinion, 1935–1971*, 1: 775. The question asked from Nov. 28, until Dec. 3, 1948, was, "What women do you admire most?" Madame Chiang ranked second; Sister Kenny and Clare Boothe Luce ranked third and fourth, respectively.

103. Ibid., p. 885. In the 1949 poll, Madame Chiang placed behind Eleanor Roosevelt, Sister Kenny, Clare Boothe Luce, and Helen Keller.

Chapter Six

1. For more on this, see Schaller, *The U.S. Crusade in China, 1938–1945*, chap. 5.

2. China revisionists and Luce supporters have argued, quite unconvincingly, that Luce had trouble deciding whether or not to publish Buck's article and in the end acquiesced only because he did not want to be criticized for giving the wrong impression to the American people about China. This argument has been made by Elson, *The World of Time Inc.*, p. 120, and also by Neils, *China Images in the Life and Times of Henry Luce*, pp. 104–6. Both these writers seem to find Buck's article far more critical of Chiang and his government than it really is; indeed, it blames the United States, not Chiang or the Nationalist government, for conditions in China. Moreover, as Elson notes, Time Inc.'s policy on China did not change, although the possibility of such a change was considered. Like many of Luce's supporters, Elson and Neils indicate that Luce had an open mind when it came to China because he talked about changing policy at one point or another. But Luce did not change his policy, because he could not. As Elson points out, Time Inc.'s policy toward the Soongs stayed the same. Luce said, "It ill befits us . . . to go sour on them" (Time Inc. memo quoted in Elson, pp. 121–22). Even John K. Fairbank, however, one of the most respected American scholars on Sino-American relations, misread Buck's article, writing that it, along with a piece by Hanson Baldwin in the *New York Times* and another by T. A. Bisson in *Far Eastern Survey*, jolted Americans out of their sentimental feelings about China in the summer of 1943; see Fairbank, *Chinabound*, p. 253. Americans did eventu-

ally receive a vastly different picture of China, but that would not come until General Joseph Stilwell's dismissal in the fall of 1994; and even then, the acrimony and unfavorable publicity over Stilwell's dismissal must be kept in the context of the larger effort to portray the Chinese in a favorable light.

3. Pearl S. Buck, "A Warning About China," *Life*, May 10, 1943, pp. 53–54.

4. This last comment foreshadowed similar tactics used during the Cold War to suggest that the Kremlin looked favorably upon certain American (in)actions. For all Luce's supposed balance in publishing Buck's article, it should be noted that in a biographical sketch on the writer that accompanied the article, *Life* displayed its insidious and subtle talent for disparaging people with whom it did not agree. The sketch mentioned Buck's maiden name, Sydenstricker, as if to suggest complete and total knowledge of the particular subject. It also took note of the fact that Buck was married for a second time; Luce publications often mentioned divorce in such a way as to cast moral aspersions—truly ironic given Luce's divorce of his first wife so that he could marry Clare Boothe. Third, *Life* pointed out that Buck had not been in China since 1934, although it quickly added that her understanding of the Chinese people was considerable. And at the end of the sketch, *Life* pointed out that Buck did not find fault with China for the conditions there; rather, *Life* approvingly noted that she placed "the blame where it belongs": on the United States and the nation's inability "to understand the necessity of helping China."

5. As quoted in Halberstam, *The Powers That Be*, p. 78.

6. For example, see Knightley, *The First Casualty*, pp. 277–79, and Fairbank, *Chinabound*, p. 253.

7. Hanson W. Baldwin, "Too Much Wishful Thinking About China," *Reader's Digest*, Aug. 1943, pp. 63–67.

8. Ernest O. Hauser, "China Gets Ready to Win," *Saturday Evening Post*, Feb. 26, 1944, p. 97.

9. Diary-type entry for May 27, 1943, Willauer Papers, box 5.

10. Currie's comment is worth quoting in full: "Madame hit the bell when she first came to Washington and addressed both houses of Congress. Since then, however, the reaction is becoming more unfavorable. She has nothing particularly new to say in her many speeches and they are becoming increasingly erudite. The New York Times on March 28, reporting on her big speech in San Francisco, had a sub-heading as follows: 'CITES HUSSITE COLLAPSE.' The speech itself contained many pearls. I liked this one: 'The present Nazi and Shintoistic indoctrinations of mendacity and deceit I attribute to the disjunctive reasoning of warped minds, and they cannot endure; for only the truth and the conviction of the truth of human postulates can withstand the onslaughts of time and violence.'" Letter, Currie to Vincent, Mar. 29, 1943, p. 1, Currie Papers, box 1.

11. Memo, "Some Reflections on Sino-American Relations," June 9, 1942, pp. 2–3, Currie Papers, box 5.

12. Letter, Currie to Vincent, May 13, 1942, Currie Papers, box 1.

13. Currie Papers, box 3.

14. "Confidential Resumé of Interchange Between the President and Congressman Walter H. Judd Concerning Madame Chiang Kai-shek," n.d., schedule A, Soong Papers, box 30. The memo indicated that Roosevelt assumed his remarks were confidential, but that Judd passed them along to T.V. "as a matter of friendship."

15. For more on the Wallace mission to China, see Schaller, *U.S. Crusade in China*, pp. 160–64.

16. *WP*, July 10, 1944, p. 3. *Washington Post* columnist Hope Ridings Miller, who had written effusively about Madame Chiang during her 1943 visit, repeated much of Pearson's information in her column of Aug. 8, 1944, with greater details about Chiang's romantic liaisons. But, she concluded: "Americans can count on it that with or without more material assistance than America is giving now, Chiang will emerge recognized as China's man of Destiny. How much better then, it would be to help him achieve his ideal of a united and progressive China." Newspaper clipping, Price Papers, box 2.

17. Schaller, *U.S. Crusade in China*, pp. 134–37.

18. Letter, Alsop to Hopkins, Mar. 1, 1943, pp. 11, 19, Hopkins Papers, box 331.

19. Ibid., p. 18.

20. Chennault himself did not hesitate to press his case to Roosevelt. In a letter to Harry Hopkins early in 1944, Chennault insisted that if his forces had adequate supplies they could take "a heavy and perhaps crippling toll of Japan's air power." See letter, Chennault to Hopkins, Feb. 8, 1944, Hopkins Papers, box 331.

21. Letter, Alsop to Hopkins, May 7, 1943, Hopkins Papers, box 331.

22. Memo, with attachment, Currie to Hopkins, Apr. 13, 1943, Hopkins Papers, box 331.

23. Memorandum, Currie to Hopkins, with complete and uncensored report of the Henan famine by Theodore H. White attached, May 28, 1943, Hopkins Papers, box 331.

24. White, *In Search of History*, p. 154.

25. Theodore H. White, "Until the Harvest Is Reaped," *Time*, Mar. 22, 1943, p. 19.

26. For more on Operation Ichigo, see Ch'i, *Nationalist China at War*, pp. 68–81.

27. White and Jacoby, *Thunder Out of China*, pp. 177–78.

28. Schaller, *U.S. Crusade in China*, pp. 159–60. See also Ch'i, who notes (p.80), "The only bright spot in China's military performance in 1944 was the expeditionary force in Burma" under Stilwell's command.

29. Schaller, *U.S. Crusade in China*, pp. 164–75.

30. Memo, Hopkins to the President, with attachment, Sept. 8, 1944, Map Room Files, box 165.

31. Memo, Davies to Hopkins, Dec. 31, 1943, p. 1, Hopkins Papers, box 334.

32. "The China Crisis," *NYT*, Nov. 1, 1944, p. 22.

33. "China's Crisis," *NYT*, Nov. 2, 1944, p. 18. Emphasis mine.

34. "Topics of the Times," *NYT*, Nov. 4, 1944, p. 14. This piece went on to discuss whether it was more accurate to characterize Chiang as a reactionary or as a conservative. "Now there is no question that on domestic issues Chiang is conservative," the *Times* said, and it noted that on his treatment of the Chinese Communists, Chiang had been called a "Fascist." "Chiang is a 'reactionary,'" the *Times* conceded, "but he has refused to bargain with Japan."

35. "A Crisis, Not a Failure," *NYT*, Nov. 4, 1944, p. 14.

36. "Dilemma Over China," *WP*, Nov. 2, 1944, p. 8.

37. Barnet Nover, "Chiang as Leader," *WP*, Nov. 2, 1944, p. 8.

38. Brooks Atkinson, "Stilwell Recall Bares Rift with Chiang," *NYT*, Oct. 31, 1944, pp. 1, 4.

39. Harold Isaacs, "One Man's Fight Against Corruption: Story Behind the Stilwell Incident," *Newsweek*, Nov. 13, 1944, pp. 44–47.

40. Harold Isaacs, "Ignorant Men and Modern Weapons: The Inside Story of the Chinese Army," *Newsweek*, Nov. 20, 1944, pp. 44–48.

41. Thoburn Wiant's article appeared under the title, "China in Dictator's Grip," *NYT*, Nov. 1, 1944, p. 2; and as "Chiang's Fear of China's Reds Saps His War," *WP*, Nov. 1, 1944, p. 1.

42. *Christian Century*, Nov. 15, 1944, p. 1.

43. "Censorship and Stupidity," *Wall Street Journal*, Nov. 1, 1944, p. 6.

44. "The Truth About China," *Chicago Daily Tribune*, Nov. 3, 1944, p. 12.

45. Raymond Moley, "Last Minute Scares," *Wall Street Journal*, Nov. 3, 1944, p. 6.

46. Pearl S. Buck, "'The Darkest Hour' in China's History," *New York Times Magazine*, Dec. 17, 1944, pp. 9, 45–46.

47. Letter, Price to Generalissimo, Nov. 16, 1944, Price Papers, box 1.

48. Draft of a memo, Price to Chiang Kai-shek, Feb. 4, 1945, Price Papers, box 1.

49. Currie's memo to Roosevelt notes of Isaacs's evaluation, "I don't imagine, however, it could have passed the Army censors to get to Newsweek." See memorandum, Currie to the President, with seven-page attachment, Jan. 17, 1945, President's Secretary File, box 27.

50. All the quotes are from two reports to General of the Army George C. Marshall from Dan I. Sultan, Feb. 13, 1945, pp. 1–4, and Albert C. Wedemeyer, dated Feb. 16, 1945, pp. 1–4, President's Secretary File, box 27.

51. Kimball, *The Juggler*.

52. *F.D.R.: His Personal Letters, 1928–1945*, p. 1468.

53. Truman, *Memoirs*, 2: 60. Truman also noted that Roosevelt's build-up of China was pushed because "he looked to the future and wanted to encourage the Chinese people" (p. 62).

Chapter Seven

1. For more on this line of thought, see Hodgson, *America in Our Time*, pp. 18–20; GNP figures are from p. 20.

2. All figures are from the appropriate year of *N. W. Ayer & Son's Directory of Newspapers and Periodicals.*

3. Goldman, *The Crucial Decade and After*, pp. 5–6.

4. For more information on the Truman administration's decision to support Chiang, see Schaller, *The U.S. Crusade in China*, chap. 12, especially, pp. 274–89.

5. Letter, Charles Warner to Mr. Forrestal Secretary of War [*sic*], n.d., but sometime in Nov. 1945, Forrestal Papers, box 63.

6. For more on the popular sentiment, see Goldman, pp. 28–32; see also, Steele, *The American People and China*, pp. 31–32.

7. Letter, James Adams to Luce, Nov. 21, 1945, attached to letter, Luce to Forrestal, Nov. 27, 1945, Forrestal Papers, box 63.

8. *Life*, Nov. 19, 1945, p. 37.

9. White, *In Search of History*, p. 241.

10. Ibid., pp. 245–54.

11. Letter, Baker to Johnson, May 30, 1947, Johnson Papers, box 18. United China Relief changed its name to United Service to China after the war and went under that title at the time of Baker's writing.

12. Letter, Price to Madame Chiang Kai-shek, Jan. 21, 1947, Price Papers, box 1.

13. As quoted in Halberstam, *The Powers That Be*, p. 85. Luce was obviously wrong in his recollection. Marshall first went to China in December 1945, nearly a year before White's and Jacoby's book was published in the fall of 1946. Marshall may have read it while he finished up his mission late in 1946, but he could not have set foot in China with it in his hand.

14. White, *In Search of History*, pp. 254–57.

15. All figures are from the appropriate year of *N. W. Ayer & Son's Directory of Newspapers and Periodicals.* In 1945, *Time* had a circulation figure of 1,181,523 and was published on every continent except Antarctica. *Life*'s figure was 4,040,300; *Fortune*'s was 180,791. The figures for *Time, Life,* and *Fortune* for 1946 were, respectively, 1,554,323; 4,699,688; and 188,000.

16. Eric Hodgins interview, Eisenhower Project, Columbia Oral History Collection.

17. *Time*, Sept. 3, 1945, p. 30.

18. For more on the assistance provided by the United States to the Nationalist government, see Department of State, *United States Relations with China*, pp. 311–12. See also, Spence, *The Search for Modern China*, pp. 484–85; Feis, *The China Tangle*, p. 362; Schaller, *The United States and China in the Twentieth Century*, pp. 109–12; Tsou, *America's Failure in China, 1941–1950*, pp. 305–11. Tsou discusses the limitations of the American assistance, but at one point concludes, "Despite these self-imposed limits, American actions achieved spectacular results" (p. 308).

19. *Time*, Sept. 3, 1945, p. 30.

20. Special Report for Time, Inc. by Alfred W. Jones, Sept. 17, 1945, p. 47, UCR-USC Papers, box 46.

21. Ibid., p. 90.   22. Ibid., p. 47.

23. Ibid., p. 48.   24. *Life*, Sept. 3, 1945, p. 28.

25. See Spence, *Search for Modern China*, pp. 491–98.

26. For more on the different strategies pursued by the Nationalist forces and the Chinese Communists, see ibid., chap. 18. See also, Eastman, *Seeds of Destruction*, chap. 7; and Sheridan, *China in Disintegration*, pp. 269–79.

27. For more on Chiang's postwar strategy, see Eastman, chap. 7. For the recommendations of American military advisers in China, see *United States Relations with China*, pp. 312–14.

28. *Time*, Nov. 19, 1945, p. 30.

29. *Life*, Nov. 19, 1945, p. 36.

30. The differences between Cantonese and Mandarin are so significant as to make them different languages. Other dialects within China vary as much, making *Life*'s claim silly.

31. *Time*, Dec. 10, 1945, p. 18. As late as October 1945, Luce planned to run a cover story on Hurley, but the general's precipitous resignation evidently squashed that idea. See Swanberg Papers, box 17. Swanberg's notes are from the John Shaw Billings Papers, entry dates for Oct. 24.

32. For assessments on Hurley's sanity, see Schaller, *U.S. Crusade in China, 1938–1945*, p. 291. See also MacKinnon and Friesen, *China Reporting*, pp. 141–44.

33. Memo, Wedemeyer to Chiang Kai-shek, Dec. 12, 1945, schedule A, T. V. Soong Papers, box 34.

34. "What Should Be Our Policy in China?" America's Town Meeting, Dec. 27, 1945, Judd Papers, box 35.

35. Ibid. There are no page numbers because the transcript of the program is in tearsheet form.

36. Millis, ed., *The Forrestal Diaries*, p. 113.

37. *Time*, Dec. 31, 1945, p. 29.

38. *Life*, Dec. 17, 1945, pp. 107–8.

39. Ibid., p. 116. See also, *Life*, Dec. 24, 1945, p. 24.

40. *Life*, Dec. 17, 1945, pp. 116–18.

41. Letter, Garside to Luce, Nov. 16, 1945, UCR-USC Papers, box 48.

42. Memorandum, Garside to James Crider, Dec. 13, 1945, pp. 1, 3, UCR-USC Papers, box 48.

43. Press release of statement by McConaughy, Nov. 15, 1945, p. 1, UCR-USC Papers, box 52.

44. Letter, Luce to Eric Johnston, Jan. 18, 1946, UCR-USC Papers, box 48.

45. Documents that partially record this change include, Points in Favor of New Name for United China Relief, n.d.; letter, McConaughy to Dr. Grady Gammage, July 30, 1946; letter, Edison to Farley, July 29, 1946; and Results of Conference consisting of six members of UCR, n.d.; all from UCR-USC Papers, box 69. The results of the conference also listed five campaign slogans, including "There's a China in your future."

46. Letter, McConaughy to Gammage, July 30, 1946, UCR-USC Papers, box 69.

47. For more on Chinese actions in Vietnam immediately after World War

II, see Kahin, *Intervention*, pp. 18–20. Chinese Communist rule has not been much different. The latest example came in 1979 when China tried to punish Vietnam for its failure to act properly. See Chanda, *Brother Enemy*, pp. 356–62.

48. As quoted in Karnow, *Vietnam*, p. 153.

49. See W. Cohen, *America's Response to China*, pp. 55–58, 73; Varg, *The Making of a Myth*, pp. 98–99. For an account of anti-Christian and anti-missionary sentiment in China for an earlier time period, see P. Cohen, *China and Christianity*, and also Hunt, *The Making of a Special Relationship*.

50. All quotes from Meeting—June 14, 1946, p. 1, UCR-USC Papers, box 55.

51. All quotes are from Speakers' Kit, n.d., but sometime after the reorganization; UCR-USC Papers, box 64. McConaughy's statement also used the historical analogy technique, comparing America's early history and the problems faced by the young republic with the situation in postwar China in an effort to draw out the common links between the two nations.

52. Discussion of UCR 1946–1947 Movie Program, July 31, 1946, p. 1, UCR-USC Papers, box 50. This was during the time the name change was being considered, thus the use of UCR.

53. Preshowing remarks for *Bridge to Yinhsi*, n.d., UCR-USC Papers, box 55.

54. All quotes are from Post-showing Remarks, n.d., UCR-USC Papers, box 55.

55. Memorandum, Helen Cornelius to Wayland Towner, Mar. 25, 1947; and an unsigned, undated memorandum, probably Mar. 7, 1947; both in UCR-USC Papers, box 55.

56. Results of the Poll Taken at Town Hall, Dec. 2, 1946, UCR-USC Papers, box 55. The breakdown is as follows: 45.6 percent, excellent; 28.1 percent, very good; 17.5 percent, good; 3.5 percent, fair; 5.3 percent, poor. Another question found that nearly 95 percent of the audience rated the entire evening's program as good, very good, or excellent.

57. Post-showing Remarks, UCR-USC Papers, box 55.

58. In answering the question, "In the progress and welfare of which 2 or 3 countries do you think Americans ought to be particularly interested, outside of North and South America?" Pottstonians responded in the two surveys as follows: China, 23 percent and 25 percent; Great Britain, 16 percent and 15 percent; Germany, 15 percent and 14 percent; the Soviet Union, 13 percent and 16 percent; and France, 13 percent and 14 percent. *Public Opinion Survey*, no. 1, November 1946, polls no. 2 and no. 3, UCR-USC Papers, box 55.

59. Preshowing remarks for *Bridge to Yinhsi*, n.d., UCR-USC Papers, box 55. Also included in a USC press release on Mar. 10, 1947.

60. Memo, H. Cornelius to W. Towner. Points Covered at the Meeting of the Pottstown Poll in Wayland D. Towner's Office, February 11th, Feb. 14, 1947, UCR-USC Papers, box 55. Emphasis in text is mine.

61. Memo, Cornelius to Towner, Mar. 4, 1947, ABMAC Papers, box 81.

. 62. Pottstown Project, Jan. 15, 1947, findings section, p. 1, UCR-USC Papers, box 55.

63. Ibid., p. 2.

64. See *Time*, Mar. 25, 1946, pp. 28–30.

65. For more on the negotiations and the situation in China, see Department of State, *United States Relations with China*, pp. 136–52, hereafter cited as *The White Paper*. See also, Melby, *The Mandate of Heaven*, pp. 86–164. Melby had a large hand in writing *The White Paper*, and his account closely parallels it.

66. Eastman, *Seeds of Destruction*, p. 159. For more on the number of arms, the amount of ammunition, and the value of the services provided by the United States after V-J Day, see *The White Paper*, pp. 354, 1048–53.

67. Henry R. Lieberman, *NYT*, Sept. 11, 1947, p. 17. This report, dated four months after the embargo was lifted, suggests Chiang's confidence, for one assumes that he would not have made such a statement had his troops been in need of arms or ammunition.

68. *The White Paper*, p. 176; Melby, p. 178.

69. *Time*, July 1, 1946, p. 35. 70. *Time*, Sept. 30, 1946, p. 38.

71. *Time*, Oct. 21, 1946, p. 36. 72. *Time*, Oct. 28, 1946, p. 42.

73. *Time*, Nov. 18, 1946. 74. *Time*, Nov. 11, 1946, p. 37.

75. *Life*, Sept. 2, 1946, p. 36. As has already been noted, the Soviets did assist the Communists in certain ways, but their aid was far less than that of the United States for Chiang.

76. *Time*, Sept. 16, 1946, p. 35. 77. *Life*, Sept. 2, 1946, p. 37.

78. *Time*, Sept. 16, 1946, p. 35. 79. *Life*, Oct. 7, 1946, p. 37.

80. *Time*, Dec. 23, 1946, p. 34.

Chapter Eight

1. For more on the rapidly changing situation in China after 1945, see Spence, *Search for Modern China*, chap. 18. See also, Bianco, *Origins of the Chinese Revolution*, chap. 7. For an evaluation of the relative strengths and weaknesses of the Communists and Nationalists, see Sheridan, *China in Disintegration*, pp. 271–79.

2. Spence, *Search for Modern China*, pp. 507–8.

3. O. Edmund Clubb, "Chiang Kai-shek's Waterloo: The Battle of the Hwai-hai," *Pacific Historical Review*, Nov. 1956, as cited in Bianco, p. 177 n. 23.

4. On Chiang's personal interventions, see Tucker, *Patterns in the Dust*, pp. 65–66 and n. 23, p. 242.

5. Bianco estimates that the Communists captured 230,000 rifles when Manchuria fell. Both Spence and Bianco list the number of Guomindang troops who were killed, captured, or deserted during the Manchurian fighting at 400,000. Bianco adds another 550,000 for the battle of Hwai-hai. See Bianco, pp. 177–78; and Spence, *Search for Modern China*, p. 507.

6. For more on the rampant inflation, see Spence, *Search for Modern*

China, pp. 498–504. Spence points out that, although the Nationalist government's reform in the late summer of 1948 temporarily halted the upward spiral, the government refused to commit itself to a fiscally responsible program, and thus by early 1949 the effort had been for naught. The Shanghai wholesale price index rose from a base of 100 in Aug. 1948 to 1,921 in Dec. and to 40,825 in Feb. 1949; see the table on p. 504.

7. Memo, Garside to Crider, Dec. 13, 1945, pp. 1–3, UCR-USC Papers, box 48.

8. Total receipts for 1946 amounted to $6,998,408.53. Total disbursements were $6,785,032.36. Both figures from Financial Statements, UCR-USC Papers, box 36.

9. Total receipts for the years are as follows: 1947, $1.46 million; 1948, $660,055; 1949, $587,706; 1950, $267,934. All are from Financial Statements, UCR-USC Papers, box 36. The situation became so bad that UCR-USC merchandising division began to lose money starting in 1947. From a net profit of $40,000 in 1945, that division's activity fell to a net loss of $459.98 in 1947. The losses continued in 1948 and reached nearly $6,000 in 1949. See USC Merchandising Activity, UCR-USC Papers, box 37.

10. Final Report, Connecticut Headquarters, United Service to China, Inc., by William P. Spear, Oct. 15, 1947, UCR-USC Papers, box 80.

11. All material from an unsigned memo to Edison, Mar. 10, 1947, pp. 1–6, UCR-USC Papers, box 34.

12. Blank appeal letter, Apr. 21, 1947, UCR-USC Papers, box 50.

13. Form letter, addressed to Mr. A. Blank, Blank Street, Blank City, Apr. 21, 1947, UCR-USC Papers, box 50.

14. Letter, Judd to the China Relief Legion, July 9, 1948, pp. 1–2, UCR-USC Papers, box 39.

15. Résumé of Statement by Ambassador Bullitt in the House of Representatives, Committee on Foreign Relations, Aid to China, Mar. 2, 1948, p. 4, Smith Papers, box 96.

16. Statement of Major General Claire Chennault, U.S. Army (Retired) to the Senate Armed Services Committee, May 10, 1949, p. 13, Smith Papers, box 98.

17. Letter, Judd to Witter Bynner, May 17, 1949, pp. 1–2, UCR-USC Papers, box 93.

18. Survey of Mail Appeals by United Service to China, May 1, 1948–April 8, 1949, pp. 1–3, UCR-USC Papers, box 48.

19. Letter, Garside to Luce, June 26, 1948, UCR-USC Papers, box 48.

20. Telegram, Edison to Smith, n.d., UCR-USC Papers, box 34.

21. "China on the March," with a talk by William C. Bullitt, recording of a broadcast over CBS radio, Mar. 20, 1941, 10:15–10:45 P.M., phonograph no. 1, ABMAC Papers.

22. *Time*, Jan. 17, 1949, p. 17. These comments were made by Bullitt on Dec. 24, 1948, before a joint congressional committee investigating aid to China. See Report by Consultant William C. Bullitt to the Joint Committee

on Foreign Economic Cooperation Concerning China, p. 13, Smith Papers, box 98.

23. May, *Homeward Bound*, p. 98.

24. *Life*, July 29, 1946, p. 85; see also, May, p. 98.

25. *Life*, July 29, 1946, p. 87.

26. John McPartland, "Portrait of an American Communist," *Life*, Jan. 5, 1948, p. 75. For more on the idea that women's sexuality could represent aberrant, abnormal, and unhealthy behavior, see May, *Homeward Bound*, pp. 60–64, 71; for more on the anti-Communist aspect of these fears of women's independent sexuality, see pp. 92–101.

27. Earl Cressy, "China Marches Toward the Cross" (New York, 1938), p. 62, UBCHEA Papers, box 458. Cressy finished the sentence by comparing communism with the sexual aberrations of the Tantric sect of Buddhism. For a slightly more elaborate discussion, see Ch'en, *Buddhism in China*, pp. 325–28.

28. Father Raymond de Jaegher, "The True Story of Chinese Communism," *Fu Jen Magazine*, June 1948, Judd Papers, box 184.

29. *Time*, Jan. 5, 1948, pp. 18–19.

30. Smith, U.S. Policy in China, n.d., Smith Papers, box 98.

31. Introduction to America's World Task Under President Truman, n.d., Smith Papers, box 98.

32. Herrymon Maurer, "The Tyrannous Decade," *Fortune*, Feb. 1948, p. 156.

33. Ibid., p. 119.

34. Ibid., p. 114. Tuchman, *Stilwell and the American Experience in China*, p. 220, mentions Corcoran's lobbying activities. For a slightly more substantial treatment, see Lash, *Dealers and Dreamers*, pp. 461–62. Lash points out that Corcoran's brother, David, was the president of China Defense Supplies. See also, Thomas G. Corcoran Papers, Library of Congress.

35. White, *In Search of History*, p. 126. See also, Halberstam, *The Powers That Be*, p. 85.

36. Halberstam, p. 87. For a general assessment of Guomindang lobbying activities in the United States after 1945, see Tucker, *Patterns in the Dust*, pp. 75–78, 143–44.

37. Interview with Wesley Bailey, Swanberg Papers, box 18.

38. *Life*, Mar. 29, 1948, p. 28.

39. Letter, Frederick Anderson to Judd, Jan. 8, 1948, Judd Papers, box 36. Judd's comments were part of the Town Meeting Program, "What Should We Do in China Now?" Jan. 6, 1948. Another listener warned Judd away from the Lincoln analogy, calling it "a boomerang."

40. The NBC radio discussion was part of the University of Chicago's Round Table. Nov. 11, 1948, Judd Papers, box 36.

41. *Life*, Mar. 29, 1948, p. 28.

42. *Time*, Mar. 29, 1948, p. 30. For another mention of Luce's magazines, see Purifoy, *Harry Truman's China Policy*, p. 66. For Acheson's remarks, see Acheson, *Present at the Creation*, p. 219.

43. *Time*, Mar. 29, 1948, p. 31.

44. Ibid.

45. Ibid., p. 29.

46. Acheson, *Present at the Creation*, p. 219.

47. This includes covers in which Chiang shared the space with others such as his wife. The covers are from the following dates of *Time*: Oct. 26, 1931 (with Madame Chiang), Dec. 11, 1933, Feb. 24, 1936 (with Joseph Stalin, Puyi, and Emperor Hirohito), Nov. 9, 1936, Jan. 3, 1938 (with his wife as man and woman of the year), June 1, 1942, Sept. 3, 1945, and Dec. 6, 1948. Time Inc. also published covers of Madame Chiang Kai-shek alone (*Life*, June 1941, and *Time*, Mar. 1, 1943). Zhen Zheng made the cover of *Time* on June 16, 1941; a *Life* cover of May 16, 1938, showed a young Chinese soldier; and although Ginger Rogers made the cover of *Life* on Mar. 2, 1942, that issue had a long, well-illustrated article on Chiang. This does not include the numerous other articles on China in *Fortune*, and the others on the American generals who served in China during the war.

48. *Time*, Dec. 6, 1948, p. 27.

49. Cort, *The Sin of Henry R. Luce*, p. 100. A random sampling of *Life* bears out the heavy and consistent interest in stories relating to farming or the Midwest.

50. Quoted in Halberstam, *The Powers That Be*, p. 48.

51. Quoted in Goldman, *The Crucial Decade and After*, p. 116.

52. *Time*, Feb. 7, 1949, pp. 19–24. Luce himself had noted the contrast in appearance between Chiang and Mao when he visited China in the fall of 1945. Luce wrote of Mao, "His sloppy blue-denim garment contrasted sharply with his host's snappy be-ribboned uniform." See Oct. 8, 1945, entry, Swanberg Papers, box 17.

53. *Time*, Dec. 6, 1948, p. 28.

54. Ibid., p. 31.

55. Letter, Roots to Smith, Aug. 27, 1949, Smith Papers, box 98.

56. "Strategy Number 6: Giving the Patriots of China and India an Ideology to Inspire the Millions, Multiply Men of Moral Fibre in their Governments, and Win the Battle for the Mind of Asia," p. 3. Draft chapter for *Reader's Digest* by Roots, Smith Papers, box 98.

57. Letter, Twitchell to Smith, July 9, 1949, Smith Papers, box 98.

58. Letter, Twitchell to Smith, June 28, 1949, Smith Papers, box 98.

59. Letter, Twitchell to Smith, Sept. 18, 1949, Smith Papers, box 98.

60. Letter, Roots to Smith, June 28, 1949, Smith Papers, box 98.

61. Far Eastern Problems Facing the United States, Report of Visit to the Far East, Sept. and Oct. 1948, by Smith, Nov. 21, 1949, Part II, p. 2, Smith Papers, box 98.

62. Letter, Roots to Smith, Aug. 27, 1949, p. 2, Smith Papers, box 98.

63. Senator Smith Calls for Positive U.S. Policy to Help 'Rebuild' China, press release to newspapers June 30, 1949, p. 2, Smith Papers, box 98.

64. Draft of a statement for NBC on China by Senator H. Alexander Smith, Dec. 1, 1949, p. 1, Smith Papers, box 98. Smith's son-in-law, Ken Twitchell,

had noted the previous July that the Chinese Nationalists still afforded them an opportunity to pursue an ideological policy since so many men within the government knew "the power of God-directed life and the need for moral standards in the fabric of the nation." Letter, Twitchell to Smith, July 23, 1949, Smith Papers, box 98.

65. Letter, Smith to Twitchell, Apr. 27, 1949, Smith Papers, box 98. Smith repeated his determination not to advocate military assistance to Chiang's government for use on the mainland after his trip to Asia in the fall of 1949. See, Far Eastern Problems Facing the United States, Report of Visit to the Far East, Sept. and Oct. 1949, by Smith, Nov. 21, 1949, Part III, pp. 3–4, and Part V, p. 4, Smith Papers, box 98.

66. Draft of a memo submitted to Acheson, Jan. 31, 1949, p. 3, Smith Papers, box 98.

67. Address by John Foster Dulles at the twenty-fifth anniversary dinner of the China Institute in America, May 18, 1951, Smith Papers, box 105. Luce served as the toastmaster and Dean Rusk also addressed the gathering. It must be kept in mind that Kennan thought the key to America's foreign policy in Asia had to be Japan and not China. See, for example, Gaddis, *Strategies of Containment.*

68. George F. Kennan, "The Sources of Soviet Conduct," originally published in *Foreign Affairs*, July 1947, reprinted in *Foreign Affairs*, Spring 1987. Quote is from p. 868.

69. Some of the other pro-Chiang enthusiasts were Senators Styles Bridges (Rep., N.H.), William Jenner (Rep., Ind.), Patrick McCarran (Dem., Nev.), and Joseph McCarthy (Rep., Wis.).

70. Diary entry for Aug. 25, 1950, Smith Diaries, Smith Papers.

71. Letter, Van Dusen to Smith, Dec. 17, 1948, Smith Papers, box 98.

72. Quoted in Jessup, ed., *The Ideas of Henry Luce*, pp. 196–97.

73. Hobson, *God and Mammon*, p. 6.

74. Spence, *To Change China*, p. 291.

75. Interview with Henry P. Van Dusen, John Foster Dulles Oral Histories, Mudd Library.

76. Letter, Luce to Stimson, Jan. 15, 1948, Stimson papers, reel 119. See also, Stimson and Bundy, *On Active Service in Peace and War*, p. 539. The offending statement in Stimson's magazine article was as follows: "Had Chiang Kai-shek permitted [General Joseph] Stilwell to carry out his training program on the scale and in the manner that Stilwell originally planned, he must surely have found himself, at the end of the war, with a vastly stronger army, of whose military reputation there could have been no doubt. Such support for Stilwell would have required a vigorous purge of the incompetent and the dishonest in Chiang's military entourage. . . . It would also have required a shift in Chiang's whole attitude, which remained throughout the war what Stilwell had described in 1942 as that of an ignorant, suspicious, feudal autocrat with a profound but misconceived devotion to the integrity of China and to himself as her savior." In response to Luce's letter, Stimson wrote that his major problem with Chiang during the war was his refusal to cooperate

toward achieving a common goal; Chiang seemed more interested in pursuing his own strategy. "My disappointment with Chiang Kai-shek," Stimson wrote, "was indeed largely the result of my very great hopes for China under his leadership in the war." See Stimson to Luce, Mar. 31, 1948, Stimson Papers, reel 119.

77. Thomas S. Matthews interview, Columbia Oral History Collection.

78. The phrase "the misery of China" is from Luce's letter to Stimson dated Apr. 20, 1948, Stimson Papers, reel 119.

79. Halberstam, *The Powers That Be,* p. 86.

Chapter Nine

1. Owen Lattimore speaking at a Round Table Discussion on American Policy Toward China Held in the Department of State, Oct. 6–8, 1949, p. B-22, Judd Papers, box 194. Some of the other participants were John K. Fairbank, William Herod (formerly associated with UCR), George Marshall, Nathaniel Peffer from Columbia University, Edwin O. Reischauer, John D. Rockefeller III, and Harold Stassen.

2. Said, *Orientalism,* pp. 1–2.

3. Hunt, *Ideology and U.S. Foreign Policy,* p. 176.

4. Tucker discusses the application of containment to various areas around the globe, but not to mainland China, in *Patterns in the Dust,* p. 14.

5. All figures are from Gallup, *The Gallup Poll: Public Opinion, 1935–1971:* 1: 728, 774, 852.

6. Harold R. Isaacs, "Sources for Images of Foreign Countries," in Small, ed., *Public Opinion and Historians,* p. 97.

7. Dower, *War Without Mercy.* The MacArthur material is on p. 303; the quote is from p. 309, but see his epilogue more generally.

8. Tucker, *Patterns in the Dust,* pp. 197–201; Cumings, *The Origins of the Korean War,* chap. 1; Gaddis, *Strategies of Containment,* chaps. 2–3 for a discussion of George F. Kennan, containment, and its implementation.

9. *Gallup Poll, 1935–1971,* 1:773, 955.

10. Ibid., pp. 852–53.

11. Telegram, Judd to Chiang Kai-shek, July 30, 1949, Judd Papers, box 163.

12. John F. Melby Oral History Interview, p. 168, HSTL. The phrase "keen to publish" is from Newman, "The Self-Inflicted Wound," p. 144.

13. Memo for the President (from Dean Acheson with attachment), July 8, 1949, President's Secretary Files, box 173, HSTL.

14. Memo of Conversation with the President, July 25, 1949, Acheson Papers, box 64, HSTL. Acheson wrote in his memoirs that he suffered from the "frustrated schoolteacher" syndrome with regard to *The White Paper* in that he tried to convince the American people that the situation within China was "beyond the control of the government of the United States" through a careful and reasoned explication of the facts. See *Present at the Creation,* pp. 302–3.

15. Francis Russell Oral History Interview, pp. 13, 16, 22, 23, 26, 27, 29, 42, HSTL. Certain historians have emphasized the disdain Dean Acheson personally, and members of the Truman administration more generally, had for public opinion, suggesting that public opinion ultimately did little to influence or restrain actions that the administration wished to take. Thomas Paterson, *On Every Front*, to cite one example, says, "President Truman charted his own foreign policy course and successfully persuaded the reluctant to walk his path" (p. 115). Though certainly true to a large extent, that does not mean that Truman and his advisers, including Dean Acheson, did not understand the importance of selling their policies to the public and Congress. In the case of postwar relations with China, in 1949 the administration found itself facing a storm of criticism for losing China to the Communists. Despite the patent lack of merit to such an accusation, Truman and his advisers still felt it a good idea to assemble and publish *The White Paper*, an act that speaks to the importance given to the public's perception of events. Joseph Jones, discussing the subject of selling policies in his history and analysis of the Truman Doctrine, says "On this occasion the policy-operations officers were among the most effective in analyzing strategic and political considerations. There is a major lesson in public administration here, for there is no question that the information officers, with their sensibilities attuned to the public, made a powerful contribution to the Truman Doctrine." See *Fifteen Weeks*, p. 150.

16. Russett, "Doves, Hawks, and U.S. Public Opinion," pp. 515–16.

17. Charles Collingwood, CBS News, Aug. 7, 1949, pp. 1–5. Quotes are from pp. 1, 3, respectively, Bruce Smith Papers, Hoover Institution.

18. Freeland, *Truman Doctrine and the Origins of McCarthyism*, p. 341. Tucker expresses much the same idea: "Having once utilized global rhetoric . . . the White House and State Department found it impossible to channel the militancy the rhetoric engendered." See *Patterns in the Dust*, p. 11.

19. *Time*, Aug. 15, 1949, pp. 11–13. For a particularly insightful contemporaneous assessment of *The White Paper*, see Richard W. Van Alstyne, "The White Paper and China," *Current History* 17 (Oct. 1949): 193–201. Van Alstyne argued that the Truman administration's main purpose in issuing the *White Paper* was to "present an inquest on China," but such an investigation allowed others to do the same with respect to American policy toward China. He also pointed out that the administration sought to explain how circumstances in Asia differed from those in Europe, and why actions in support of Europe could not apply equally well in China; but as Van Alstyne asked, "Why did it take the State Department until July 30, 1949 to arrive at this conclusion?" For a historical analysis that asserts that issuing *The White Paper* was a major blunder, see Newman, "The Self-Inflicted Wound," pp. 141–56. Newman also covers more of the press reaction to *The White Paper*.

20. "China Whitewash," *Wall Street Journal*, Aug. 8, 1949, p. 4; and "Confessions of Failure," *Chicago Daily Tribune*, Aug. 8, 1949, p. 24.

21. Judd's remarks can be found in a guest column he wrote for the *Buffalo*

Evening News, Aug. 17, 1949, Judd Papers, box 37. Knowland's speech, delivered on Sept. 26, 1949, appears as part of the *Congressional Record*, Judd Papers, box 194.

22. Collingwood, p. 1, Bruce Smith Papers.

23. Letter, W. B. Pettus to Judd, Aug. 25, 1949, Judd Papers, box 200.

24. For letters to Judd after the incident involving Angus Ward, see Judd Papers, box 199.

25. Cumings, *The Origins of the Korean War*, 2:17. In discussing how China could quickly come to mean so much to the political scene, Cumings argues (p. 107): "China, little known to most Americans, an opaque, inscrutable vastness, could become 'China,' an issue that people could be mobilized around because it stood for nothing in the American mind and therefore could stand for everything—it was a tabula rasa on which the right-wing and the expansionists could write."

26. Form letter, Judd to past USC contributors, Aug. 11, 1950, UCR-USC Papers, box 93.

27. Letter, Garside to Edison, May 4, 1950, UCR-USC Papers, box 34.

28. Bachrack, *The Committee of One Million*, deals with the activities of Judd, Garside, and others in the post-1949 period. Also of use here are Judd's and Garside's Papers at the Hoover Institution.

29. The Rutgers University Forum, Jan. 3, 1950, p. 3, Smith Papers, box 211. The subject for the forum was America's "Far Eastern Policy" and the program was broadcast eight times over thirteen different radio stations in New Jersey from Jan. 3 to 15, 1950. Emphasis mine.

30. Letter, Fitch to "dear Friends," Apr. 25, 1950, Right Wing Pamphlet Collection, box 9.

31. Atterbury letter, n.d., Right Wing Pamphlet Collection, box 10.

32. Open Letter to the President, Mar. 28, 1951, pp. 2, 3, Right Wing Pamphlet Collection, box 10. An earlier report by the China Emergency Committee written by Mary Fine Twinem emphasized the same supposed connection: "China's first Christian President is no second to America's Washington and Lincoln as a great praying man, walking humbly with his Lord." Right Wing Pamphlet Collection, box 9.

33. Clare Boothe Luce, "The Mystery of American Policy in China," June 14, 1949, pp. 5–20, Baruch Papers, box 86.

34. Clare Boothe Luce converted to Catholicism shortly after the death of her daughter in January 1944.

35. Collingwood, p. 1, Bruce Smith Papers.

36. Luce, "The Mystery of American Policy in China," pp. 17–20.

37. Ibid., p. 19. Many conservatives have seen liberal naïveté as one of the major ills afflicting certain policymakers. In a 1982 letter to Walter Judd, Madame Chiang made reference to the "soft-headed, the naive, and the liberal groupies of the world." Mar. 6, 1982, Judd Papers, box 163.

38. The 1968 figure is from Gallup, *The Gallup Poll: Public Opinion, 1935–1971*, 3: 2105. The latter figure is from Gallup, *The Gallup Poll: Public*

232   *Notes to Pages 183–85*

Opinion, 1972–1977, p. 129. See also Russett, "Doves, Hawks, and U.S. Public Opinion," p. 536, for a graph of the rapid change in public opinion toward Communist China from 1967 to 1973. Chang, *Friends and Enemies*, chap. 9, analyzes the beginnings of this turnaround during the Johnson administration.

    39. Gallup, *The Gallup Poll, 1935–1971*, 1: 508–9; 2: 1007.

    40. Gaddis, *Strategies of Containment*, pp. 295–98. See also notes taken by White House Chief of Staff H. R. Haldeman of a meeting held on July 13, 1971, Haldeman files, Nixon Papers Project, National Archives, box 44. I thank Michael Schaller for bringing these notes to my attention. Henry Kissinger's memoirs are of additional interest. On the impact the China visit would have on North Vietnam, he wrote, "The visit of an American emissary to Peking was bound to spark a geopolitical revolution; the effect on Hanoi alone would be traumatic." See, Kissinger, *The White House Years*, p. 691. Despite his reputation as a calm strategist, even Kissinger became caught up in the excitement over reestablishing contact with China. He wrote of his first flight to China in July 1971, "Only some truly extraordinary event, both novel and moving, both unusual and overwhelming, restores the innocence of the years when each day was a precious adventure in defining the meaning of life. This is how it was for me as the aircraft crossed the snow-capped Himalayas, thrusting toward the heavens in roseate glow of a rising sun" (p. 742). Arthur Waldron made an apt comparison between Kissinger's rhetoric and statements made by "radical" American students on traveling to China at the same time. See his article, "Bullish on Beijing," *New Republic*, Apr. 9, 1990, pp. 20–25, especially p. 24. Immediately following the announcement of Nixon's visit to China, B. A. Garside wrote a letter to Nixon in which he was very critical of the denouement. His final objection was, "Whatever transient benefits the President may hope to gain from this adventure will be buried beneath the overwhelming disasters it will create." See Garside's letter to Nixon, July 15, 1971, p. 2, Garside Papers, box 4. Walter Judd, though now retired, still commanded enough clout to warrant a telephone call from President Gerald Ford as he prepared to visit China in December 1975. One administration official noted that Judd had "quite a following not only in Congress, but across the country as being a very strong spokesman in China policy." This must be kept in perspective, however, since Judd originally wanted a personal meeting but settled for the telephone conversation. Memo, Marsh to Scowcroft, Nov. 27, 1975, CO 34-2 PRC, 11/1/75–4/30/76, CO 34-1-CO 34-2, box 13, Gerald R. Ford Library.

    41. Hunt, *Ideology and U.S. Foreign Policy*, chap. 3. For the polling data on fifty years after Pearl Harbor, see Gallup, Jr., *The Gallup Poll: Public Opinion, 1991*, pp. 240–44; and *The Gallup Poll: Public Opinion, 1992*, p. 28.

    42. Dower, *War Without Mercy*, chap. 5. Dower also mentions the growing tide of anti-Japanese sentiment within the United States during the 1980's in his epilogue.

    43. Crichton, *Rising Sun*, p. 336. Emphasis mine. Morton also says, "As

our economic power fades, we are vulnerable to a new kind of invasion" (p. 252). Two different characters in the book state that the Japanese are "the most racist people on the planet," a highly dubious assertion given that there is no standardized test for assessing the collective racism of a people. I do not mean to ignore the brutal nature of the Japanese occupation of various Asian nations earlier in the century, particularly in Korea and China, where the Japanese army committed horrible acts of mass rape, torture, and murder. But how does one compare those actions with the German campaign to exterminate Jews, or the legacy of American slavery and treatment of Indians?

44. Crichton's work is clearly a type of that wonderfully American tradition, the Jeremiad. It is most reminiscent of an earlier best-seller that was also made into a movie, Lederer and Burdick, *The Ugly American*. John Hellmann ties this novel to the New Frontier of the Kennedy administration in his excellent analysis; see *American Myth and the Legacy of Vietnam*, chap. 1. *Rising Sun*, like *The Ugly American*, casts blame in two directions: inwardly it finds a weak and soft America gladly selling its vital high-tech industries to the Japanese. Outwardly, the novel exhumes the notion of a monolithic Japan bent on world domination, this time through economic means rather than military ones. *The Ugly American* found the same softness domestically but depicted an external menace led by Soviet-directed communism.

45. Charles M. Crowe, "Christianity and Capitalism," reprinted from the *Christian Advocate*, Apr. 19, 1951, Right Wing Pamphlet Collection, box 10.

46. Andrew Tanzer, "'The mountains are high, the emperor is far away,'" *Forbes* 5 (Aug. 1991): 70.

47. Sheryl WuDunn, "Booming China Is a Dream Market for West," *NYT*, Feb. 15, 1993, p. 1.

48. Sheryl WuDunn, "China Village Prospers But Retains Old Ways," *NYT*, Jan. 17, 1993, p. 8. Another article by the same author on Chinese purchases of one square inch of U.S. soil stated, "The mania reflects the infatuation with most things American." See "Chinese Buy American Dream by the Inch," *NYT*, Jan. 29, 1993, p. 1. The idea behind the scheme was to purchase one-acre plots and subdivide them into one-inch squares for sale as novelty items to Chinese. Some Chinese received the impression that purchasing them would allow the owner to obtain a visa to visit his or her land.

49. Tanzer, "'The mountains are high, the emperor is far away,'" p. 72.

50. *Business Week*, Dec. 24, 1990, p. 82.

51. WuDunn, *NYT*, Jan. 17, 1993, p. 8.

52. Fergus M. Bordewich, "China's Daring Underground of Faith," *Reader's Digest*, Aug. 1991, pp. 33–38.

53. Tanzer, "'The mountains are high, the emperor is far away,'" p. 71.

54. *National Review*, Apr. 27, 1992, p. 18.

55. Conable, Jr., and Lampton, "China: The Coming Power," p. 134.

56. Lynn Chu, "The Chimera of the China Market," *Atlantic*, Oct. 1990, p. 64.

57. Tucker, "China and America," pp. 91–92.

58. Waldron, "Bullish on Beijing."

59. Geraldine Guiness, "An Appeal from China," May 2, 1890, Student Movement Publications, box 554.

60. Spence, *To Change China*, p. 292.

61. Joseph Kraft, "America's China Myths," Feb. 22, 1972, Judd Papers, box 196.

62. W. Walton Butterworth, "China in Mid-Revolution," address, May 10, 1950, p. 1, Butterworth Papers, box 3.

Bibliography

Manuscript Collections, Oral Histories, and Archives

Dean Acheson Papers, Harry S. Truman Library, Independence, Missouri
Joseph and Stewart Alsop Papers, Library of Congress
American Bureau for Medical Aid to China Papers, Rare Book and Manuscript Library, Butler Library, Columbia University
Bernard Baruch Papers, Seely G. Mudd Manuscript Library, Princeton University
W. Walton Butterworth Papers, George C. Marshall Library and Archive, Lexington, Virginia
Claire Chennault Papers, Hoover Institution on War, Revolution, and Peace, Stanford University
China Records Project, Yale Divinity School Library
Thomas G. Corcoran Papers, Library of Congress
Lauchlin Currie Papers, Hoover Institution on War, Revolution, and Peace
John Foster Dulles Papers, Seely G. Mudd Manuscript Library
James V. Forrestal Papers, Seely G. Mudd Manuscript Library
B. A. Garside Papers, Hoover Institution on War, Revolution, and Peace
Joseph C. Green Papers, Seely G. Mudd Manuscript Library
Harry L. Hopkins Papers, Franklin D. Roosevelt Library, Hyde Park, New York
Edward and Lotta Hume Papers, Sterling Memorial Library, Yale University
John Raymond Hutchinson Papers, Hoover Institution On War, Revolution, and Peace
Indusco, Inc. Papers, Rare Book and Manuscript Library, Butler Library
William Richard Johnson Papers, Yale Divinity School Library
Walter Judd Papers, Hoover Institution On War, Revolution, and Peace

Wellington Koo Papers, Rare Book and Manuscript Library, Butler Library
Walter Lippmann Papers, Sterling Memorial Library
Dwight D. Macdonald Papers, Sterling Memorial Library
George C. Marshall Papers, George C. Marshall Library and Archive
Missions Pamphlet Collection, Yale Divinity School Library
National Achives, Washington, D.C.
Oral History Collection, Butler Library
Frank W. Price Papers, George C. Marshall Library and Archive
Right Wing Pamphlet Collection, Sterling Memorial Library
Franklin D. Roosevelt Papers, Map Room File, Roosevelt Library
Franklin D. Roosevelt Papers, Official File, Roosevelt Library
Franklin D. Roosevelt Papers, President's Personal File, Roosevelt Library
Franklin D. Roosevelt Papers, President's Secretary File, Roosevelt Library
Laurence Salisbury Papers, Hoover Institution on War, Revolution, and Peace
Bruce M. Smith Papers, Hoover Institution on War, Revolution, and Peace
H. Alexander Smith Papers, Seely G. Mudd Manuscript Library
T. V. Soong Papers, Hoover Institution on War, Revolution, and Peace
Henry L. Stimson Papers, Sterling Memorial Library
Anson Phelps Stokes Papers, Sterling Memorial Library
Archives of the Student Volunteer Movement, Yale Divinity School Library
W. A. Swanberg Papers, Rare Book and Manuscript Library, Butler Library
Harry S. Truman Papers, Oral History Collection, Truman Library
Harry S. Truman Papers, President's Personal File, Truman Library
Harry S. Truman Papers, President's Secretary's File, Truman Library
Harry S. Truman Papers, White House Central File, Truman Library
Archives of the United Board for Christian Higher Education in Asia, Yale
    Divinity School Library
United China Relief–United Service to China Papers, Seely G. Mudd Manu-
    script Library
Whiting Willauer Papers, Seely G. Mudd Manuscript Library
C. E. A. Winslow Papers, Sterling Memorial Library
Yale-in-China Association Papers, Sterling Memorial Library

Published Government Documents

CONGRESS

Senate

Committee on Foreign Relations. *Economic Assistance to China and Korea:
    1949–50.* Washington, D.C.: Government Printing Office, 1974.
———. *Sino-American Relations: One Year After the Massacre at Tianan-
    men Square.* 101st Cong., 2d sess., 1990.
Committee on Foreign Relations and Armed Services. *Hearings: Military
    Situation in the Far East.* 82d Cong., 1st sess., 1951.

Committee on the Judiciary. *Morgenthau Diary (China), Volumes I and II.* 89th Cong., 1st sess., 1965.

EXECUTIVE BRANCH

Department of State. *Foreign Relations of the United States,* 1895. Washington, D.C., 1896.

———. *Foreign Relations of the United States,* volumes as cited for the years 1931–49. Washington, D.C., 1946–78.

———. *Foreign Relations of the United States, 1942, China,* and *1943, China.* Washington, D.C., 1956, 1957.

———. *Foreign Relations of the United States. The Conferences at Cairo and Teheran, 1943.* Washington, D.C., 1961.

———. *United States Relations with China, with a Special Reference to the Period 1944–1949.* Washington, D.C.: Department of State Publications, 1949.

Contemporary Periodicals and Newspapers

Asia
Chicago Tribune
Christian Century
Christian Science Monitor
Current History
Fortune
Hibbert Journal
Life
Los Angeles Times
Missionary Review of the World
New Republic

New York Herald-Tribune
New York Times
The Outlook
San Francisco Chronicle
Saturday Evening Post
Smithsonian
Time
U.S. News & World Report
Vogue
Washington Post

Other Sources: Primary and Secondary

Acheson, Dean. *Present at the Creation: My Years in the State Department.* New York: W. W. Norton, 1969.

Anderson, George L., ed. *Issues and Conflicts: Studies in Twentieth Century American Diplomacy.* Lawrence: University of Kansas Press, 1959.

Ayer, N. W., and Son. *N. W. Ayer & Son's Directory of Newspapers and Periodicals.* Philadelphia: N. W. Ayer & Son, 1938, 1941, 1944, 1945, 1947.

Bachrack, Stanley D. *The Committee of One Million: The "China Lobby" and U.S. Policy, 1953–1971.* New York: Columbia University Press, 1976.

Barnett, A. Doak. *China on the Eve of the Communist Takeover.* New York: Praeger, 1963.

Barrett, David D. *Dixie Mission: The United States Army Observer Group in Yenan, 1944.* Berkeley: Center for Chinese Studies, China Research Monographs, University of California, 1970.

Baughman, James L. *Henry R. Luce and the Rise of the American News Media*. Boston: Twayne, 1987.

Belden, Jack. *China Shakes the World*. New York: Monthly Review Press, 1949.

Bercovitch, Sacvan. *The Puritan Origins of the American Self*. New Haven, Conn.: Yale University Press, 1975.

Berkov, Robert. *Strong Man of China: The Story of Chiang Kai-shek*. Boston: Houghton Mifflin, 1938.

Bertram, James M. *First Act in China: The Story of Chiang Kai-shek*. New York: Viking, 1938.

Bianco, Lucien. *Origins of the Chinese Revolution, 1915–1949*. Translated from the French by Muriel Bell. Stanford, Calif.: Stanford University Press, 1971.

Billington, Rosamund, Sheelagh Strawbridge, Lenore Greensides, and Annette Fitzsimons. *Culture and Society: A Sociology of Culture*. London: Houndmills, 1991.

Blum, John Morton. *From the Morgenthau Diaries: Years of Urgency, 1938–1941*. Boston: Houghton Mifflin, 1965.

Blumenthal, Sidney. *Pledging Allegiance: The Last Campaign of the Cold War*. New York: HarperCollins, 1990.

Bohn, Thomas William. *An Historical and Descriptive Analysis of the "Why We Fight" Series*. New York: Arno Press, 1977.

Borg, Dorothy, and Waldo Heinrichs, eds. *Uncertain Years: Chinese-American Relations, 1947–1950*. New York: Columbia University Press, 1980.

Borg, Dorothy, and Shumpei Okamoto, eds. *Pearl Harbor as History: Japanese-American Relations, 1931–1941*. New York: Columbia University Press, 1973.

Buck, Pearl S. *The Good Earth*. New York: John Day, 1931.

———. *My Several Worlds*. New York: John Day, 1954.

Burke, James. *My Father in China*. London: Michael Joseph, 1945.

Burns, Edward McNall. *The American Idea of Mission: Concepts of National Purpose and Destiny*. New Brunswick, N.J.: Rutgers University Press, 1957.

Bush, George. *Public Papers of the Presidents: George Bush*, Book 1. Washington, D.C.: Government Printing Office, 1990.

Bush, George, with Victor Gold. *Looking Forward*. Garden City, N.Y.: Doubleday, 1987.

Carnegie, Dale. *Dale Carnegie's Biographical Roundup: Highlights in the Lives of Forty Famous People*. New York: Forest Hills Publishing Co., 1944.

Chafe, William. *The American Woman: Her Changing Social, Economic, and Political Roles, 1920–1970*. New York: Oxford University Press, 1972.

Chanda, Nayan. *Brother Enemy: The War After the War*. New York: Collier Books, 1986.

Chang, Gordon. *Friends and Enemies: The United States, China, and the Soviet Union, 1948–1972*. Stanford, Calif.: Stanford University Press, 1990.

Ch'en, Kenneth. *Buddhism in China: A Historical Survey.* Princeton, N.J.: Princeton University Press, 1964.

Chennault, Claire Lee. *Way of a Fighter.* New York: G. P. Putnam's Sons, 1949.

Chern, Kenneth S. *Dilemma in China: America's Policy Debate, 1945.* Hamden, Conn.: Archon Books, 1980.

Ch'i, Hsi-sheng. *Nationalist China at War: Military Defeats and Political Collapse, 1937–1945.* Ann Arbor: University of Michigan Press, 1982.

Chiang, May-ling Soong. *China Shall Rise Again.* New York: Harper & Brothers, 1940.

Chiang Kai-shek. *China's Destiny.* New York: Macmillan, 1947.

Clurman, Richard M. *Beyond Malice: The Media's Years of Reckoning.* New Brunswick, N.J.: Transaction Books, 1988.

Cohen, Bernard C. *The Press and Foreign Policy.* Princeton, N.J.: Princeton University Press, 1963.

Cohen, Paul A. *China and Christianity: The Missionary Movement and the Growth of Chinese Antiforeignism, 1860–1870.* Cambridge, Mass.: Harvard University Press, 1963.

Cohen, Warren I. *America's Response to China: An Interpretative History of Sino-American Relations.* 3d ed. New York: Columbia University Press, 1990.

———. "The History of American-East Asian Relations: Cutting Edge of the Historical Profession." *Diplomatic History* 9 (Spring 1985): 101–12.

Conable, Barber B., Jr., and David M. Lampton. "China: The Coming Power." *Foreign Affairs* 71 (Winter 1992–93): 133–49.

Cort, David. *The Sin of Henry R. Luce: An Anatomy of Journalism.* Secaucus, N.J.: Lyle Stuart, 1974.

Crichton, Michael. *Rising Sun.* New York: Ballantine, 1992.

Crow, Carl. *China Takes Her Place.* New York: Harper & Brothers, 1944.

———. *Four Hundred Million Customers.* New York: Halcyon House, 1937.

———. *I Speak for the Chinese.* New York: Harper & Brothers, 1937.

Cumings, Bruce. *The Origins of the Korean War. Vol. 2, The Roaring of the Cataract, 1947–1950.* Princeton, N.J.: Princeton University Press, 1990.

Dallek, Robert. *The American Style of Foreign Policy: Cultural Politics and Foreign Affairs.* New York: Knopf, 1983.

———. *Franklin D. Roosevelt and American Foreign Policy, 1932–1945.* New York: Oxford University Press, 1979.

Daugherty, William E. "China's Official Publicity in the United States." *Public Opinion Quarterly* 6 (Spring 1942): 70–86.

Davies, John Paton. *Dragon by the Tail: American British, Japanese, and Russian Encounters with China and One Another.* New York: W. W. Norton, 1972.

Dower, John. *War Without Mercy: Race and Power in the Pacific War.* New York: Pantheon, 1986.

Eastman, Lloyd E. *Seeds of Destruction: Nationalist China in War and Revolution, 1937–1949.* Stanford, Calif.: Stanford University Press, 1984.

Eddy, Sherwood. *Pathfinders of the World Missionary Crusade.* Freeport, N.Y.: Books for Libraries Press, 1945.

Elson, Robert T. *Time Inc. An Intimate History of a Publishing Enterprise, 1923–1941.* New York: Atheneum, 1968.

———. *The World of Time Inc. The Intimate History of a Publishing Enterprise. Vol. 2, 1941–1960.* New York: Atheneum, 1973.

Epstein, Joseph. "Henry Luce and His Time." *Commentary* 44 (Nov. 1967): 35–47.

Fairbank, John K. "'American China Policy' to 1898: A Misconception." *Pacific Historical Review* 39 (Nov. 1970): 409–20.

———. *Chinabound: A Fifty-Year Memoir.* New York: Harper & Row, 1982.

———. "The Problem of Revolutionary Asia." *Foreign Affairs* 29 (Oct. 1950): 101–13.

Feaver, John H. "The China Aid Bill of 1948: Limited Assistance as a Cold War Strategy." *Diplomatic History* 5 (Spring 1981): 107–20.

Feinberg, Joel. *Harm to Self: The Moral Limits of Criminal Law.* New York: Oxford University Press, 1986.

Feis, Herbert. *The China Tangle: The American Effort in China from Pearl Harbor to the Marshall Mission.* Princeton, N.J.: Princeton University Press, 1953.

Fielding, Raymond. *The American Newsreel, 1911–1967.* Norman: University of Oklahoma Press, 1972.

———. *The March of Time, 1935–1951.* New York: Oxford University Press, 1978.

Freeland, Richard M. *The Truman Doctrine and the Origins of McCarthyism: Foreign Policy, Domestic Politics, and Internal Security, 1946–1948.* New York: Knopf, 1972.

Friedrich, Otto. "There Are oo Trees in Russia: The Function of Facts in Newsmagazines." *Harper's* 229 (Oct. 1964): 59–65.

Fussell, Paul. *Wartime: Understanding and Behavior in the Second World War.* New York: Oxford University Press, 1989.

Gaddis, John Lewis. *Strategies of Containment: A Critical Appraisal of Postwar American National Security Policy.* New York: Oxford University Press, 1982.

Gallup, George H. *The Gallup Poll: Public Opinion, 1935–1971.* 3 vols. New York: Random House, 1972.

———. *The Gallup Poll: Public Opinion, 1972–1977.* 2 vols. Wilmington, Del.: Scholarly Resources, 1978.

Gallup, Dr. George, Jr. *The Gallup Poll: Public Opinion, 1991.* Wilmington, Del.: Scholarly Resources, 1992.

———. *The Gallup Poll: Public Opinion, 1992.* Wilmington, Del.: Scholarly Resources, 1993.

Gamson, William, and Andre Modigliani. "Media Discourse and Public Opinion: A Constructionist Approach." *American Journal of Sociology* 95 (July 1989): 1–37.

Gardner, Lloyd C. *Architects of Illusion.* Chicago: Quadrangle, 1970.

Gasster, Michael. *China's Struggle to Modernize.* 2d ed. New York: Knopf, 1983.

Goldman, Eric. *The Crucial Decade and After: America, 1945–1960.* New York: Vintage Books, 1960.

Griffith, Robert. *The Politics of Fear: Joseph R. McCarthy and the Senate.* Lexington: University of Kentucky Press, 1970.

Guimond, James. *American Photography and the American Dream.* Chapel Hill: University of North Carolina Press, 1991.

Hahn, Emily. *The Soong Sisters.* New York: Doubleday, 1941.

Halberstam, David. *The Powers That Be.* New York: Knopf, 1979.

Hartmann, Susan M. *The Home Front and Beyond: American Women in the 1940s.* Boston: Twayne, 1982.

Heininger, Janet E. "Private Positions Versus Public Policy: Chinese Devolution and the American Experience in East Asia." *Diplomatic History* 6 (Summer 1982): 287–302.

Hellmann, John. *American Myth and the Legacy of Vietnam.* New York: Columbia University Press, 1986.

Hersey, John. "Henry Luce's China Dream." *New Republic,* May 2, 1983: 27–32.

Herzstein, Robert E. *Henry R. Luce: A Political Portrait of the Man Who Created the American Century.* New York: Scribner's, 1994.

Hobson, J. A. *God and Mammon: The Relations of Religion and Economics.* New York: Macmillan, 1931.

Hodgson, Godfrey. *America in Our Time.* New York: Vintage Books, 1978.

Hoopes, Roy. *Ralph Ingersol: A Biography.* New York: Atheneum, 1985.

Horsman, Reginald. *Race and Manifest Destiny: The Origins of American Racial Anglo-Saxonism.* Cambridge, Mass.: Harvard University Press, 1981.

Hu, Shih. "China in Stalin's Grand Strategy." *Foreign Affairs* 29 (Oct. 1950): 11–40.

Hull, Cordell. *The Memoirs of Cordell Hull.* New York: Macmillan, 1948.

Hunt, Michael H. *Ideology and U.S. Foreign Policy.* New Haven, Conn.: Yale University Press, 1987.

———. "Internationalizing U.S. Diplomatic History." *Diplomatic History* 15 (Winter 1991): 1–11.

———. *The Making of a Special Relationship: The United States and China to 1914.* New York: Columbia University Press, 1983.

———. "Pearl Buck—Popular Expert on China, 1931–1949." *Modern China* 3 (Jan. 1977): 33–64.

Hunter, Jane. *The Gospel of Gentility: American Women Missionaries in Turn-of-the-Century China.* New Haven, Conn.: Yale University Press, 1984.

Iriye, Akira. *Across the Pacific: An Inner History of American–East Asian Relations.* New York: Harcourt, Brace & World, 1967.

———. "Culture and Power: International Relations as Intercultural Relations." *Diplomatic History* 3 (Spring 1979): 115–28.

Bibliography

———. "The Internationalization of History." *American Historical Review* 1 (Feb. 1989): 1–10.

Isaacs, Harold R. *No Peace for Asia*. New York: Macmillan, 1947.

———. *Scratches on Our Minds: American Images of China and India*. New York: John Day, 1958.

———. *The Tragedy of the Chinese Revolution*. 2d rev. ed. Stanford, Calif.: Stanford University Press, 1961.

Jessup, John K., ed. *The Ideas of Henry Luce*. New York: Atheneum, 1969.

Johnson, Chalmers A. *Peasant Nationalism and Communist Power: The Emergence of Revolutionary China, 1937–1945*. Stanford, Calif.: Stanford University Press, 1962.

Jones, Joseph M. *Fifteen Weeks*. New York: Viking, 1955.

Kahin, George McT. *Intervention: How America Became Involved in Vietnam*. New York: Doubleday, 1986.

Kaplan, Amy, and Donald E. Pease, eds. *Cultures of United States Imperialism*. Durham, N.C.: Duke University Press, 1993.

Karnow, Stanley. *Vietnam: A History*. New York: Penguin Books, 1993.

Kennan, George F. (Originally published under the pseud. "X"). "The Sources of Soviet Conduct." Reprinted in *Foreign Affairs* 65 (Spring 1987): 852–68.

Kimball, Warren F. *The Juggler: Franklin Roosevelt as Wartime Statesman*. Princeton, N.J.: Princeton University Press, 1991.

Kirby, William C. *Germany and Republican China*. Stanford, Calif.: Stanford University Press, 1984.

Kissinger, Henry. *The White House Years*. Boston: Little, Brown, 1979.

Knightley, Phillip. *The First Casualty: From the Crimea to Vietnam. The War Correspondent as Hero, Propagandist, and Myth Maker*. New York: Harcourt Brace Jovanovich, 1975.

Kobler, John. *Luce: His Time, Life, and Fortune*. Garden City, N.Y.: Doubleday, 1968.

Koen, Ross Y. *The China Lobby in American Politics*. New York: Macmillan, 1960.

Kopkind, Andrew. "Serving Time." *New York Review of Books*, 11 (Sept. 12, 1968): 23–28.

Koppes, Clayton R., and Gregory D. Black. *Hollywood Goes to War: How Politics, Profits, and Propaganda Shaped World War II Movies*. Berkeley: University of California Press, 1987.

LaFeber, Walter. *The New Empire: An Interpretation of American Expansion, 1860–1898*. Ithaca, N.Y.: Cornell University Press, 1963.

Lash, Joseph P. *Dealers and Dreamers: A New Look at the New Deal*. New York: Doubleday, 1988.

Latourette, Kenneth Scott. *The American Record in the Far East, 1945–1951*. New York: Macmillan, 1952.

Leahy, William D. *I Was There*. New York: McGraw-Hill, 1950.

Lederer, William J., and Eugene Burdick. *The Ugly American*. New York: W. W. Norton, 1958.

Levine, Steven I. *Anvil of Victory: The Communist Revolution in Manchuria, 1945–1948.* New York: Columbia University Press, 1987.
———. "A New Look at American Mediation in the Chinese Civil War: The Marshall Mission and Manchuria." *Diplomatic History* 3 (Fall 1979): 349–75.
Lutz, Jessie G. *China and the Christian Colleges, 1890–1950.* Ithaca, N.Y.: Cornell University Press, 1971.
———. *Christian Missions in China: Evangelists of What?* Lexington, Mass.: D. C. Heath, 1965.
McClellan, Robert. *The Heathen Chinee: A Study of American Attitudes Toward China, 1890–1905.* Columbus: Ohio State University Press, 1971.
McCormick, Thomas J. *China Market: America's Quest for Informal Empire, 1893–1901.* Chicago: Quadrangle, 1967.
Macdonald, Dwight. *Discriminations: Essays and Afterthoughts, 1938–1974.* New York: Grossman, 1974.
MacKinnon, Stephen R., and Oris Friesen. *China Reporting: An Oral History of American Journalism in the 1930s and 1940s.* Berkeley: University of California Press, 1987.
Marchand, Roland. *Advertising the American Dream: Making Way for Modernity, 1920–1940.* Berkeley: University of California Press, 1985.
Masland, John W. "Missionary Influence Upon American Far Eastern Policy." *Pacific Historical Review* 10 (Sept. 1941): 279–96.
May, Elaine Tyler. *Homeward Bound: American Families in the Cold War Era.* New York: Basic Books, 1988.
May, Ernest R., and John K. Fairbank, eds. *America's China Trade in Historical Perspective: The Chinese and American Performance.* Cambridge, Mass.: Harvard University Press, 1986.
Melby, John F. *The Mandate of Heaven: Record of a Civil War, China 1945–49.* New York: Anchor Books, 1971.
Miller, Basil. *Generalissimo and Madame Chiang Kai-shek: Christian Liberators of China.* 3d ed. Grand Rapids, Mich.: Zondervan, 1943.
Millis, Walter, ed. *The Forrestal Diaries.* New York: Viking, 1951.
Nagai, Yonosuke, and Akira Iriye, eds. *The Origins of the Cold War in Asia.* New York: Columbia University Press, 1977.
Naquin, Susan, and Evelyn D. Rawski. *Chinese Society in the Eighteenth Century.* New Haven, Conn.: Yale University Press, 1987.
Neils, Patricia. *China Images in the Life and Times of Henry Luce.* Savage, Md.: Rowman & Littlefield, 1990.
———. *United States Attitudes and Policy Toward China: The Impact of American Missionaries.* Armonk, N.Y.: M. E. Sharpe, 1990.
Newman, Robert P. *Owen Lattimore and the "Loss" of China.* Berkeley: University of California Press, 1992.
———. "The Self-Inflicted Wound: The China White Paper of 1949." *Prologue* 14 (Fall 1982): 141–56.
Ninkovich, Frank. "Cultural Relations and American China Policy, 1942–1945." *Pacific Historical Review* 49 (Nov. 1980): 471–98.

————. "Interests and Discourse in Diplomatic History." *Diplomatic History* 13 (Spring 1989): 135–61.
North Carolina's "China Connection," 1840–1949: A Record. North Carolina China Council, 1981.
Paterson, Thomas G. "If Europe, Why Not China? The Containment Doctrine, 1947–49." *Prologue,* Spring 1981: 19–38.
————. *On Every Front: The Making of the Cold War.* New York: W. W. Norton, 1979.
————. "Presidential Foreign Policy, Public Opinion, and Congress: The Truman Years." *Diplomatic History* 3 (Winter 1979): 1–18.
Peck, Graham. *Two Kinds of Time.* Boston: Houghton Mifflin, 1950.
Pogue, Forrest C., ed. *George C. Marshall Interviews and Reminiscences for Forrest C. Pogue.* Lexington, Va.: George C. Marshall Research Foundation, 1991.
Purifoy, Lewis McCarroll. *Harry Truman's China Policy: McCarthyism and the Diplomacy of Hysteria, 1947–1951.* New York: New Viewpoints, 1976.
Rabe, Valentin H. *The Home Base of American China Missions, 1880–1920.* Cambridge, Mass.: Harvard University Press, 1978.
Reed, James. *The Missionary Mind and American East Asia Policy, 1911–1915.* Cambridge, Mass.: Council on East Asian Studies, Harvard University, 1983.
Reston, James. *The Artillery of the Press: Its Influence on American Foreign Policy.* New York: Harper & Row, 1966.
Romanus, Charles F., and Riley Sunderland. *Stilwell's Command Problems.* Washington, D.C.: Department of the Army, 1956.
————. *Stilwell's Mission to China.* Washington, D.C.: Department of the Army, 1953.
————. *Time Runs Out in CBI.* Washington, D.C.: Department of the Army, 1959.
Roosevelt, Franklin D. *F.D.R.: His Personal Letters, 1928–1945.* Edited by Elliot Roosevelt. 3 vols. New York: Duell, Sloan and Pearce, 1970.
————. *The Public Papers and Addresses of Franklin D. Roosevelt, 1933–1945.* Edited by Samuel I. Rosenman. 13 vols. New York: Harper & Brothers, 1938–50. Special reference to vols. 1941–1944/45.
Rosenberg, Emily. "Gender," in "A Round Table: Explaining the History of American Foreign Relations." *Journal of American History* 77 (June 1990): 116–24.
————. *Spreading the American Dream: American Economic and Cultural Expansion, 1890–1945.* New York: Hill & Wang, 1982.
Rupp, Leila J. *Mobilizing Women for War: German and American Propaganda, 1939–1945.* Princeton, N.J.: Princeton University Press, 1978.
Russet, Bruce. "Doves, Hawks, and U.S. Public Opinion." *Political Science Quarterly* 105 (Winter 1990): 515–38.
Said, Edward W. *Orientalism.* New York: Vintage Books, 1978.
Schaller, Michael. *The United States and China in the Twentieth Century.* New York: Oxford University Press, 1979.

———. *The U.S. Crusade in China, 1938–1945.* New York: Columbia University Press, 1979.

Schram, Stuart. *Mao Tse-tung.* Baltimore: Penguin Books, 1967.

Scott, Joan W. "Gender: A Useful Category of Historical Analysis." *American Historical Review* 91 (Dec. 1986): 1053–75.

Seagrave, Sterling. *The Soong Dynasty.* New York: Harper & Row, 1985.

Sheridan, James E. *China in Disintegration: The Republican Era in Chinese History, 1912–1949.* New York: Free Press, 1975.

Sherwood, Robert E. *Roosevelt and Hopkins: An Intimate History.* New York: Harper & Brothers, 1948.

Shewmaker, Kenneth E. *Americans and Chinese Communists, 1927–1945: A Persuading Encounter.* Ithaca, N.Y.: Cornell University Press, 1971.

Short, K. R. M., ed. *Film and Radio Propaganda in World War II.* Knoxville: University of Tennessee Press, 1983.

Small, Melvin, ed. *Public Opinion and Historians.* Detroit: Wayne State University Press, 1970.

Smedley, Agnes. *Portraits of Chinese Women in Revolution.* Edited with an Introduction by Jan MacKinnon and Steve MacKinnon; with an Afterword by Florence Howe. New York: Feminist Press, 1976.

Snow, Edgar. *Red Star Over China.* New York: Random House, 1938.

Spence, Jonathan D. *The Search for Modern China.* New York: W. W. Norton, 1990.

———. *To Change China: Western Advisors in China, 1620–1960.* New York: Penguin Books, 1980.

Steele, A. T. *The American People and China.* New York: McGraw-Hill, 1966.

Steuck, William. *The Wedemeyer Mission: American Politics and Foreign Policy During the Cold War.* Athens: University of Georgia Press, 1984.

Stimson, Henry L., and McGeorge Bundy. *On Active Service in Peace and War.* New York: Harper & Brothers, 1948.

Stross, Randall E. *The Stubborn Earth: American Agriculturalists on Chinese Soil, 1898–1937.* Berkeley: University of California Press, 1986.

Stuart, John Leighton. *Fifty Years in China: The Memoirs of John Leighton Stuart.* New York: Random House, 1954.

Sues, Ilona Ralf. *Shark's Fins and Millet.* Garden City, N.Y.: Garden City Publishing Co., 1944.

Susman, Warren I. *Culture as History: The Transformation of American Society in the Twentieth Century.* New York: Pantheon, 1973.

Swanberg, W. A. *Luce and His Empire.* New York: Scribner's, 1972.

Swidler, Ann. "Culture in Action: Symbols and Strategies." *American Sociological Review* 51 (Apr. 1986): 273–86.

Thomson, James C., Jr. *While China Faced West: American Reformers in Nationalist China, 1928–1937.* Cambridge, Mass.: Harvard University Press, 1969.

Thomson, James C., Jr., Peter W. Stanley, and John Curtis Perry. *Sentimental Imperialists: The American Experience in East Asia.* New York: Harper & Row, 1981.

Thorne, Christopher. *Allies of a Kind: The United States, Britain, and the War Against Japan, 1931–1945.* Oxford: Oxford University Press, 1978.

Truman, Harry S. *Memoirs.* Vol. 1, *Year of Decisions.* Vol. 2, *Years of Trial and Hope, 1946–1952.* Garden City, N.Y.: Doubleday, 1955, 1956.

Tsou, Tang. *America's Failure in China, 1941–1950.* Chicago: University of Chicago Press, 1963.

Tuchman, Barbara W. *Stilwell and the American Experience in China, 1911–1945.* New York: Bantam Books, 1970.

Tucker, Nancy Bernkopf. "China and America: 1941–1991." *Foreign Affairs* 70 (Winter 1991–92): 75–92.

———. *Patterns in the Dust: Chinese-American Relations and the Recognition Controversy, 1949–1950.* New York: Columbia University Press, 1983.

Tuveson, Ernest Lee. *Redeemer Nation: The Idea of America's Millennial Role.* Chicago: University of Chicago Press, 1968.

Utley, Freda. *Last Chance in China.* Indianapolis: Bobbs-Merrill, 1947.

Van Dusen, Henry P., ed., *The Spiritual Legacy of John Foster Dulles.* Freeport, N.Y.: Books for Libraries Press, 1960.

Van Slyke, Lyman P. *Enemies and Friends: The United Front in Chinese Communist History.* Stanford, Calif.: Stanford University Press, 1967.

Vandenberg, Arthur H., Jr., ed. *The Private Papers of Senator Vandenberg.* Boston: Houghton Mifflin, 1952.

Varg, Paul A. *The Making of a Myth: The United States and China, 1897–1912.* Westport, Conn.: Greenwood Press, 1980.

———. *Missionaries, Chinese, and Diplomats: The American Protestant Missionary Movement in China, 1890–1952.* Princeton, N.J.: Princeton University Press, 1958.

———. "Sino-American Relations Past and Present." *Diplomatic History* 4 (Spring 1980): 101–11.

Wainwright, Loudan. *The Great American Magazine: An Inside Story of Life.* New York: Knopf, 1986.

Wakeman, Frederic, Jr. *The Fall of Imperial China.* New York: Free Press, 1975.

Waldron, Arthur. "Bullish on Beijing." *New Republic,* Apr. 9, 1990, 20–25.

Wedemeyer, Albert C. *Wedemeyer Reports!* New York: Henry Holt, 1958.

West, Philip. *Yenching University and Sino-Western Relations, 1916–1952.* Cambridge, Mass.: Harvard University Press, 1976.

Westerfield, H. Bradford. *Foreign Policy and Party Politics: Pearl Harbor to Korea.* New Haven, Conn.: Yale University Press, 1955.

White, Donald W. "The 'American Century' in World History." *Journal of World History* 3 (Spring 1992): 105–27.

White, Theodore H. *In Search of History.* New York: Harper & Row, 1978.

———, ed. *The Stilwell Papers.* New York: William Sloane Associates, 1948.

White, Theodore H., and Analee Jacoby. *Thunder Out of China.* New York: William Sloane Associates, 1946.

Wiebe, Robert H. *The Search for Order, 1877–1920.* New York: Hill & Wang, 1967.

Williams, William Appleman. *The Contours of American History.* New York: World, 1961.

―――. *The Tragedy of American Diplomacy.* 2d ed. New York: Dell, 1972.

Williams, William Appleman et al., eds. *America in Vietnam: A Documentary History.* Garden City, N.Y.: Doubleday, 1985.

Willkie, Wendell. *One World.* New York: Simon & Schuster, 1943.

Winfield, Betty Houchin. *FDR and the News Media.* Urbana: University of Illinois Press, 1990.

Woodside, Alexander. *Vietnam and the Chinese Model: A Comparative Study of Nguyen and Ch'ing Civil Government in the First Half of the Nineteenth Century.* Cambridge, Mass.: Harvard University Press, 1971.

Young, Marilyn Blatt. *The Rhetoric of Empire: American China Policy, 1895–1901.* Cambridge, Mass.: Harvard University Press, 1969.

Index

In this index an "f" after a number indicates a separate reference on the next page, and an "ff" indicates separate references on the next two pages. A continuous discussion over two or more pages is indicated by a span of page numbers, e.g., "57–59." "Passim" is used for a cluster of references in close but not consecutive sequence.

Library of Congress Cataloging-in-Publication Data

Jespersen, T. Christopher
American images of China, 1931–1949 / T. Christopher Jespersen
    p. cm.
Includes bibliographical references and index.
ISBN 0-8047-2596-9 (cl.)   :   ISBN 0-8047-3654-5 (pbk.)
1. China—Foreign public opinion, American history—20th century.
2. Public opinion—United States—History—20th century.   3. Luce, Henry
Robinson, 1898–1967—View on China.   I. Title.
DS744.5.J47   1996
951.04—dc20
95–19565 CIP

♾ This book is printed on acid-free, recycled paper.

Original printing 1996
Last figure below indicates year of this printing:
05   04   03   02   01   00   99